Southie Won't Go

Southie Won't Go

A Teacher's Diary of the Desegregation of South Boston High School

Ione Malloy

UNIVERSITY OF ILLINOIS PRESS
Urbana and Chicago

© 1986 by the Board of Trustees of the University of Illinois
Manufactured in the United States of America
C 5 4 3 2 1

This book is printed on acid-free paper.

Library of Congress Cataloging-in-Publication Data

Malloy, Ione, 1931-
  Southie won't go.

  Bibliography: p.
  Includes index.
  1. South Boston High School—History—20th century.
2. Malloy, Ione, 1931-   . 3. High school teachers—
Massachusetts—Biography. 4. School integration—
Massachusetts—Boston—History. 5. Busing for school
integration—Massachusetts—Boston—History. 6. Busing
for school integration—Law and legislation—United
States. I. Title.
LD7501.B677M35   1986   373.744'61   85-16563
ISBN 0-252-01276-3

Contents

Generally speaking, except for the special needs and bilingual classes, the whole place was devoid of the youthful spontaneity that one associates with a high school. It was not just a matter of one race not speaking to or paying attention to students of another race, but of their saying little and seeming to pay little attention to fellow students of the same race. The students appeared to be calm compared to many of the non-uniformed personnel, nor did they seem inclined to exchange hostile glances or prone to give offense. They simply seemed to be the victims of constant cynical surveillance unconcerned, uninvolved and cowed.

> *Text of U.S. District Judge W. Arthur Garrity's rationale for placing South Boston High School under federal court receivership on December 9, 1975*

There is very abundant research literature that a school administrator can affect the educational environment powerfully, and in a very short time—more or less overnight. . . . We [Dentler and Scott]° were advising before, during and after on the nature of urban high schools in general—and of Boston in particular—for months.

> *Robert A. Dentler, December 17, 1975*

° Robert A. Dentler and Marvin Scott, deans of the Boston University Graduate School of Education, were appointed by the court to act as "experts" on the plan to desegregate the Boston schools.

South Boston High—
Before Desegregation

South Boston High School
Not a building
A small world
Enclosed
In youth
Reared with
Spukies & television
Saluting the flag
Carson beach
Summertime sand castles
Graduates
Of
Broadway matinees
The confessions & confirmations
The Kennedys
St. Pat's parade
Crowded corner
Liquor stores
Youth,
Reared in
Traditional American spirit
To win
The war—the football game
City kids
Whose mothers didn't go to college
Whose fathers fought in yesterday's wars
And came back and some who didn't
And the sons are now fighting
The wars they never started
Nor understand
A small world

Cut off from
The mayor's Boston
By the detour sign
On the still broken
Summer street bridge
Nearly surrounded
By water
Islanders
Hating & fearing & judging
The unknown
South Boston High School
Only a reflection of
The town
Like other towns, times
People.

student poem

Preface

I did not anticipate the advent of busing in Boston in 1974 with poised pen, ready to chronicle. Not a diarist, I have, however, long been impressed by the dynamic impact of accumulated daily minutiae — whether in Samuel Pepys's *Diary*, Daniel Defoe's *A Journal of the Plague Year*, Brendan Behan's autobiographical novel, *Borstal Boy*, or in a film like *Celeste*, an account of the eccentric employer Marcel Proust from the point of view of his housekeeper's kitchen routine. Not until October 1974, after the Rabbit Inn incident, did I realize that what Dr. William J. Reid, the headmaster of South Boston High School, had been told — "Everything will be all right if the buses get through the first day" — did not apply to South Boston. Instead, South Boston High School was gradually becoming the focal point of resistance to court-ordered busing in Boston. I began to keep a diary.

Unlike Elizabeth Huckaby's *Crisis at Central High*, an administrator's journal of the desegregation of the Little Rock high school from 1957 to 1958, *Southie Won't Go* is from a teacher's point of view — a tenured teacher in the Boston public schools. I tried to record events objectively, letting the people and occurrences at the high school speak for themselves, and to frame these daily situations in the larger historical setting — who (politician or statesman) said what, and when.

Southie Won't Go covers three school years, from 1974 to 1977: the events preceding, leading to, and culminating in the receivership of South Boston High School on December 9, 1975, and then the immediate aftermath of that decision.

I later condensed the manuscript to half its original size, inserting student compositions under the appropriate dates and adding clarifying information as needed, and I summarized most of the third year, 1976–77, because my diary entries had been short and uneventful. When in 1980 I first read the 1,163 pages of testimony given during the six-day federal court hearings on which Judge W. Arthur Garrity based his decision to place South Boston High School in receivership, I added a transcript of the testimony in greatly abbreviated form.

Prior to these receivership hearings, teachers at South Boston High School had felt that their colleagues "would be exonerated of the unjust allegations brought against them." They were not. Their protest to Judge Garrity provoked only one reply from him, a report on his "findings and conclusions on South Boston High School," then silence. Furthermore, in 1981, Judge Garrity's paid, court-appointed desegregation advisers, Robert Dentler and Marvin Scott, in their published account of the Boston desegregation case underscored their contempt for that faculty at South Boston High School, describing them as "natives of South Boston whose ignorance and hostility matched that of the street-corner toughs."

Of Judge Garrity's decision to place South Boston High School in receivership, Dr. Reid said, "I don't think Judge Garrity acted as impartially as the blindfold of justice would require." A reader of this chronicle can now judge the validity of Dr. Reid's comment. It is my hope that this diary will balance the historical record, and that it will be the final memorial to that faculty, now long dispersed.

All student names have been changed or, in a few cases, abbreviated, except Michael Faith's, whose name was almost a household word at the time.

Grateful acknowledgment is made to the following authors, publishers, and agents for permission to reprint copyrighted material:

Abt Books, for excerpt from *Schools on Trial* by Robert A. Dentler and Marvin B. Scott. Copyright 1981. Reprinted by permission.

Random House, Inc., for excerpt from *Light in August* by William Faulkner. Copyright 1950. Reprinted by permission.

Tribune Company Syndicate, Inc., for excerpt from "Jimmy Breslin on Boston," published in the *Boston Globe*, September 8, 1975. Reprinted by permission.

Doubleday & Company, Inc., for "What Is Black?" from *Hailstones and Halibut Bones* by Mary O'Neill. Copyright © 1960 by The Curtis Publishing Co. Reprinted by permission.

World's Work, for "What Is Black?" by Mary O'Neill from *Hailstones and Halibut Bones.* Copyright © 1961 by Mary Gibbons O'Neill. All rights reserved. First published in Great Britain in 1962 by World's Work.

The *Boston Phoenix,* for excerpt from "Kennedy on Racism, Violence, and the American Flag" by Howard Husock. Copyright 1976. Reprinted by permission.

The *Boston Globe* and the *Boston Herald,* for excerpts from articles listed in the Bibliography. Reprinted by permission.

Excerpt from "Presentation to the Massachusetts Legislature" by James S. Coleman. March 30, 1976. Printed by permission.

The *Boston Globe,* the *Boston Herald,* the *Pilot,* UPI/Bettmann, Wide World Photos, Inc., and the Massachusetts State Police for photographs from their film archives. Published by permission.

Dean Yarborough for the photograph from his extensive collection on South Boston High School, and Stanley Forman for his Pulitzer Prize photograph. Published by permission.

I am also grateful to my many friends for their help and encouragement, especially Dr. Marie T. Hayes, formerly head of the English department, South Boston High School, and Professor Dolores Burton, Boston University; to Homer Jenks, assistant managing editor, the *Boston Herald,* and Professor Celia Millward, Boston University, for their careful reading of the work in progress; and to my father, for his steady illumination, both critical and spiritual, of the word and the way.

Introduction

Though I've seen the world from the summit of Mt. Fuji and climbed the heights of academia at Austin, Texas, to earn a Ph.D. in English, the radius of my tether has been narrow.

Across from Boston Latin School, where I now teach—the oldest public school in the United States and one year older than Harvard—is Roxbury Community College. In that building, which assumed several aliases—recently State College at Boston and earlier the Girls' Latin School—I earned respectively a master's degree in education and a high school diploma; later, at Boston College, a few miles west, a master's degree in English. Around the corner is Emmanuel College, where I majored in English and minored in Latin. It is just a short subway ride away from the townhouse in the Back Bay where in 1937 my father, for whom the Great Depression was "academic," founded Stratford School for girls. We lived there in the quondam servants' quarters on the top floor behind locked doors with the ever-present and ominous caveat to my four brothers and two sisters: "Shhhhhhhhhh. They'll *hear* you."

As we grew up, the cultural trove of the city was our daily constant: the Children's Room of the Boston Public Library, the Museum of Natural History (now Bonwit Teller's), the Exeter Street Theatre, Arthur Fiedler and the Boston Pops Esplanade concerts. In winter we sledded in the alleys behind Commonwealth Avenue and ice-skated on the Lagoon of the Public Garden. Summertime brought sailing on the Charles River and swimming at Carson Beach in South Boston. On rainy days we picnicked on the floor of the great basement townhouse kitchen with its butler's pantry and dumbwaiter connecting now to school offices above. Summertime also meant processing thousands of direct mail pieces to prospective Stratford School students—stuffing and stamping envelopes—or, if we were not wary enough to refuse a ride, waiting endless hours in the family car while my father interviewed prospects in nearby communities. By the time I was in college, the school had changed names and direction, becoming the first junior college in Boston, and the family had moved to suburban Newton, the "Garden City."

I began teaching by substituting in the Boston public schools and simply stayed on, accepting my first assignment—untrained for it—to a first grade in Dorchester. Six years later, although I had survived a brief floundering passage using the "look-say" method of teaching reading and was sailing smoothly and soundly on a new phonetic course, I opted out of the first-grade classroom, whose numbers never dropped below forty-four (including several students with learning disabilities awaiting an opening in special class). Thus, between November 30 and December 1, 1964, I rocketed from teaching reading to six-year-olds to instructing shop boys at Hyde Park High School about the aesthetics of *The Yearling*. Dr. William J. Reid, the assistant headmaster, was my strong support. "Don't quit," he advised me, when the shop boys threw pennies at the light fixtures if I turned my back to write on the blackboard.

The following year Dr. Reid became the sixth headmaster at South Boston High. When I transferred there five years later, I had come full circle again. From the school site on Dorchester Heights, the strand of Carson Beach was visible below.

Growing up in the Back Bay, I had found stability in cultural institutions, not in the transient population of the neighborhood Prince School I attended nor at the Girls' Latin School, which attracted a student population citywide. South Boston, by contrast, was a neighborhood remarkable for the natural beauty of its location on the Atlantic seacoast and the strong cohesiveness of its people. What it meant to grow up in such a community was an experience I could appreciate now only as an adult outsider peering through a glass darkly.

Behind South Boston High School, on a rise commanding "a great part of the town and almost the whole harbor," ° juts the white marble Dorchester Heights National Monument, 124 feet high, marking the exact center of the colonial fortification ordered by General George Washington in the winter of 1776. From this dominance, surrounded by water on three sides— the Fort Point Channel on the west and Boston Harbor on the north and

---

° George Washington to the American Congress, Feb. 26, 1776, in *Official Letters to the Honorable American Congress . . .* (London, 1795), 1: 97.

east — Washington mustered several thousand men and a show of strength that forced the evacuation of Boston Harbor on March 17, 1776. The code word on that night the cannons were stealthily hauled up the Heights was "Boston," and the reply, in honor of Washington's many Irish soldiers, was "Saint Patrick."

Today Evacuation Day is celebrated on the tight little peninsula of South Boston with a St. Patrick's Day Parade, shamrocks, and green beer.

Although one of the earliest settlements in New England, by 1810 the peninsula still numbered only 354 inhabitants. After 1843, when the first free bridge from the city proper to South Boston opened, the population increased rapidly. By 1870, what had once been intended as a spacious, aristocratic residential area bustled with almost 40,000 residents. They gave their loyalty to family, church, community, and country, living modestly in the rows of three-decker—mostly wood and some brick—houses that stretched away from the monument in neat streets labeled alphabetically from Broadway Station out to City Point and numerically, First to Eighth, from one side of the peninsula to the other. They sent sons to the wars, their surnames on the military roster reflecting the waves of immigration: Irish, Poles, Lithuanians, Italians, Germans, Greeks, and Albanians. In the Vietnam War they lost twenty-five young men who had rallied to their country's flag because "that's the way we were brought up."

The South Bostonians survived the Great Depression with little difficulty, having little to lose. While Back Bay society sold their antique Louis XIV furniture and their brownstone townhouses along Commonwealth Avenue and Marlborough and Beacon streets and moved to suburban Dover and Beverly in the late 1920s and 1930s, many South Bostonians moved to Dorchester and West Roxbury, to the more affluent parts of Boston, or to towns along the South Shore. At the end of World War II, with the advent of GI mortgage loans, the outward migration increased. Those South Bostonians who remained, many of them city workers and public utility employees, set their aspirations away from the industrial Lower End to the Upper End of the peninsula, the Point, where the "high" Irish lived, in carefully renovated homes with a command of the ocean. A minority of the total population, the Irish remained the largest of the ethnic groups in a community that supported Polish and Greek churches, a Lithuanian church and newspaper, an Albanian cathedral, and at least three Protestant churches. From their ranks, over the years, they sent the first American gold medalist to the Olympics, a cardinal to Rome, and the first Catholic Speaker to the U.S. Congress.

Isolated from the rest of the city, the people of South Boston worked together to solve their problems. They blocked the conversion of Carson Beach on Day Boulevard into an amusement park, devised clean-up campaigns, and planned together—in a never very successful effort—to improve the access bridges to their community. "Southie" meant strong community pride, a fierce loyalty to one another, a distrust of any change, and—among some—a suspicion of those who might be different.

This togetherness is both South Boston's greatest strength and greatest weakness, Dr. Reid told the commencement audience of 1974, the last before the impact of desegregation. He described how secure he felt when his daughter, class of 1972, went out at night and was "passed along" from corner to corner by her friends, the "street-corner society" of South Boston. Strength and weakness. I felt, listening to Dr. Reid, that he was trying to warn the community that "we take care of our own" was an inadequate ideal. Three months later, when the world closed in and South Boston High School became the focal point of resistance to court-ordered busing, I would hear, over and over, "We just want to be left alone."

While traditionally the public Latin or parochial schools attracted the children of the financially more comfortable, more ambitious, or prestigious families, South Boston High reached out to potential athletes and to the children from the poorer families in one of the four community housing projects—Columbia Point, Old Colony, D Street, and Mary McCormack—and beyond to nearby sections of Dorchester, including Uphams Corner and Savin Hill. No other high school in the city had on its roster so large a number of children from families on welfare. For these young people, many of whom never left the community except to serve in the armed forces, South Boston High was the place to be, where the action was, where they made their friends—many they kept for life. For most, Dr. Reid said, the high school experience was the happiest time of their lives.

A rambling, three-story yellow brick building with a half basement, built at the turn of the century in Colonial style, South Boston High over the years expanded roughly to the shape of the letter "C," as the school adapted to community needs, adding programs in business, cooking, sewing, and sheet metal, including machine shop practice, welding, and auto body repair. Under Dr. Reid's administration, the school day stretched from 8:00 A.M. until 4:15 P.M. to accommodate the student body, which grew from 1,400 students in 1965 to 2,200 in 1973, two-thirds of them from South Boston proper and one-third from the Dorchester area. To accommodate 420 ninth graders, the L-Street Bathhouse at the end of Carson Beach, site of the mid-winter skinny-dipping rite of the octogenarian "Brownies," was annexed to the high school. Of the more than 400 seniors graduated each year, about 16 percent, most of them the first in their families, went on to degree-granting institutions.

One last item: In the ten years from 1964 to 1974, only three black students attended South Boston High. Two were sisters. One of them had no trouble, the other claimed to have been pushed down the stairs. The third was a girl who became quite well accepted by her classmates and was graduated with the class of 1973. One day before graduation the senior, a light-complexioned minority student, invited her friend to play the piano at the school assembly. The guest, a black girl, was doused with a bucket of water. Within five minutes, the unheard-of occurred: An informant gave Dr. Reid the name of the culprit.

In the days just before desegregation, teachers agreed, "Dr. Reid is the only one who could handle this school." Of medium height and solidly built, with a shock of white hair and rough eyebrows that matched his sometimes gruff manner, Dr. Reid was a strong leader. He was a commander in the naval reserve and had earned a doctorate in American history. He was fair, honest, firm, even tough, qualities he liked in Southie students. "They're not sea lawyers," he said. "If they've done something, they'll say so." My own talisman to the Southie student I took from an old Southie math teacher when I transferred there from Hyde Park High in 1970: "You can push the students, but don't push them too hard, because then they'll just go the other way."

On June 21, 1974, the last day of the school year, Federal District Court Judge W. Arthur Garrity, ending months of speculation and uncertainty, ruled that the rights of the plaintiff class of black students and parents had been and were being violated by the defendant School Committee of the City of Boston in its management and operation of the public schools, and enjoined the School Committee for failing to comply with the timetable implementing the racial balance plan of the Massachusetts State Board of Education. He ordered the short-term plan of the board of education, involving only part of the city, be adopted until a citywide busing plan could be devised with the approval of the Boston School Committee. Phase 1 would begin in September.

Weeks earlier, in anticipation of that decision, Dr. Reid had explained to the assembled student body the projected South Boston–Roxbury High Paired School Complex desegregation plan. Freshmen would attend classes at the Hart-Dean Annex a few blocks away and at the L-Street Annex on Day Boulevard. Sophomores would remain at South Boston High, integrating with black sophomores bused from Roxbury and Columbia Point; the South Boston High School junior class would be bused to Roxbury to desegregate Roxbury High, and the senior class at both high schools could choose either high school. It was like the hostage system of the Middle Ages, whereby the princes of opposing crowns were kept in rival kings' courts as a preventive against war, he explained. Still, there was the advantage for the juniors that they would be together with their friends.

During those last weeks of the school year, voluntary sensitivity courses on race relations were offered in the city schools and at the high school. In chitchat before the meeting, one of the black teachers, who had transferred to South Boston High from Roxbury High, stated that if there were any race riots in the fall, she would stay home. She had been through them three years before at Roxbury High, and once was enough. Though peacefully integrated, after the riots Roxbury High had become an all-black school. This was new information to me, but, no doubt, not to the South Boston and Roxbury communities. To talk of hostages, then, was not unrealistic. In another sensitivity meeting, attended by Dr. Reid, a black woman who had grown up in South Boston shared her experiences with us. I asked her what black people hoped to gain from the busing, since transporting students between Roxbury and South Boston simply exchanged students of one working-class background to another. "Do you just want to break a color barrier?" She answered, "Yes." She did not like the poor discipline in any of the Boston schools, however, and sent her children to private schools in Braintree.

In May a group of teachers at the projected paired-school complex, hoping to alleviate fear of the unknown, arranged for an exchange of students between Roxbury and South Boston highs, providing transportation in their own cars. About twenty students from each high school took part—the white students from South Boston greeted at Roxbury High by large welcoming banners; the black students from Roxbury conducted around South Boston High School and to classes by a core group of white students.

In addition, English teachers at South Boston High School tried to persuade their students to obtain consent forms from their reluctant parents to participate in an interracial human relations seminar weekend on Cape Cod, a neutral site. The object was to bring black student leaders from Roxbury High together with white student leaders from South Boston High, so that they could set a positive direction in student thinking and attitudes

in case of mandatory desegregation. Before summer vacation began, Chuck
Williams, the head of the psychology department at South Boston High,
and three other teachers had one successful weekend with students, among
them Michael Faith, a senior at South Boston High, but there were no
funds for any more. By December of the following year, Michael would
be in the hospital on the danger list, the victim of a racial confrontation.

Some of the South Boston High faculty also went to Roxbury High in
June to meet after school with teachers and students. As I looked at the
murals, dioramas of the black struggle, with black athletes and patriots, I
reflected what a difficult psychological adjustment it would be for the
Southie students in an environment so foreign to their own backgrounds,
and unprepared by educational experience, to go from an almost all-white
community to one that was 80 percent black.

If the desegregation decision had been made before the end of the school
year, perhaps more would have been done to prepare for September 1974.

During the summer Judge Garrity heard and denied a petition to exempt
high school seniors from the desegregation plan and let them graduate from
the high schools that they had been attending. As a result, South Boston
High School lost from the senior class eighty-six members who lived outside
the new district. The seniors would set an example for all the schools, Judge
Garrity said, since they had "more at stake," including diplomas and recommendations for jobs and colleges. For mixups in class rings and yearbooks
already subscribed for, he suggested a refund or a "swap-off." Looking
ahead to the new school year, he observed, "So I think this is all going to
work out, but it's going to take a great deal of understanding and sacrifice
and suppression of personal preferences in order to be done successfully."

But if Judge Garrity was sanguine, the newspapers were sending out
alarm signals: "School Integration: 10 Days to Go," "Busing to Split Up
Athletic Teams," "Boston Officials Outline Plans for Safe Busing," "Hicks
Pleads for Peace on First Day of School."

In September, before school began, teachers made plans to meet at
Dorgan's Restaurant on Day Boulevard, facing the Columbia Point housing
project across the bay, if the white students succeeded in ringing the buses
as they had promised, and neither black students nor teachers could get
through to the school. Dr. Reid asked that no black teacher leave the school
unless accompanied by someone known to the community. One afternoon
a group of us, black and white teachers and transitional aides, walked
happily down the hill to Dorgan's Restaurant for lunch, where we discussed

jocularly how much money the aides would receive for riding the buses, like "sitting ducks," between South Boston and Roxbury.

The opening of Boston schools was postponed a week. Then South Boston students boycotted them—by white consensus rather than by conscious organization, although City Councilwoman Louise Day Hicks and Boston School Committee President John Kerrigan had urged parents to protest peacefully by keeping their children off the buses and out of the schools. Tom Atkins, president of the Boston branch of the National Association for the Advancement of Colored People (NAACP), suggested that the parents be prosecuted. However, parents had only to say that they were concerned for the safety of their children, and they had sufficient legal cause to keep them home.

On September 12, the first day of school, I arrived early. Curiosity seekers, cameramen, and over 100 Boston police were already there—in front of the school and strung out along G Street, the bus route to the Heights. One man on the sidewalk held a Progressive Labor party sign welcoming blacks, urging unity between black and white working classes; another held a sign: FIGHT RACISM, FIGHT THE BOSSES. From my homeroom window on the front second floor, I watched a crowd of several hundred gather—a few students Dr. Reid recognized, young adults, neighbors, clergy, parents, and several vociferous viragoes.

At last the first yellow bus topped the hill and pulled to the front of the school. There was a roar of disapproval from the crowd. Another bus topped the hill. I heard a rock hit one bus, the crowd shouting approval. "Get those niggers out of our school." Then a shout warned the police, who had moved the crowd well back from the iron gate entrance to the building, "You won't be here all the time."

Police Commissioner Robert diGrazia escorted the black youngsters into the school.

One white girl, Kathryn, enrolled in my homeroom the first day. She pointed out her father standing on the street corner; he stayed there all day. Martin, a black boy from Columbia Point, came, too. I held out my hand to him. His hand was cold.

At the faculty meeting at the end of the day, Dr. Reid was pleased. "Everything will be all right if the buses get through the first day," he had been told.

Outside in the school yard, young Southie boys kicked at the Progressive Labor party sign, now abandoned on the pavement.

Total attendance for the day at South Boston High School was 124: 56

blacks, 68 whites; the anticipated enrollment was 1,300. Total attendance at the L-Street Annex was 92: 77 blacks, 15 whites; the anticipated enrollment was 600.

At the L-Street Annex buses were stoned as they pulled away from the school. Six black children, a monitor, and a bus driver were hurt by flying glass.

The politicians responded. From Freedom House in Roxbury, Tom Atkins advised black parents not to send their children to schools in South Boston. Mayor Kevin White banned groups of three or more persons from congregating near or around Boston schools, under penalty of arrest.

Beginning on September 13, the second day of desegregation, school buses in and out of South Boston were escorted by motorcycle police.

The violence that met the first yellow bus as it topped Dorchester Heights was indicative of the deep rift desegregation had torn in the community, a rift that only widened as time passed. By December the logistics of Dorchester Heights would become a real threat to the safety of the black students. South Boston was to be the "most difficult" desegregation case the Justice Department had ever encountered.

In the days that followed, while we waited for the boycott to end, I taught a unit in humor to my all-black sophomores. I hoped they could learn to laugh at the people who held up bananas as they passed by in the school buses or carried signs reading "Take a Roxbury bus." I began one class by asking, "Did you see anything humorous on TV last night?" A boy answered, "Yes, the whites." Then he apologized.

Black students, arriving at the high school after having run the gauntlet of jeers and curses shouted at the buses, often released their fear in obscenities. A senior boy who heard them in the adjoining room slammed the door shut. Another senior, who was upset last spring about the "niggers" coming to the high school, walked around stiffened by fear like a wooden soldier. I wondered, "Are the most prejudiced the most afraid?" He did not finish his senior year.

As the boycott extended into weeks, Massachusetts Commissioner of Education Gregory Anrig appeared on television, ordering the students back: "You've made your point. Now get back to school." But Southie juniors, mostly from a working-class background with few traditions of a college education, were legally able to quit, and many had. Others had gone to live with relatives in the suburbs or enrolled in private schools. Of the 550 white students in the junior class, only thirteen were to enroll at Roxbury High.

Improvements at the high school came gradually. At first, when the buses were simply emptied, black students without a school program who did not belong in the school and had just come along for the fun were sent to the school library for the day. There, for bravado, some boasted loudly about robbing whites and beating up police. They gathered at the windows and watched the crowds outside the school. When I asked a black aide to help move them from the windows, he yelled at them, "Do you want to be shot? Get away." Under the strain, the librarian's eyes became bloodshot from ruptured blood vessels. At a faculty meeting, one teacher objected, "I'm tired of seeing 30-year-old 'students' with book bags walking into this school." Finally the library was closed, and programs were checked before the buses emptied and students were allowed inside.

One afternoon, while I was assigned to a study class in the school cafeteria, members of the Home and School Association of South Boston High, disturbed about reports of graffiti in the girls' lavatories, passed through on an inspection tour of the school. One looked at me with such hatred that I was frightened. Another stopped to talk. Anne, a black girl in my sophomore English class, came over and sat near me to hear what the parent said. The woman, patting Anne on the knee, calling her "Dear," told her she knew Anne did not want to be at the high school either. After the parents left, the girls were upset. Anne was angry because one of them had used "nigger." Anne then talked about the bus ride to the high school, the old women in their nightdresses who stood on the streets and gave them the finger. "If that was my mother," she said, "I'd take her inside before she caught cold and give her a nice hot drink. And the little kids that say 'Kill the niggers!'" she exclaimed. "They don't even know what they're saying. If that was my little brother, I'd slap his behind."

Jackie, one of my black sophomore girls, came to class one day, sat down, and exulted, "Today was a good day." "Why's that?" I asked. She said, "Nobody gave me the finger, held their nose, or yelled at us in the buses today."

Wednesday, October 2, was the first riot. I was working with a sophomore English class on the third floor, waiting our turn to go to lunch at the tail end of the staggered lunch period. Dr. Reid's voice on the intercom suddenly broke into the class: "Black students to the south side of the building, white students to the north, and all teachers return to their homerooms." Our harmonious little group was suddenly split apart by fear of unidentified danger. We had no idea what had happened or where, what was coming at us, or from what direction. Since we were on the south side of the building, I left the black students there and went back to my homeroom on the second floor front. Members of the Boston Tactical Patrol Force— 30 of them in the building for the first time—ran down the stairs past me toward the screams bellowing up the stairwell from the basement cafeteria. Then the first of our many long waits began, two hours in the homerooms until the buses arrived early at 1:00.

After school the faculty met with Dr. Reid in the assembly hall to assess the riot that had begun in the cafeteria. Dr. Reid explained. A scuffle broke out near the water cooler; it was broken up by the teachers. Then a white boy knocked a black student's lunch tray into the air, and the cafeteria became a scene of flying lunch trays—milk, cake, spaghetti—the floor slick with spaghetti sauce. In the melee Dr. Reid was knocked to the floor. There were approximately 200 students in the cafeteria at the time; most did not take part in the disturbance. Order was restored in the cafeteria within minutes, but rumor of the trouble spread like a fireball through the building, and incidents broke out everywhere. "It was mass hysteria," one teacher explained.

Dr. Reid tallied the casualties: One teacher's wallet had been stolen. Another had been locked in a room, another chased down the corridor by a black student shouting, "You honky white bitch." The nurse had been banged on the arms with book bags by students crowding into her office. Joanne Leonard, a young teacher, had slipped on the spaghetti, fallen backward, and sprained her back and neck; another male teacher had ducked the flying food trays by squatting under a cafeteria table. In addition to several teachers and aides, seven students were injured, one of them a black girl who had been kicked in the hip and was taken to Boston City Hospital. Two black girls were arrested on charges of assault and possession of dangerous weapons. The white boy who had provoked the riot was suspended.

But I saw none of the violence. I only momentarily contributed to Police Commissioner diGrazia's alarm by clattering noisily down the stairs in my leather sandals to the now empty cafeteria to pick up a plastic spoon, so I could eat my yogurt while we waited for the buses.

Attendance was down the next day: from a high of 504 on Wednesday, October 2 (294 whites, 194 blacks, 16 others), down to 311 on Thursday, October 3 (145 whites, 158 blacks, 8 others).

On Saturday, October 5, I attended the annual *Globe* Book Fair, where I met Miss Marjorie Gibbons, the librarian from the South Boston branch of the Boston Public Library. She described the National Boycott Day antibusing march of over 7,000 people down Broadway in South Boston on Friday, October 4. She said, "I've never seen anything like it, very peaceful and silent. It was like a funeral march. It gave me the most eerie feeling."

James Michener talked briefly about the alienation of city and suburb caused by busing. Bearing out his remarks, the Hyde Park section of Boston was now talking about seceding from the city. The headmaster of Charlestown High also ruefully remarked that Charlestown had become a part of Boston by just 150 votes; except for that small margin, Charlestown High would not now be facing busing.

On Sunday, October 6, political activist Angela Davis, addressing the Book Fair audience, asked them to meet at a hall in Jamaica Plain, a mixed area of Boston, to rally against racism in South Boston. A carefully groomed, almost all-white audience gave her a standing ovation.

During the weekend there were ominous rumblings and sketchy TV newscasts about confrontation with the police at the Rabbit Inn bar in South Boston.

On Sunday night 1,000 men and women from South Boston protested outside police headquarters, alleging police brutality at the inn on Saturday night. The police, they claimed, had demolished the restaurant and "busted the heads" of several patrons of the tavern. Two persons had been arrested, and twelve others treated for head cuts and bruises at Boston City Hospital.

Representatives Ray Flynn and Michael Flaherty from South Boston, together with Mrs. Virginia Sheehy, an official of the South Boston Home and School Association, met with Police Superintendent Joseph Jordan to demand the withdrawal of the Tactical Patrol Force from South Boston.

When I arrived at the high school on Monday morning, I knew the year would not be "desegregation as usual." I began keeping a diary.

Phase 1 Desegregation, 1974–75

Monday, October 7, 1974

Martin looked over my shoulder as I filled out the daily racial census form in my homeroom: Number of Blacks, Number of Whites, Other Minorities. "What's this?" he asked, displeased. "That's what it's all about — desegregation. How many blacks, how many whites," I answered, as I filled in the racial counts in the proper squares.

Besides my sophomore homeroom, which met briefly at the beginning and end of the day, primarily for an attendance check, I had been assigned two racially mixed sophomore classes, one all-white senior class, a study period in the cafeteria, and two administrative periods in the school library.

My senior class, still bristling with anger about the Saturday night beating raid by the Boston Tactical Patrol Force on the Rabbit Inn patrons, claimed that the TPF had cleared the street before the raid. According to reports in the *Globe,* the barman at the Rabbit Inn had received a telephone call warning about the raid, presumably in retaliation because several TPF officers had been injured in a scuffle there the previous night, but he had ignored the call. At 8:10, in response to a telephoned request for help, two police cars were sent to the Rabbit Inn. The first police car to arrive was waved away by the TPF, according to a police officer at nearby station 6, and the second car followed. Contradictory police reports claim TPF responded to two officer-in-trouble calls recorded at 8:22 and 8:24 in the police department's operations center.

Father Arthur DiPietro, the unofficial chaplain of South Boston High, told me he had been at the Rabbit Inn and seen the TPF, their badges removed from their riot helmets, beat with their sticks on women and children, then jump in their cars and speed away. The women came out of the Old Colony housing project across from the inn with clubs, screaming for the police to appear so they could return blow for blow with them. Father DiPietro had never seen people as angry as these women.

At the high school the Boston TPF sat at the table next to us in the faculty cafeteria annex, playing cards for money. They had no sympathy for the raid victims; the bar was the hangout of the Mullen gang and of hoods—truckers and gangsters who had taunted them with "Fuck the police" in antibusing protests since school began. When Rosalie Packard, a teacher who had grown up in South Boston, got up to leave, she said loudly so they could hear, "Well, I have to go now. I don't want to get caught in a gambling raid."

Most black students did not come to South Boston High School today. Instead the buses were detoured by NAACP President Tom Atkins to the Columbia Point campus of the University of Massachusetts, where seminars had been arranged to "increase student awareness of the political and educational history of desegregation in the Boston schools," and "to find out from the students' perspective just how school personnel and police in their roles were responding to the situation." According to Ophie Franklin, NAACP seminar coordinator, interviewed in the *Herald*, "These facts are essential in requesting federal marshals." Dr. Bernard Shulman, associate superintendent for the South Boston–Roxbury Paired School Complex, gave his permission and was there to oversee "the efforts of more than fifty black community leaders, who included Atkins, Elma Lewis [founder and director of the Elma Lewis School of Fine Arts, Roxbury], Ellen Jackson [organizer and director of the Institute on Schools and Education at Freedom House, Roxbury], and Model Cities Administrator Paul Parks."°

However, according to the radio report, the students lost interest, scuffles broke out among about twelve students, and the buses were called early to take them home at 12:30. The students allegedly tore up the library and stole two pocketbooks. The University of Massachusetts then terminated the agreement to receive the buses of black students, an arrangement which had proved unbeneficial to all, a University spokesperson said.

I drove near the Rabbit Inn on my way home. I was surprised by the crowd of police and residents who had collected there. Shortly after I left, a black man, André Yvon Jean-Louis, a Haitian immigrant now living in Dorchester, stopped for a red light at the intersection there. Infuriated

° Boston *Herald American*, late ed., Oct. 7, 1974, p. 3.

bystanders broke the windows of his car. He ran for a house, but was beaten with a lead pipe before he could be rescued. A policeman fired two warning shots. Four or five hundred police were called to the corner, then clashed with the mob in a near riot.

Tuesday, October 8

On the televised news last night, Mayor White said he could no longer contain the situation in Boston. He wanted federal troops to enforce federal law on busing. The black community supported him.

At the high school, there were about eight armed Boston police on each floor, reading newspapers and books and talking to girls.

No black students attended school today. There were eight white seniors in my class, and one white boy, Sam, in my sophomore college English class. I asked him if his peers hassled him at all about coming to school. He said, "No," but he didn't hang around with the kids in the neighborhood anyway. Last week he had been sitting with some blacks in the cafeteria, but the white seniors called him over and warned him not to sit with blacks or they would get him in the next lunchroom riot. He sat by himself now. The next two years, he said, he would elect to go to Roxbury High. Nobody would bother him there.

At about 1:00 P.M. I heard from a Boston policeman with a walkie-talkie that English High, as yet free from racial tension, had exploded. A false alarm had sounded, and most of the black students then left the school. They were told by school administrators not to return, and made their way home breaking windows and smashing car windshields of whites driving by.

There was trouble at Technical High also. Bars in Roxbury were ordered closed. The bars had already been ordered closed in South Boston. Driving to work that morning in Southie, I had noticed for the first time the wizened men in shabby gray coats leaning against the buildings along Broadway — the bar addicts with no place to go.

Wednesday, October 9

Dorgan's Restaurant burned down last night, another South Boston tradition gone. Politicians from around the state, both Democrat and Republican, had gathered there on St. Patrick's Day for a corned-beef-and-cabbage luncheon, spiced with political wit and lampoons, and presided over by the incumbent state senator from Southie. The celebration was canceled last year as a protest against busing—popularly dubbed "The WASP Revenge."

From my window on the second floor, I could see a trickle of black students surrounded by about forty police walking up police-lined East 6th Street. The fire engine trucks, whose hoses had been pouring water into the smoking shell of the restaurant, had blocked the bus route at the end of the street, but my first thought was of black Roxbury leader Bill Owens, who had called on other leaders—without response—to join with him in a walk through the streets of South Boston. On TV he said: "We're going to go to school in South Boston, work there and live there, and the people of South Boston better accept that." Angry white students were quoting him today.

There were a few white students in my classes today, but no blacks. Sally, a sophomore, was in school because a boycott would do no good, she said, and her mother planned to move before the end of the year anyway, to a place where she would not be bused.

Evening TV pictured about 200 blacks in gangs roaming the streets bordering Roxbury, smashing windows of cars, breaking into a TV store. A white man had his car stoned, then was set upon by thirty-five youths and beaten unconscious. A wide-eyed commentator reported that the mood of the city was one of growing hatred and fear; that Mayor White, with whom he had spent the day, had to enforce a law he didn't agree with and hadn't been given the tools to enforce: The very fabric of the city was being torn apart.

Judge Garrity said he did not like the community leaders of South Boston inflaming sentiments; nothing would change the law but an amendment to the Constitution, and no amount of boycotting would help. The only federal troops Boston could have, he said, were the thirty-four marshals under his jurisdiction, together with National Guard and suburban police. Governor Francis Sargent reported he had tossed the ball to Mayor White, who could send for the troops if he needed them. The governor would do his part and stand by. People are afraid of unskilled troops coming into the city and panicking in a crisis. Representative Ray Flynn of South Boston asked that no police be sent. The people would prove they could handle the situation, he said.

President Gerald Ford told a televised press conference he didn't believe in forced busing "to achieve racial balance as a solution to quality education" and "respectfully" disagreed with the judge's (Garrity's) order.

Thursday, October 10

Because of the change in command from Boston to state police at
the high school, the buses were delayed one hour. Boston Police Commissioner Robert diGrazia met the state police outside the high school gate.
Although usually he wears cherry red trousers and red necktie with a white
floral design, today he was dressed in suit and tie for the funeral of a
policeman who suffered a heart attack after being struck in the chest by
a missile while he was on duty at an antibusing demonstration in South
Boston.

Four hundred fifty state troopers will be in South Boston; the Boston
police will patrol the rest of the city. After lining up three-deep in front
of the high school, the state police marched off single-file and lined the
streets along the bus approach. The North Cafeteria will be their command
post and staging area in the high school. The troopers will be stationed in
the lunchrooms, gyms, shops, at the stairwells, and in the corridors of all
four floors of the building—eight men to a floor—so they can have eye-
to-eye contact with one another. They have military and tactical-police
training and discipline, and a reputation for being tough. They seem a
little nervous with the students, but they will get used to them.

In my sophomore class there were only three students—two white boys,
one of them an immigrant from Sicily, and Janice, a black girl, who had
to sneak out to school because her mother didn't want her to go. Earlier
in the year Janice had talked about her belief in the ideals of Martin Luther
King, that there would be integration one day, and her own dream of the
world as one community with everyone owning a piece of it. Now she was
bitter. Now, she said, she realized that whites didn't want blacks to have
a chance at jobs, and wanted to keep them down. The blacks were ruining
their own community. They were frustrated. Their leaders told them to go
to school, then to stay home, then took them to the University of Massachusetts and talked about nothing. They're tired of talking and getting
nowhere, so they're stoning and beating up whites when they drive through
their neighborhoods—"even my friends." Some kids are depressed and
don't want to go to school anymore. They feel they have been used as
political pawns, and when Atkins ordered them back to school today, only
a few would come, she said. But she was going to get an education and a
college degree.

Janice will be leaving South Boston High soon. Her house has been condemned. I'll miss her. She has a tender and perceptive nature. She was the heart of the class.

From my homeroom window at the end of the day the white students watched the black students board the buses in the shadow of a white K-9 wagon flanked by police, standing with legs apart. The students pointed out one black girl they liked—"she's funny"—and one they didn't. White students may leave the school only after the buses have left.

On my way home I passed the Old Colony Housing Project near the Rabbit Inn and the Gavin Middle School. State troopers now lined the corners and the streets facing the project. Some troopers stationed on the roofs scanned the area with binoculars. Below, two little girls stood with their doll carriages talking to a trooper.

Mayor White again demanded federal troops to enforce a federal order; he will not implement the second part of a desegregation order until he has federal guidelines on how to implement it; he is angry with President Ford for giving the antibusing element false hope, thus fanning violence. The antibusing groups have resolved not to give Cardinal Humberto Medeiros a penny in contributions until he relaxes the guidelines for transfer of white students to parochial schools.

Monday, Columbus Day

Yesterday 700 blacks marched to a rally on Boston Common. One student speaker, who said she attended South Boston High because "they don't want me there," was cheered.

Today a "mystery ride" of 1,000 antibusing cars from South Boston demonstrated outside the Sheraton Hotel in Copley Square, where a Democratic fund-raiser was in progress, then proceeded to Pier 4 Restaurant on the waterfront, where political leaders Senator Edward Kennedy, Congressman Robert Drinan, Speaker John McCormack, and gubernatorial nominee Michael Dukakis were dining. They held Kennedy political prisoner inside for two hours, until 10:30 P.M., when enough people had left so that a passageway could be forced for him.

John Boone, black state corrections commissioner, appealed to the citizens of Boston on evening television. His eyes were reading prompter cards, but he made sense. He said what a policeman on duty at Hyde Park High had already told me: People were beginning to see the inequalities that segregation produces; kids belong in schools, not boycotting; kids not in school could become involved in dope, crime, and sex; and they could end up on a long bus ride to Walpole or Bridgewater state prisons, where it wouldn't matter in the least what race or color they were. "Wouldn't kids be better off in school than standing on the corners yelling 'nigger,' and getting involved in drugs and sex?" the policeman had asked.

Tuesday, October 15

Attendance was down. My largest class had twelve students. As usual, the first class of the day lasted only twenty minutes because the buses were late again.

During morning coffee break, Ruby Spriggs, a black faculty member, complained, "It is degrading and humiliating to have to take the guarded bus up the hill." She criticized the NAACP leaders for accepting the Phase 1 busing plan, as well as Garrity and Commissioner Anrig for not considering the South Boston–Roxbury communities. "Probably they are bright Harvard boys from the suburbs," she mocked.

Hyde Park High closed at 11:00 A.M. today. There were eight incidents. One student walking past a group of blacks said to his friend, "I think I've been stabbed. What do I do?" He is in Carney Hospital with a knife wound in the abdomen. Evening television reported the buses had left Hyde Park High with black students waving knives from the rear.

From my homeroom at the end of the day, we could see crowds milling around outside, angry now, since they had heard about the incidents at Hyde Park High. They were moved back by the police. After the students had left, a custodian came in to empty the wastebasket. He told me what had happened at Hyde Park. Angrily he warned, "The police are here now, but they won't always be here. We'll come in here and clean them out."

Governor Sargent alerted the Massachusetts National Guard, who were moved, 450 strong, to armories in and near Boston. An angry Mayor White, who hadn't been alerted to the move beforehand, met with Senators Edward Brooke and Edward Kennedy at City Hall.

Wednesday, October 16

Although a state police cruiser was stationed at the entrance to the Thomas Park circle behind the high school, I expected little violence today because it was raining hard. Attendance was down—only one black and two white students in my homeroom. An intercom bulletin instructed teachers to take umbrellas (potential weapons) from students and hold them until the end of the school day.

When I called parents of absentee youngsters during my free period, they told me they wanted nothing more than to send them, but they were afraid. One woman said, "I don't want to send my child to be killed."

In mid-morning class, a male teacher called me out of my room. He cautioned, "There is a warning of trouble for period 4. Watch yourself." Then he left. There were three minutes left until the bell. I packed my things together while the class continued their values discussion of Paul Zindel's teen novel *Pigman*. Before the bell I cautioned, "Stay out of the corridors and go directly to your classes."

The police in riot helmets stood and watched in the corridors. Assistant Headmasters Tony Gizzi and Jim Corscadden patrolled as a team, walking swiftly, looking to either side of the corridors.

The day passed without incident, although the mood of the school was ugly. Shock waves from the stabbing at Hyde Park High have charged the atmosphere here with violence. A small black boy wearing elevator shoes told me his shoes were good for kicking in a riot.

At the faculty meeting after school, teachers debated what penalty should be given to students found with weapons. Should the punishment for possession of a weapon be as severe as for cutting classes? What constituted a weapon—the long-toothed plastic and steel combs—the picks—the blacks carried? What about a math compass? A pair of scissors? It was decided that the Biracial Parents Council should draw up the list. Anyone found carrying weapons would have to appear with a parent at this council before being allowed back in school. One teacher proposed the installation of a metal detector at the front entrance. The faculty voted to make ID picture cards compulsory for all students, despite possible objection from the black community.

On my car radio going home I listened to black representative Royal Bolling, Democrat from Dorchester, compare desegregation in the South with the North. The difference was ignorance and fear, he said. In the North there were greater economic, sociological, and political differences between whites and blacks. There was no single leader whites and blacks could turn to. Cardinal Medeiros had taken a hard line, but he was rejected by the whites; thus he could serve neither blacks nor whites.

Judge Garrity, perhaps uneasy about rumors of the Mafia blowing up the tunnels under Boston Harbor, now says he will probably forego busing to East Boston. A Southie High administrator of Italian background, who no longer wears ties because "they can be used to strangle," commented, "They better not fool around with those people." A trooper sitting near me in the cafeteria study said, "Over there they'll use bullets."

Thursday, October 17

All was calm today.

I suggested to two white girls in my homeroom, before the buses arrived, that their parents might want to join the high school's Biracial Parents Council, one of the court-mandated committees elected at each school citywide to monitor desegregation and advise the court. The council would, I said, be discussing vital topics like: Is a hair pick a weapon? The girls had no doubt that the combs are weapons, used to scratch. After the bused students arrived, I again suggested the council and its possible watch-dog function. Black students replied: "Nobody is going to take my comb away, weapon or no weapon." The white girls listened, their faces pinched.

On evening TV, black students from Hyde Park High charged that their teachers, assuming black students had not done their homework, would ask more questions of the whites than of the blacks; they would not teach if the whites were not in class and would let the black students sit and talk or look out the window. They demanded that half of the sixty police stationed in the school building be black. They complained that, whereas before just their satchels and bags had been searched, now the staff gave students a body search. As I listened to the allegations of the Hyde Park High students, I reflected how wise Dr. Reid had been when he told our staff to conduct classes whether we had one student or twenty, and by no means to double up with another teacher in order to have more free periods. Sometimes classes had consisted only of tutoring a single student, but teachers always taught. Then, when aides or parents or students complained to the media or in public assemblies that the students weren't being taught, I, at least, suffered no damage to my self-esteem because I knew it wasn't true.

Mayor White on TV characterized Boston as "in the eye of a hurricane," but able to survive. Antibusing advocates are urging a financial boycott— of Cardinal Medeiros's annual charity fund, Filene's and Jordan Marsh's department stores, the United Way—and they'll think of others—to "bring the city to its knees."

Friday, October 18

In my homeroom the black boys sat around my desk and thumbed through my papers. They seem to want to touch and be close. The librarian, Mrs. Betty Rains, said she had noticed this, too. Their parents were not interested, they said, in being part of the biracial council. The white students said their parents would consider it.

In class Dawn protested the use of a multiple-choice question that included "black sheep of the family." She asked what the phrase meant.

Going down to my study assignment in the basement cafeteria after lunch, I noticed black students blocking the staircase, some hanging over bannisters, others as if stationed along the steps. I stood there, telling them to move along. Two white students pushed their way up the stairs. When a teacher brought a trooper over, I continued to the study.

The mood of the study was ugly, but there were two troopers and several teachers in the cafeteria. The young black gym teacher, his arms adorned with silver-twisted snake bracelets, sat with the black students to help relieve tension. Today the troopers commented, "This place is like a time bomb. Any minute it can blow up." The newspapers and media report the schools are calm.

After school I called a parent to ask why her daughter hadn't yet come to school. She replied she was afraid. Her oldest daughter, who bought a ring and had had her yearbook picture taken, was now at a preparatory school. I suggested the parent come to the high school and look around. There were eight police on every floor; I went to school every day, and nobody had been hurt seriously. She ought to save her money for college. The woman seemed very despairing. Another parent, whose daughter had been assigned to my homeroom, was on ABC national news, talking about the effect of busing. She had loved the high school and the teachers, and now her children couldn't go. She felt the church had deserted them; she didn't attend anymore.

In the evening I went to a Drinan-for-Congress party at a home in suburban Newton. Father Drinan arrived shortly after I did at 8:30 P.M. I cornered him almost immediately about busing in Boston, since I had gone there deliberately to politick. He said, "I know all that. Stop nagging me. What do you want me to do?" Then he hustled off. Later he apologized for being abrupt. I said, "I don't mind. I have had great admiration for your honesty in the Congress." He does have real warmth and moves around at a party like a practiced cocktail-party goer.

After his talk later, he asked for questions. I asked his opinion on busing. He answered indirectly, telling how he had received mail from all over the world about busing in Boston. There was another question; then I raised my hand again. Regretting perhaps his abruptness earlier, he singled me out again.

I said, "I'd like you to make a statement on how you feel about the

Supreme Court decision that there should be no busing imposed on the suburbs of Detroit—a five to four decision."

He mentioned METCO (Metropolitan Council for Educational Opportunities), founded in 1966 to bus inner-city blacks to suburban schools, then said, "I don't agree with the decision. It was wrong."

I raised my hand again, but he ignored me.

Later, while the black maid cleared away the dishes, I talked with a member of the Boston Vigil for Peace and Education. Their handout resolves they will demonstrate each school day "until the present tense school situation becomes peaceful." I told her that her group's prayer vigil around Boston City Hall was ridiculous. There had to be a change in the busing plan before there could be peace. She became angry.

Saturday, October 19

There was a march today of 400 or 500, mostly white probusing adults (representing tenant groups in Boston and United Labor Action), from Copley Square in the Back Bay to the State House. They carried huge red banners for the working class, both whites and blacks, and signs against school committeeman John Kerrigan and City Councilwoman Louise Day Hicks: HICKS AND KERRIGAN HAVE TO GO. They handed out leaflets and shouted slogans as they walked with a fury to match the gusting wind and their passions.

There was an antibusing car rally at Kelly's Field, Hyde Park. The cars were decorated with American flags. The speakers talked about "our President Ford."

Sunday, October 20

Tonight Governor Sargent announced that the National Guard would be kept on because there was "fear everywhere you go in the city."

The probusing advocates speak benignly of peaceful integration and peaceful dissent through the courts.

Wednesday, October 23

All white students at South Boston High met in the assembly hall, as ordered by Judge Garrity, but refused to elect a white caucus for the mandated biracial council.

Scuffles broke out in the cafeteria during lunch. There were eighteen suspensions—more, said Assistant Headmaster Harold Goorvich, than in his entire history at South Boston High. One aide received a broken nose from a black student he was escorting to the office. Michael Faith attacked a black student in the office and had to be pulled off by a trooper. Mike will be arraigned in court. What has happened to him between last spring and now?

When I hustled some students along in the corridor, one boy complained, "You're my English teacher and you're acting like a cop."

Jasmin, a black sophomore, came late to class. She got in trouble with a white teacher, she said. "No white teacher is going to put his hands on me." Then almost cross with herself, "I don't even know myself why I acted the way I did. I want to get out of this school." I asked no questions; I felt sorry for her. "People sometimes act," I said, "then have to analyze what they've done to find out why they did what they did."

After school, while the walkers, the white students living in South Boston, waited in the homeroom for the bused students to leave, Kathryn recounted to her classmates how a white girl had come to typing class carrying a handful of her own hair, pulled out by some black kids.

At the faculty meeting at the end of the day, the teachers proposed to Dr. Reid that there should be no more segregated meetings of either black or white students. For the first time Dr. Reid showed annoyance about the court order. "That's the law. You protest to Judge Garrity," he said. "Of course the students get worked up at these meetings."

Thursday, October 24

All black students at South Boston High assembled, as ordered by Judge Garrity, in the auditorium and, while the police peered through the upstairs balcony window at them, elected a black caucus. The white students printed a "White Student Caucus Statement," giving, among their reasons for not complying with the court order to form a biracial committee, "We do not want to comply with the second court order of a biracial committee, when we do not agree with the first court order of desegregation." Some teachers suggested that the students didn't write the statement themselves, but I know the senior class officers. They are clever, and at least one of them — Meg — is a capable writer.

My sophomore class that meets during lunchtime was quite nasty. One threatened to punch me in the mouth if I sent him a conduct slip for coming late. I ignored him. During class I showed the film version of George Orwell's *Animal Farm*, which the students enjoyed, since they enjoyed the book. One boy told me the number of Bluebell's puppies was incorrect; one puppy short. I'm always surprised to find what students look for in a film. He had watched the film and counted the puppies. One student exclaimed, "It's like what's happening in this school with the police."

The white students are becoming, it seems, more hostile. They are openly critical and derogatory.

Friday, October 25

My lunch period class came in subdued, angry that I had sent them cut slips for not returning to class yesterday after the lunch break.

Malcolm, who has given me trouble coming in late with no textbook, complained that the white students "make noises when the blacks come into the classroom, and make fun of us." I asked, "They don't do that in this room, do they?" Then I said, "You're pioneers. It's always hard for the first. Emotions take a long time to change and adjust, and you just have to accept that fact." Sally, the only white girl in class today, commented, "About eight years."

During my study assignment in the cafeteria, the trooper sat down at a bench across from me. He was frustrated that he would probably have to be "sitting around" at South Boston High for the rest of the year when he wanted to "be out on the job investigating cases." The troopers are moved from floor to floor and have been instructed not to talk to the teachers or students because they might get too familiar; but what can you do for five hours? Trooper Richard Jennings, whom I occasionally talk to, came down later, reporting there had been "another pattycake," his term for the student scuffles he contrasted with "a stabbing a day at Walpole State Prison." I am beginning to conclude that many incidents are self-dramatization, and I plan not to magnify them to myself.

After school the walkers were waiting in the homeroom for the bused students to finish boarding the buses. For the first time they were talking with amused interest about some black student. I said, "Who knows? By next year you'll be so well adjusted that you'll be off to Roxbury." Kathryn, who came to school the first day, said, "No way!" During the first scuffle she was chased by a black student with a knife. She had decided not to return and had lifted the phone to call the high school, when her mother told her, "Think it over."

Dr. Reid also, I heard, is beginning to get the idea that South Boston youngsters will never go to Roxbury.

In my homeroom there is now an enrollment of three white girls—Kathryn, Debbie, and Agnes; one white boy—James; and two black boys—

Jeffrey and Martin. Their way of communicating so far is for the black students to write Spanish on the board and translate for the white students.

Mayor White's press information center for rumor control, set up to separate fact from fiction in school rumors for any anxious parent who called, and operating since September 12, closed.

Citizens of South Boston are collecting antibusing signatures for petitions to Senators Brooke and Kennedy.

Saturday, October 26

An antibusing protest caravan of cars drove to Commissioner Anrig's house in suburban Needham. They demonstrated peacefully. One man rang the bell to deliver a message to Dr. Anrig, but there was no response. They left signs behind that read, "Anrig has the intelligence of a flea," and more ominously, "We have a surprise for you."

Sunday, October 27

The *Pilot,* Catholic archdiocesan newspaper, published a sensitive editorial, asking, "Please don't make it impossible." The article criticized the Catholic Racial Justice Conference in Chicago, which had condemned the "white people of South Boston as racists." The *Pilot* said, "It was unjust, and simply not true."

Another motorcade of cars boldly flying huge American flags demonstrated again at the home of Commissioner Anrig. This time a deputy was allowed to enter. Later Dr. Anrig told a newsman, "There are serious flaws with the present busing plan. I've said that over and over in every public speech I've made, but it's the duty of the Boston School Committee to come up with a good plan this December." The constitutional rights of little black children have been denied, he said, and must be remedied by busing.

The police would not allow another contingent of cars through to Judge Garrity's house in suburban Wellesley.

Monday, October 28

Antibusers again rallied at Marine Park, South Boston. On the bandstand was a sign

Welcome to Boston.
The city is occupied
A boycott exists

1774   1974

> A tyrant Reigns
> Law is by Decree
> The people are oppressed

Another sign read: BETTER NOT TO BE EDUCATED THAN NOT TO BE FREE.

My homeroom is steady, but the white students glare when the two black boys take my attention. Today I asked Martin to stop marking on the blackboard. I encouraged, "Be a good boy." Then I remembered how Mr. Fred Van Schyndel, an auto-body teacher, had tried to catch a black student in the assembly hall while the aides only watched. Mr. Van Schyndel called, "Stop that boy." A black aide came over and, instead of helping Fred, told him he didn't like his using the word "boy." Remembering, I caught my breath, but Martin didn't seem offended, and I hadn't intended any offense.

On my way down to the cafeteria study I again saw black students standing on either side of the steps, holding out a foot so the white student had to squeeze by, then kicking him. The troopers noticed me standing and watching, and moved over.

Again in homeroom after school the white boys and girls were hostile, complaining that the black kids left first all the time while they had to wait until the buses had gone. I asked them if they knew why. They were silent. They were upset because the black kids had promised to put on masks and come over to South Boston to haunt them on Halloween. I mentioned that Halloween had originated in Ireland; that the original pumpkin was an Irish potato with the eyes and nose carved out, and that the Irish brought the traditions of Halloween to America after the Great Famine immigration in the 1840s. They were intrigued, and diverted.

Thursday, October 31. Halloween

Dr. Reid called me to his office late in the day. Obviously pleased, he waited while I read a letter notifying me of a $4,000 National Defense Education Act grant for the Irish literature proposal I had written a year ago, placed on "hold" by the Massachusetts Board of Education until South Boston High should be desegregated and just now released. My hope had been to change the self-image of the South Boston youth by giving him a sense of his cultural roots so he could stand strong; I had hoped over the years, perhaps, to create a mini-Irish cultural renaissance in South Boston.

"The letter has no meaning," I said, and losing control, left the letter on his desk and rushed out. It was almost time for the end-of-school final bell. I was able to return to the homeroom for dismissal. Then I waited until I thought everyone had left the school, and left by the side stairs.

But Dr. Reid was still waiting at the front door with a plainclothes detective. He asked what the matter was. Again I said, "It has no meaning." But my control was lost. I left him abruptly, passing the last two cars of state troopers in the schoolyard. There could be no Irish cultural renaissance if the students abandoned the school.

Friday, November 1

During the day I had a chance to observe Thomas Park behind the high school—a five-acre sloping hill of lawn and trees dominated by the white obelisk of the Dorchester Heights Monument. There are just a few police there now. There are no longer dogs snarling at any youngster who mounts the hill to the monument and no police chasing them away.

It's the small infringements on privileges that frustrate the students. For instance, students can't leave the study for any reason—even to go to the lavatory. One girl came up to me for permission to go to her locker. I said, "No." She might get in trouble. I asked, "What if someone jumped you in the locker room?" Worried, she replied, "Those girls said they're going to get me. They called me Linda, and that's my sister's name. That's why I wanted to go." I asked, "What if I had let you go? Then they came up, told me they wanted to go to their locker, too, and I said, 'Yes.' They'd be out there after you."

The state police may be changed in two weeks. A teacher commented, "When the police leave, I leave." A pile of lead steel strips was found near the upstairs landing. The strips possibly came from the shop, since everyone is checked before coming into the school building. Yesterday a piece of bannister was hurled down the stairwell. No one was hurt, but someone could have been killed.

During my senior English class I asked the students to write on the subject, "The Utopian Society." Marlene called out, "It has no blacks." I answered, "You sound like Hitler." I then read the following compositions from two black sophomore girls. I told the seniors, "This is a sensitivity session. These compositions represent the utopian society as two black girls see it. Put yourselves in their place." I read:

Composition 1

Where everybody thinks of each other as equal human beings. Not by race, creed, or color or by how smart you are or how pretty you look. By you being yourself and not what people want you to be. For people to get equal opportunity in finding a job and moving into a new neighborhood where there are mostly blacks or whites or another race. People should think of others as they think of themselves.

Composition 2

A land with no war, no killing, a sweet clean environment. A land where all animals are equal and really equal. A place where everyone is treated alike. Noone hates anyone ever. Noone is looked down upon. Everyone believes in one religion. And everything and everyone is allowed to grow free. And where there is no, absolutely no law.

Another thoughtful composition was by a white sophomore boy from the D Street project in the Lower End.

The utopian society for man would be a world of no hate or cruelty. A place where you come and go to inner space or outer space for no cost at all. Where every one speaks one language and there is no ruler or law makers. Make it a combination of very old times and medieval times and modern times. There would be natural death at around 190 with no change in age after hitting maturity. Drugs and vacinations to conquer diseases and deformities.

Lawrence, a black student in my sophomore class, told me he had been interviewed on radio and had put in a good word for me. He said he had expressed a belief in "equal rights for men and women." Paraphrasing from *Animal Farm*, I commented, "Men and women are equal, but men are more equal than women."

After school I talked with an assistant superintendent at school headquarters, who speculated there would be a change in the South Boston–Roxbury pairing next year because the "politicians have gotten to Judge Garrity and Senator Kennedy."

Sunday, November 3

The media commented on the relative calm in the schools. Some officials speculated on the reasons. School Superintendent William Leary is "hopeful" but "apprehensive." Police Commissioner diGrazia said it's "heavy police presence" calming things down. The deputy mayor said people are getting "weary." I think Superintendent Leary is most correct.

There was another antibusing rally of 8,000 protesters in Charlestown today.

Monday, November 4

Two more white students enrolled in my homeroom. The girls were talking about a black aide, Mrs. Pam. They can say anything to her, they said. It's as if she isn't black. They can say, "I hate niggers," and she doesn't care. She just laughs. I asked, "Don't you think you hurt her when you talk like that?" They didn't answer.

I saw Dr. Reid outside his office today and promised to write an Irish literature curriculum to get the best use from the NDEA grant. He seemed pleased. I felt sorry I had added to his burdens and hoped he could now put me out of his mind.°

Tuesday, November 5, Election Day

Only 5 percent of the white student body came to school: National Boycott Day. It must be like a whiplash to the black students, and black teachers, too, to find the school all black again and think, as they must, that it is a rejection of them—if any of them had thought things were going better.

During my study assignment in the cafeteria I talked with a substitute teacher. Compared with some other Boston schools he had been to, South Boston High is heaven, he said. When he goes around as a substitute in a black school, the students ask him, "Do you come from South Boston?" He answers, "Does every white have to come from South Boston?" If the students won't pay attention to him, he tells them he won't teach them. They retort, "Would you teach us if we were white?"

While we were talking, he had been scanning the newspaper. Suddenly he pointed to the write-up of an incident he had witnessed involving a black substitute history teacher beaten by a gang of boys on G Street near the high school. The black teacher had been walking ahead to the public bus stop when suddenly a can of tonic hurtled at him. A boy kicked the black teacher from behind, scattering his books. Then the gang of boys closed in around him. A car stopped. A white man got out and admonished, "One to one," but did nothing. Uncertain whether to go back for police or to stay and help the black man, now being kicked at as he lay on the ground, the white substitute teacher decided to stay and help. Afterward he urged the victim to press charges. "I want to be safe myself when I walk the streets in Roxbury, and I'd like someone to come to my aid if I were being beaten." He has been assigned to the high school to look for the boys and identify them to the FBI.

I asked, "Describe the boy and see if I recognize him." He said, "He

° My *Curriculum Guide: Irish Literature and Related Arts* was published by the Boston Public Schools in 1977. It was microfilmed by the Massachusetts Board of Education and is available through ERIC (ED 176 331-CS 205 196).

looks like a leprechaun, short, with a beard that goes around his face." I knew him immediately—the boy a trooper had picked out as a leader and troublemaker, someone he'd like to "stuff in a barrel" in a riot, the same boy the black students had pointed out to me from the homeroom window, and one I had been watching.

The sub said, "He'll carry the emotional scars for life." I asked, "Who, the boy?" because they are both victims.

In homeroom I told Martin, "I have a present for you." It was just a plastic bank book cover for his class program, which students must carry with them for identification, but he was very pleased.

In today's national elections, two blacks were elected lieutenant-governors, the highest state office blacks have held since Reconstruction.

Wednesday, November 6

The substitute has identified six of the boys, even though the leprechaun had shaved off his beard. The sub drove around the neighborhood yesterday to identify the boys to the police. When he left the school at dismissal today, he was worried about his safety.

At the faculty meeting after school, Dr. Reid, with concern, discussed the possible reduction of the staff of ninety-nine because there are as yet only 500 students enrolled. The English and social study classes would have to consolidate for purposes of discussion, he said. I inquired, "What's the point of consolidating the classes for purposes of discussion, when the problem is that the students can't read?"

One million dollars had been made available to Boston for desegregation use before the end of June, he told us, and urged us to write proposals for the high school. His own priority was a van for the transportation of black students. He also reported that a hair pick had been judged not to be a dangerous weapon unless used as one.

Dr. Reid is a good headmaster. Yesterday he rode to the soccer game in the school bus with the integrated team from the high school.

Thursday, November 7

Last October, when South Boston residents asked for a line-up of the 200 Boston TPF in order to identify the men involved in the Rabbit Inn raid, police officials replied, "No." They could instead look through the departmental file pictures. Angry residents refused because many officers had grown beards or long hair. Now one month later, 200 photos of the

TPF in jumpsuits and riot helmets will be available for viewing and identification.

One can't blame the students for trying similar tricks as the TPF. The
"leprechaun" looks much younger now without his beard. He sits or lies
on a bench in the cafeteria during study. Father DiPietro, the unofficial
chaplain of the high school, was in today talking to him. It's heartening
to see someone trying to help.

Friday, November 8

I met Captain John Hurley, master in charge of the Hart-Dean
Annex, a few blocks away from the high school, where some of the ninth
grade students of the new South Boston–Roxbury High Paired School Complex have been assigned. He restricts the fifteen state troopers stationed at
his building to the school basement because he thinks they give teachers
a false sense of security.

The attendance at the Hart-Dean Annex today was 138 blacks, 47 whites,
and 7 others; the projected enrollment—745 students.

I prefer a safe building where one can teach without violence.

Right now the high school has to function as a school; and parents,
teachers, and students are afraid. Incidents break out in the cafeteria, as
Dr. Reid said, even with police lining the walls. If some student shoots a
bottle of milk down the table and it lands in another's lap, the student
reacts; there is a confrontation. But, with the police there, the confrontation
doesn't spread.

A police deputy told me, "Detroit has had police protection for ten
years." He was disgusted.

In sophomore English we are reading *The Execution of Private Slovik*.
One black boy, who hasn't read anything yet, said, "I'll read this," and
signed for the book. But there are other students who aren't interested in
executions, soldiers, or World War II, no matter that the criticism of our
government is as pertinent now as then.

Sunday, November 10

Three hundred Lutherans, who had gathered from all over New
England for a convention in Boston, marched downtown in support of
desegregation of the Boston public schools. They should march in their
own communities to have their own school boards take in black students
and their own city halls put up housing for poor blacks and whites to share
in their wealth and good will; but, too many, it seems, can do good only
in the abstract, not when it means giving away a piece of themselves.

Elma Lewis, founder of the School of Fine Arts, Roxbury, made an appeal on WGBH, the public classical music station, not exactly the workingman's station: "All we want is a chance for black students to sit with white students. They don't have to be friends. Just sit beside each other and learn." It sounds so simple.

Monday, November 11

The troopers were cut by about one-third today. I don't feel as steady as before. It's as if we're just learning to walk without support.

The sophomores are still reading *The Execution of Private Slovik*. Malcolm, the last reluctant scholar into class every day, is finally reading. I talked about Slovik and crime. I asked them how they felt about fewer troopers at the school. Malcolm said it didn't make any difference: When he was in the classroom below on last Friday, some white boys shot two arrows at him from Dorchester Heights, but they stuck in the window grill.

After school in homeroom, one of the girls told me she had been on a "mystery ride" last Sunday to Brighton, a part of Boston with a high percentage of college-student housing. The traffic was held up for the antibusing caravan of cars draped with Irish and American flags, horns blaring. Angered at the delay, people yelled at them, "Southie go home," giving them the finger. Then, when the police held back the motorcade so the other traffic could move, their car became separated from the other "mystery" riders and they just rode around. Her father is a Boston policeman. Her mother has sent her to school from almost the opening of school in September. In school today she was wearing a button that read, "STOP BUSING."

The Boston School Committee refused headmasters authorization to permit forty high school students—black and white—from the South, sponsored by thirty-five different community and religious groups in Greater Boston, to talk with Boston students about desegregation and busing. School committeeman John Kerrigan scoffed at the "hoax" perpetrated on Boston's schools by Charlottesville, North Carolina, where two riots broke out while the biracial group of four students from Hyde Park High was there.

Thursday, November 14

I was absent today. Very tired. There were eleven teachers out. The new lunchroom pass program, admitting students to lunch by the color of their lunch pass, was to begin, but was called off because of absentee teachers.

Friday, November 15

Consolidation of sophomore classes has begun. Now I don't have enough copies of *The Execution of Private Slovik*, which I bought at discount and will have to supplement at personal expense.

Martin, who lives at the Columbia Point housing project, came to school wearing a maroon ski cap. I advised him it would be best to take off the cap before someone told him to. He had braided his hair and hadn't done a good job; he couldn't take the hat off, he explained. I encouraged him, "It doesn't matter. You're not an expert yet, but the patterns are attractive." Martin got as far as lunch time, then was sent to the office for not removing his hat. After lunch, Martin was sent down to the cafeteria for cake and milk. He refused. He passed me without looking.

The colored lunch cards for the staggered lunch period were tried today. The plan worked. The lunchroom did not crowd up with students overstaying their lunch break, and students returned to class on time.

I was touched by the concern of a trooper. "The way you run up and down the stairs. Slow down," he warned. "I mean it." The problem is that my classes are scattered over three floors, and on both the north and south sides of the building. If I forget anything, I have to go back up or down the stairs. If I want books from the book room, or coffee, I have to go to the basement. I don't like the students to be in the room when I'm not there because it isn't safe. So I try to keep up with the schedule and run. My nickname among the troopers is "the roadrunner." A trooper asked, "Haven't you ever heard 'beep, beep' as you passed?"

This was a good week with only three reported and one unreported fights. Miss Gertrude Morrissey, guidance counselor and senior class adviser, told of the pain she felt seeing two girls after a fight, one black and one white, being escorted by a trooper to the front office, their arms twisted behind their backs.

The "leprechaun" goes to court on Saturday.

Monday, November 18

In senior English, an all-white class, we talked about color symbolism in connection with a story we're reading, Bernard Malamud's "The Magic Barrel": white for purity, innocence, and hope; red for passion, anger, and danger; black (groans from the seniors) for hopelessness, despair, and death. I pointed out that blacks have to fight color symbolism and color association by the slogan "Black is beautiful." The idea is a cliché, but for

South Boston youngsters, probably new. I read poems of color symbolism from *Hailstones and Halibut Bones,* a children's book that adults can enjoy as well. The section on black I read twice. The seniors noticed.

What Is Black?

Black is the night
When there isn't a star
And you can't tell by looking
Where you are.
Black is a pail of paving tar.
Black is jet
And things you'd like to forget.
Black is a smokestack
Black is a cat,
A leopard, a raven,
A high silk hat.
The sound of black is
"Boom! Boom! Boom!"
Echoing in
An empty room.
Black is kind—
It covers up
The run-down street,
The broken cup.
Black is charcoal
And patio grill,
The soot spots on
The window sill.
Black is a feeling
Hard to explain
Like suffering but
Without the pain.
Black is licorice
And patent leather shoes
Black is the print
In the news.
Black is beauty
In its deepest form,
The darkest cloud
In a thunderstorm.
Think of what starlight
And lamplight would lack
Diamonds and fireflies
If they couldn't lean against
Black. . . .

Wednesday, November 20

From my homeroom window I watched the school buses empty one by one, while an administrator, Mr. Gizzi, checked each student's class program to see whether the student belonged at the high school. As I watched, a girl's piercing screams rose from the front lobby. Troopers began running toward the building. Trooper squad cars blocked off G Street down the hill so the buses couldn't move. Mr. Gizzi stayed with the buses. Over the intercom the secretary's voice cried, "We need help here on the second floor. Please send help to the office." Isolated on the second floor in the front corner of the building, in a small room attached to two adjoining rooms, I again felt the terror of not knowing what was coming from what direction, feeling unable to protect myself or the students from an un-identified danger.

I have never had a desire to flee, just to protect the students, though I don't like the feeling of being trapped. I closed the door, turned out the lights, and told my homeroom students we would stay there and help each other. We waited — two white girls, Kathryn and Becky; James, a small, long-haired white boy; and Jeffrey, a black. In a few minutes the door opened. The gym teacher, carrying an umbrella, stood there with a trooper, their faces anxious. "Have you seen Jane?" they asked, then hurried away. What had happened? Why was the teacher carrying an umbrella? Who was Jane, and where might she have gone, we wondered, but there was no chance to ask. They had already shut the door behind them.

Then came a call for all teachers not assigned to homerooms to report to the front lobby. The call was repeated several times.

About forty minutes later, I was amazed when, from my window, I saw the last bus empty. Several minutes later the intercom announced that the school day would begin. Students should proceed to their first class. Instead, everyone just sat, afraid to move, paralyzed by the unknown.

There were only twenty minutes left in the first class, senior English. The seniors were upset. There had been fights in the South Cafeteria, in the third floor lavatory, and in room 303 on the third floor down the hall, they told me. Because the fights had broken out simultaneously, the seniors felt they had been planned. Just then the intercom requested custodians to report to the third floor lavatory and to the South Cafeteria. "To clean up the blood," the seniors explained.

Although the seniors wanted to discus the fights, I said we would first take a quick, objective, one-word test. I was a little angry. It was better to get their minds focused on something else. In the few remaining minutes, I let them take the Luscher color preference test and talk about the correlation of color with personality. Most of them chose yellow, red, or blue in their color preference. They are a good class.

When I passed room 303 a few minutes later, the students were pushing at the door to get out. A trooper was holding them in. I told two boys at the door to go in and help their teacher. They asked, "Help *her?*" It hadn't occurred to them that she might need their help. Jack Kennedy, administrator, passed me in the corridor, his face white and drained. I stopped in the teachers' room to comb my hair. My face in the mirror looked ghastly. It must take the body time to recover its equilibrium, even after the mind has composed itself.

As I walked around the school, and felt the mood of the school, I thought, "This school is DEATH. The mood of the school is black."

The troopers were happy, however, I was surprised to see. One said, "This is more like it. It gets the old adrenalin going."

My sophomores, a mixed class of black and white students, also wanted to talk about the incidents. They explained how the fight before school had started at the front lobby door. A black girl and a white boy were going through the front lobby—the boy first. He let the door slam on her. She screamed; a black male jumped to her defense, and the fight was on. A trooper pushed a white boy back over a desk and dislocated his shoulder. A black student on the stairs started screaming insults at the white students—among them Michael Faith—and Faith lunged for him. Fights broke out everywhere in the lobby. Students rushed down from the classrooms, or out of their homerooms to aid the secretaries when they called for help on the intercom.

Anne was upset because a trooper in the cafeteria had grabbed a black girl and called her "nigger." "Nobody calls me 'nigger,'" Anne said. "My friend got her comb and got a piece of his red meat."

I played dumb and, for the benefit of white students, said, "But I hear black kids call each other 'nigger,' and they don't seem to mind." Anne said, "Nobody's calling *me* 'nigger.' I don't care who he is." Louis, a black student who has come to school regularly in a taxi even when Atkins called for a boycott, sat back confidently in his fine pressed suit and said, "It's all right when another black person calls me a 'nigger,' but not a white person. Then it's an insult. If I don't know a person and he calls me 'nigger,' I don't say anything until I find out how he feels about me."

Anne said, "I hate this school. I don't never want to come back."

I concluded, "We all need more understanding."

We discussed *The Execution of Private Slovik,* then the class took parts reading a dramatization of *Cool Hand Luke* in *Scholastic Scope,* a high-interest magazine geared for fourth- to seventh-grade reading levels. Some of the white sophomore students had more difficulty reading than the blacks. They enjoyed the play because they can identify with the injustice and violence. There is a trooper in the building who wears tinted glasses that mirror what he sees, like the cop in the play. I can't help making sinister comparisons when I see him.

By the end of the class the students were calm. Once they have had a chance to share their thoughts and feelings about the problems around them—and I am curious, too—they can get back to work. They need their minds directed and filled with other things, but they also need to see how their fellow students feel.

I had expected it would be a bad day, but the teaching in the classes brought a tense calm to the school.

Later in the day I saw the two white girls from my homeroom, Kathryn and Agnes, with an aide, Mrs. Pam. They were shaking their heads "No." After school they told me, "Mrs. Pam would side with the black if it came to white or black."

I mentioned the incidents of the morning and concluded: "Apparently just one incident set everything off; the fear and retaliations were needless; if the first incident hadn't happened, the others wouldn't have followed." Kathryn seemed to listen.

There was a faculty meeting after school. Dr. Reid took the toll of casualties and names involved in fights. Unconsciously he wiped his brow with the classic tragic sweep of his hand and said, "I don't know what we can do. We were all at our posts doing our jobs. But if a youngster will insult and another responds with his fists, there's nothing we can do— except encourage them to watch their mouths and language."

Dr. Reid announced he would like to have an honor roll assembly for sophomores. Mrs. Marie Folkart, the oldest, most respected member of the faculty, raised her hand: She hoped he wouldn't have an assembly. Usually very deferential to her, he disagreed, "I don't know about that. I think maybe we should."

The assembly, the first this year, is scheduled for Friday, a day when attendance is the lowest.

Thursday, November 21

Whites and blacks now enter the school by separate doors.

In senior English we discussed William Faulkner's short story, "A Rose for Emily." As background, I gave a brief biography of Faulkner, mentioning how he had slept in the same bed with a black servant boy until he was in his teens, when his black friend had to move to the floor, and how traumatic the incident had been for Faulkner. I mentioned one of the themes of Faulkner, the crucifixion of the white man on the cross of the black man, and read a section on the Negro from *Light in August:*

> I had seen and known Negroes since I could remember. I just looked at them as I did at rain, or furniture, or food or sleep. But after that I seemed to see them for the first time not as people, but as a thing, a shadow in which I lived, we lived, all white people, all other people. I thought of all the children coming forever and ever into the world, white, with the black shadow already falling upon them before they drew breath. And I seemed to see the black shadow in the shape of a cross. And it seemed like the white babies were struggling, even before they drew breath, to escape from the shadow that was not only upon them but beneath them too, flung out like their arms were flung out, as if they were nailed to the cross. I saw all the little babies that would ever be in the world, the ones not yet even born—a long line of them with their arms spread, on the black crosses.

Friday, November 22

The sophomore assembly convened as planned. Classes filed to assigned seats room by room without incident. Troopers lined the auditorium. The mood was ugly.

Dr. Reid entered from the rear of the hall. As he moved down the center aisle to the stage, he urged the students to stand. He stopped at my class. Martin wouldn't stand because Siegfried, behind him, wouldn't. Then James sat down—later, he told me, because the black kids—Martin and Siegfried—wouldn't stand. Dr. Reid insisted, and I insisted, but Martin refused. Dr. Reid proceeded on. Again I thought, "This school is death."

After the pledge of allegiance to the flag, Dr. Reid lectured on the courtesy of standing when a guest comes to one's home. A few students snickered. When he alluded to the troopers, the black boys in the row behind me yelled, "Get them out." Then Dr. Reid outlined the sports plan for the winter and told the assembly, "We will be together for the year. After that I don't know. But we're here, and we had better make the best of it. And let's have a little courtesy toward one another. Let's treat each other with respect and watch what we say to one another—treat each other with a little kindness. A smile goes a long way if someone accidentally bumps you, instead of pushing back." The students listened respectfully.

Then, as both black and white students crossed the stage to accept their honor roll cards from Dr. Reid, the assembly applauded.

Students left the auditorium room by room.

During the day, girl students traveled the school in roving gangs of blacks and whites, bursting out of classes at any provocation, spreading consternation among the police. "They're in holiday mood," I told the police, dismayed at the prospect of chasing pretty girls back to classrooms.

At the end of the day in homeroom, I told Martin, "Dr. Reid has put his life on the line about desegregation because it is the law. His house in South Boston is guarded. Then he asks you to stand in the assembly, and you refuse. He is your friend, the friend of all of us, and you should know that." James said to Martin, "That's right, Dr. Reid has guards."

A neighborhood crowd chanted at Dr. Reid outside the school this morning.

Saturday, November 23

A librarian at the Boston Public Library in Copley Square told me there are enough kids in the library all day to have school there. He doesn't know where they come from.

Monday, November 25

The number of troopers in the building was increased instead of decreased, contrary to what the troopers had anticipated Friday when I talked to them.

The two black boys—Martin and Jeffrey—and one white girl, Kathryn, were present in my homeroom today. Expecting a boycott, I was surprised to see any white students in school until I learned that a walkout of white students was anticipated at 9:45 A.M., when the parents, now gathering on the sidewalk, planned to walk in to protest the presence of steel combs in the school.

Walkers (or white students) were permitted to leave by the side doors, if they preferred, so as not to be identified and, perhaps, intimidated by the now divided community. In South Boston families once friends are now enemies, since half support the antibusing boycott and the other half feel they have to educate their children.

Television cameras recorded Dr. Reid facing the protesters outside the building in the morning sunshine. He told them, "The black parents have elected no biracial council; the white students have elected none; the white parents have elected none. And frankly, the number of fights last week made me afraid."

In class Anne described the walkout. "The white kids said, 'See you Tuesday, niggers.' If the black kids had a walkout, I'd go, too. The white kids have to go, or they'll get beaten up." Gretchen, a diligent and intelligent white student, who had attended the advanced classes of the New York public schools, listened. I give her extra reading and reports because she is highly motivated. Besides Gretchen, there were five black students in the class.

I left school at the end of the day by the front lobby staircase, passing the Greek frieze laboriously painted by the art teachers in neutral dark brown last September before school began. The frieze had been nightly mutilated with spray paint and daily repaired by the art department, until finally they gave up. The frieze is now hideous: The faces are black blobs, or white blobs, or faceless with black holes for eyes. Looking at them, one teacher shuddered, "The hatred is getting to me."

Tuesday, November 26

The buses came by an alternate route today because of snow and slippery streets. Surprisingly the newspapers printed the exact route of the buses. Attendance was very low.

During my study in the cafeteria, the black students suddenly started whistling, louder and louder. I know of no way to stop forty students from whistling, so I ignored them. The state trooper standing near me shook his head. "We'd have this school under control in two hours," he said, and pointed to his stick. "We won't tolerate disrespect," he said, with finality.

Beginning next Monday, the state police will be gradually replaced by Boston police. The troopers are anxious to be gone. This isn't their problem, they say. How much longer before everyone walks away from the situation? "We're counting on the people of South Boston being too poor to leave," Arthur Alexander, a black teacher, told me.

Wednesday, November 27

The day before Thanksgiving. Attendance was very low: 74 white students, 114 black students. The total number of students registered at the high school this year is 1,814.

I had asked my students, sophomores and seniors, to describe the communities where they had grown up, Roxbury or South Boston, and recreate what it is like to live there. Today we exchanged the community experiences. The students talked about themselves and learned more about one another. Nobody represented South Boston among the sophomores, since Gretchen has lived in the neighborhood only about two years. Nobody grew up in Roxbury; they were from Alabama, Georgia, Florida. For one girl this was her second desegregation experience.

Louis's Composition

Roxbury

I didn't live in Roxbury all my life, but I can describe what it's like. Roxbury is about 80 percent black. The people there, that is most of them, do not go to church. I don't believe in church myself. I think its because they realise that some man, called God, who has never been in touch with anybody on this planet, is not going to give them food and shelter. At least that's my point of view of the Religious aspects of Roxbury.

Socially the people are friendly face to face but keep your guard up. Not too many people in this no. 1 crime-rated area can be trusted. The most competitive and widly played sport is basketball. I know a few dudes, who had potential to be good ball players, turn too cool to play. I'm ashamed to say that the people of Roxbury, which is predominantly *black*, know that we were slaves and are up to this day, the difference being chains or no chains.

Financially Roxbury is made up of poor and middle-class citizens. 3 out of five familys are getting public assistance, welfare, or whatever you might call it. It's not much to talk about, but I live there.

Gretchen's Composition

New York, New York

. . . In every grade I was in, including kindergarten, I had kids of many different nationalities in my class. In my 8th grade class (my last class in New York City) I had a boy from Ecuador, another boy from Canada, two boys from Yugoslavia, one from Greece, another from India, a Chinese girl and Chinese boy, four girls from Puerto Rico, an Italian boy and Italian girl, and two black girls, one of whom I was with since Kindergarten. There was even a Persian girl in my gym class. But, would you believe that I knew no one who was Irish?

Anne's Composition

LaGrange, Georgia, and Roxbury

I was born in LaGrange Georgia and grew up there and in Roxbury. Down South the weather was nice warm hot days and long cool nights. But in Roxbury its cold in the winter and hot in the summer and in

Georgia After School you could go horse back riding and swimming. And there are farms to work on and if you love animals there are animals and the school are good the White, Black kids got along ok. But in Roxbury there is a special time to go riding and swimming and you can't walk around with your shoe's off Because people think your crazy or something. But there one thing that is Pretty about Roxbury the snow the first time I came up to Roxbury and I saw this white stuff on the walk so I was scared too walk on it But Someone told me what It was so I went on. Down South the food is good Because of the special meats like Pig feet and Buttermilk Fresh Eggs all kinds of foods. In Roxbury the people rape, kill, beat up and steal from you and it's too bad for the People that they got Roxbury is a place where I would never want my children too grow up in Because of the violence, and prsitution and dirt in the street. The Prices are so high you can't even Buy Bread and get some change Back. But in the South if your farming it's all right Because food is all over you. But one that Roxbury has a advantage over is the jobs Because in the South jobs are harder to get Because everyone is working for him or herself. But I'd rather live any place else than here because of the enviriment.

Jackie's Composition

Mobile, Alabama

I was born in Mobile Alabama. And that's where I spent most of my life. The schools are different such as — integration school houses. Things are not as bad as people say they are. And the schools have marching bands, cheerleader, majorettes, Mardi Gras, School Dances, track team for both boys & girls. And Later after my 10th grade year I was transferred to a school in Boston. It really wasn't the first time, because I like to travel alot. But anyway schools are different, when you walk along the streets people don't speak to be friendly or nice.

The seniors, all from South Boston, described their community:

Meg's Composition

South Boston, two words that exemplify so many things to the people who live here. It's a place like no other on the map; its history and its people help detail its uniqueness. It means more than a place to reside, it's a place to really live. A togetherness and community spirit are the backbone of this town.

We are a hard working people, who shun charity and we deplore phonies because we know what they say doesn't come from the heart. We are honest, sometimes too honest, but at least you always know where you stand with a "Southie" person. We carry out ethnic heritage proudly. Many people are jealous of us because you see, not many places in the world have the cohesiveness and stamina that we have. Together we decide what is right or wrong. Everyone has a comment to make about South Boston and lately we are burdened with all negative comments, but we never use our heritage or situation as an excuse to get ahead. If we climb the economic or social ladder, we do it the hard way, one rung at a time, not skipping any steps in between.

Our sports, friends, parties and school make up most of our lives. All of the articles I read say South Boston people never leave the community. Oh, I traveled and spent some summers away, but I was glad to come home again.

I am neither a "Honky," "white trash," radical or illiterate. All of these things I have been called.

I am the fourth generation South Bostonian. Due to political differences my great grandfather fled from Ireland.

. . . I would never provoke trouble, but if I am antagonized and become violated of my rights, I will go down fighting.

We will negotiate freely,

But we will not negotiate our freedom. . . .

David's Composition

South Boston as long as I've known has been a pretty good place to live. The people here are always working together to help one another. The people don't want to be selfish, they want to help. And right now these people are working together to help, help stop a man who wants to force our brothers and sisters out of their home town and travel over to a town where the crime rate is five times worse than ours is. I'm not saying there is no crime in Southie, because there is. People in Southie know there is crime in the streets. There is wherever you go, but it is not half as bad as it is in Roxbury. When I was young, I had no trouble at all from anybody. I had fights but the next day that kid and I were friends again and it's the same way all over town. Southie is a good town and still is and always will be no matter what somebody does to force us out of it.

Thursday, November 28 — Thanksgiving Day

There was no traditional South Boston–East Boston football game because potential players at South Boston High School had refused to form a football team. Chippewas, a local town team, played instead. The game was, in fact, an antibusing rally, the proceeds to be used for a legal battle against busing. Five thousand people attended at two dollars a ticket.

A yellow "school bus" was brought onto the field and emptied during half-time: out came a Pig (Police Commissioner diGrazia); a Donkey (Mayor White); a Donald Duck (Judge Garrity). Then the school bus was burned — it took a long time burning. A pizza-eating contest followed, with the Italians feeding their team and the Southies cheating by feeding their Irish terrier as well. Four antibusing leaders were awarded gold medals.

Vacation now until December 2.

Monday, December 2

The state troopers have almost all left, replaced by Boston police, mostly older men in their fifties. They seem depressed. The students have begun collecting in loose groups in corridors to talk, probably to plan. There were two fights. I noticed Michael Faith was back in school.

Tuesday, December 3

There was more collecting in the corridors.

Mr. Joseph Cronin, the retiring secretary of education for the Commonwealth of Massachusetts under Governor Sargent, interviewed on TV, stated there was no improvement in scores when students are bused from one poor section of the city to another poor section. He referred specifically to South Boston and its match, Roxbury.

Wednesday, December 4

Coming upstairs from lunch I noticed a group of troopers collected outside the nurse's room. A black boy had hit a white boy on the head with a hammer in the sheet metal room. The cut required twenty stitches. The nurse said the students give no details when they go to her, just, "I got in a fight." The South Boston students go to the Information Center after school and make out forms on what is happening at the school; it is the greatest grapevine system in the world.

Ted, a white student, came in late to my sophomore English class. He couldn't get through on time, he said, because there were about forty girls, all fighting, outside the second floor girls' lavatory. Through the ventilator in the classroom we could hear the sound of loud quarreling, emotionally charged voices.

We had been reading about ESP. Gretchen had a story to tell about a fortune-teller. Gretchen talks softly. The students couldn't hear. They asked her to repeat her story. She did and they listened, although boys aren't always interested in hearing what a girl who wears glasses and speaks softly has to say.

The class dismissal bell did not ring on time. The angry voices continued through the ventilator. The students asked me about the delay. From the front of the room I could look out into the corridor and see troopers stationed there. Again, it was hard to hold down the fear of the unknown. What was going on? Where? Why not the bell?

The bell rang finally. I went to my administrative duty in the library.

The librarian told me "Red," from Southie, had quieted rampaging boys in the library for her because she asked him to. She thinks he is a great boy, but is misunderstood. The administration is "fed up" with Red. The state troopers have told him they would "get" him outside if he didn't shape up. Apparently he got the message. He wants to go to college.

The black girls involved in the lavatory fight were in the business office filling out incident reports. Then they went home in mini-buses. The school calmed down. A black administrator, Adrienne Weston, predicted trouble on Friday because some girls had received real gouges in their cheeks.

My fifth period class was extra good. They feel that the classroom, where they know one another, is a haven in times of stress. Sally, a white girl and one of my best students, left for suburban Quincy. Her mother was "tired of busing."

After lunch, the white students walked out, milled around outside the school, and demanded a meeting with Dr. Reid.

Friday, December 6

I was trying with difficulty to get the senior class to concentrate on an analogy review in preparation for the SAT exam tomorrow. Finally I asked them what they were whispering about. Brian answered, "We're talking about the assembly next period." I asked, "What is the assembly about?" Brian replied, "We're going to give out gloves." The assembly was a white student caucus convened without parents or teachers by order of Judge Garrity to elect representatives to a biracial council.

Later, while I was using the adding machine in the front administrative office, cheers broke out in the assembly hall, followed by chants: "Here we go, Southie." The secretaries exchanged glances; our hearts fell.

I went to my sophomore English class. There were only three black students. They made up work they had missed. Dawn, a good student who wears a Swahili language button from Attica Prison and attends "Free Africa" meetings, helped me with elective blanks. She told me a nightmare she had had about busing. In her nightmare Dawn had been left behind at the high school. The buses were there, but she saw her father's truck there, too. She recognized his license plate. She went to get in his truck, but it was gone. When she went back to the buses, they were gone, too. She was afraid now she would be hanged—there had been other hangings.

I asked the other two girls if they had any nightmares. When they said "No," I told them mine. In my nightmare I had looked out the school window. There were crowds of hostile people all around the school, as there have been. Then I woke up. I told my nephew Warren about it. He commented, "You wake up and the nightmare is still there."

Again the bell did not ring. Instead, classes were dismissed individually over the intercom. Shortly afterward, there were roars from the ventilator connecting with the auditorium above. The white student body had planned to synchronize their exit from the hall with the bell for changing classes, and overwhelm by numbers — planned, and foiled. They then marched down the school corridors, shouting, "Niggers eat shit." Some spat at the black students. As I started down to the vestibule, a herd of boys charged up the stairs. A crowd is a beast; I fled back up the stairs. I was glad I was not the prey.

"They could have torn the building apart, but they didn't. They didn't want to," Mr. Jim Doherty, an administrator and former acting headmaster of English High School, commented charitably.

Some black boys in the office wanted to leave to see the action, but I refused to let them. I asked a Boston policeman, as he ran past, to order the black students to stay. He slammed the door shut, yelling at them, "What you don't see won't hurt you." But they were caged animals, they complained, becoming angry. Finally I opened the door, then left.

I saw the same black students later in the library at the windows. The angry students outside roared up at the school, "Niggers eat shit."

"Hostile beasts, cannibals," they countered, watching.

"Here we go, Southie," the students chanted from the street. The black boys mimicked them. The intercom ordered everyone away from the windows. It must be terrifying for the black youngsters, realizing they can't leave the building. They must wonder if they can get out at the end of the day.

Lunch was peaceful. There were only black students in school.

A pack of black students clustered at the cafeteria door during my study there after lunch. I didn't know them. One took milk cartons from the storage chest, slipping them in his coat as fast as a magician, so fast I could barely see him move. Another stood snapping a long, plastic ruler at my feet, barely missing them. Mr. Alexander, the black teacher also assigned to the study, stood by, silent. Three troopers leaned casually against a table, appearing not to see. The police assist only if asked to, or if there is a fight. They say the students are not afraid of them; they know they can't use their guns. Then Dr. Reid's bodyguard, Charlie Famolare, a plainclothes detective, appeared at the door. The boys left. When I went around the study cafeteria finally to take attendance, one of the black girls observed, "You look scared."

How can blacks and whites meet peacefully on Monday to go to school? What stories do they bring home to their parents and other students? The hate is building on both sides.

There was a voluntary faculty meeting after school. Dr. Reid explained that he and other members of the administration had left the white students to caucus in the auditorium while they went to Roxbury to meet with parents of the black students involved in the lavatory incident. The students had been told by the Massachusetts Advocacy to write out accounts of what had happened. He was very pleased. He said it is difficult to get the true story. All stories conflict. But if thirty or forty youngsters write out their stories as they perceive what happened, the truth sifts through. Administrators are then able to piece a story together. They had picked out two students for suspension out of the melee, two or three names. He said, "We learn."

The black community, Dr. Reid said, wanted more black police — "a reasonable request" — and would prefer state police. "That is a political question," he said, "but they may have the pull." I believe Dr. Reid would prefer state police, but it is possible to tell what he thinks only by his voice — and then only sometimes.

Mrs. Brenda Houle, a white teacher, reported she had been in the audio-visual room above the auditorium and had heard parents and their lawyer representative make inflammatory statements to the white student caucus. The teachers agreed that the parents by their presence excite the students; some of us have heard parents use derogatory terms. We requested that they stay out of the building. Dr. Reid agreed, but said he needed parents on his side, and from that point of view they were helpful to him.

The adults, we later learned, represented the South Boston Information Center. They had been invited by the senior class officers to address the white caucus about an alleged double standard of discipline at the high school. Finding them in the auditorium when he went there, Dr. Reid informed the adults and students that there would be no discussion between them under the auspices of the school until they met the judge's directive to form a biracial council. After addressing the white student caucus, Dr. Reid then left for Roxbury. When he was gone, the adults returned to the auditorium, and the caucus became a pep rally.

Today the outlines of the school department's citywide Phase 2 desegregation plan were published. According to this new "program preference plan," dividing the city into six zones, almost twice as many children will be bused (from the present 17,000 up to 31,000), but there will be parental choice of learning styles at all levels and voluntary suburban involvement. Italian mothers from East Boston, linked with Roxbury in the same zone, vowed on TV their children would not be bused. Their voices were angry. They warned they would not go through the tunnel. Apparently the tunnels under Boston Harbor to East Boston and the airport will be the focus of their resistance. They said they had visited the schools in Roxbury and that they were "dumps." All Boston schools are dumps. But do you have to be bused to a dump?

Monday, December 9

There were informal "meetings" all weekend in Roxbury, foreboding a bad day.

My white senior English class was too distracted to work on *Antigone*. There had been a fight in the girls' locker room — a basement room with dead-end corridors of lockers. A black girl hit a white girl on the head with a padlock. The blood was pouring down her face. One senior asked to leave class because administrators were taking incident reports in the hall. They were upset, too, about the SAT exam on Saturday; Meg, who had taken the exam at Northeastern University, complained that the professor next door was shouting about South Boston and desegregation. The SAT proctor left the room to warn him, but the voice kept up the strident diatribe. Meg couldn't concentrate on the test because she was listening to what the professor was saying. Another student, rather than deal with his emotions, I suppose, just guessed at the answers for part of the reading material dealing with race relations.

The class denounced the black aide, Mrs. Pam: She listens to them, then goes back to Freedom House and tells everything. She is a snake and can't be trusted. When there is a fight, she sends the black kids to "go help your sister," or she pulls blacks aside, pretends she will take them to the office, then talks to them. Mrs. Pam will be on the defensive now; she can no longer be effective with the students.

Dr. Reid started everything on Friday, they said, when he addressed the white caucus. I asked, "What did he say?" Brian answered, "He said, 'Peace on earth, good will towards men.'" I then told them how Dr. Reid had supported the Southie students at the sensitivity session for teachers last spring when we were discussing the projected desegregation order and the assets South Boston High might contribute in the process. "I think we're forgetting the greatest thing in favor of busing here," he had interjected, "and that is the basic generosity and charity of the South Boston youngster." I told the seniors, "Dr. Reid was the first one to mention it." The class was thoughtful, then Meg said, "You're right." She agreed they could be more charitable.

My black sophomore students asked me facetiously if I had my whistle. White students are now carrying whistles to summon help, if needed.

When I went to my administrative duty in the library at the end of the day, I found some South Boston parents had usurped it, ordering the librarian to leave. In turn, she took away the saucers they had removed from under her plants, telling them they couldn't smoke in the school. Some parents asked to be shown the lavatory. They asked, "Is it safe?" and asked the policeman to watch them down the hall.

"I thought they weren't coming in anymore," I commented to Jim Corscadden, assistant headmaster. He answered, "They walked in the front door."

A faculty meeting had been scheduled in the auditorium after school to discuss the problems of the day and to collate information on the incidents. Instead we found parents and some students had taken over the hall. Everyone sat; nobody spoke. While we waited for Dr. Reid, one parent, a policeman, told me significantly that he knew things I didn't know. "We should have come in here at the beginning of school and cleaned them all out," he said.

Eventually some teachers tired of waiting; others left in protest, the same who had turned up their noses earlier when Tom Boussy, faculty senate president, reasoned, "These parents are scared for their children's lives and for their homes and community." This faculty boycott proved to be a tactical error.

After school I called Northeastern University and complained to an academic dean about the administration of the SAT test last Saturday. He apologized.

Tuesday, December 10

There was a milk-and-food fight in the cafeteria at lunchtime. Two black students and one white were suspended.

There was a riot at Walpole State Prison. Prisoners in minimum security took two guards and a medic hostage.

On TV a smiling, newly elected Governor Dukakis announced he would appoint black Model Cities administrator Paul Parks to the post of secretary for educational affairs. Parks immediately announced he would work on desegregation of the city and on decentralization of the schools. It's a red flag to the city now. Where's his sensitivity?

Wednesday, December 11

The state troopers were at Walpole State Prison. Only Boston police were on duty in the high school.

Before class I saw Eileen, one of my seniors. She had a black eye from the locker-room incident on Monday morning. She was crying. She had been suspended, she said; it wasn't fair.

After my first class, I was free. I mimeographed some spelling papers, carried books from the third floor to my classroom on the first floor, then went back upstairs to pick up my papers just about bell time. I was walking just outside the front office on the second floor when I heard screams and saw black male aides running down the corridor in the opposite direction, their faces like staring gargoyles. I pushed my way through. Michael Faith was lying motionless on the floor between the auditorium doors and the front staircase. Frank, a classmate, started to cry. Dr. Reid put his arms around another. Girls stood at the door of the front office and screamed at the black students there, "You dirty pigs." The black students looked non-plussed. I shut the office door. They didn't object. I then went to the guidance office and asked Mrs. Joan Dazzi, a guidance counselor, to call an ambulance. Students were running up the stairs to see what had happened. I told them to go back and continued down to my sophomore class on the first floor. A voice on the loudspeaker ordered the white students to leave the building. One boy took a black billy club from his locker outside my classroom and hid it under his jacket. I rapped on the fire-door window, pointing toward the club. The policeman looked at me quizzically through the glass, and the boy walked on.

Only the black students—Dawn, Louis, and Jackie—were in the classroom. Jackie had her head down. She had been crying. "Why are we at South Boston High?" they asked. They didn't want to be. I told them my feelings on the busing plan: that, with eighty institutions of higher learning in the Boston area, more than any other area of the country, with all the schools of education in the city, I couldn't understand why a better desegregation plan hadn't been designed. Schools should be integrated, I said. The alternative was prisons like Attica, 75 percent black.

What had happened in South Boston wouldn't happen in the South, they said. They all agreed that the Southern cops, black and white, wouldn't stand for any nonsense, from blacks or whites.

The detectors didn't detect knives, they said. They'd seen blacks and whites with knives. I asked, "Why didn't you tell someone, me or a black aide? When you keep silent, like today, you're the ones that get hurt." They answered, "The aides are afraid themselves. They see a fight, but they're too afraid to do anything."

Dr. Reid interrupted on the intercom. Michael Faith had been stabbed in the abdomen; his condition was critical, but stable.

I looked out the window and saw the white boys coming around behind the school and down the embankment, then heard them banging on the outside door at the rear of the building, now locked. I asked the police in the corridor to send for more help, and turned out the light in the room. While we were sitting there in the dark, a big white boy came running to the door. For a few moments he stood—suspended animation, framed in the doorway—looking at us confusedly, then he ran on in "mad pursuit." We were not the enemy. I was reminded of John Keats's "Ode on a Grecian Urn." Forever will he run, but he won't catch up with the enemy.

We talked on. There were men who pretended to slit their throats when they rode by in the buses, and gave them the finger, they said. "And these are grown men! That's so childish. My mother wouldn't let me do that." I said, "I'm sorry. I just hope you don't give up hope." I mentioned the aide who predicted the whites and blacks would eventually tire of hurting each other; then they would quit fighting.

A half hour later, the students asked to work on spelling. They had been working only a few minutes when Detective Charlie Famolare, Dr. Reid's bodyguard, came to the door with a Boston policeman holding a walkie-talkie. Their faces were afraid. I had never before seen Detective Famolare with fear in his face. I was afraid then, but just said, "Let's go."

All the black students had been moved to three rooms on the second floor at the center back area of the building, the safest side, to wait for police reinforcement so they could leave. A mob of mostly young people had tried to storm the building and had been barely held off. The school buses, too, had tried twice to get through the mob, then turned back.

Mr. Van Schyndel came by and walked upstairs with us. The youngsters were calm. They are already philosophers.

The teachers' duty was to keep the black students in the assigned rooms and away from the windows so they would not see outside and become hysterical. Some students played cribbage and Scrabble; some sat or stood quietly; others played hangman at the blackboard with Mary Colvario and Sue Diamond, teachers. Some became sick, asking for aspirins. I brought magazines from the library to them. I gave Malcolm some gum. He chuckled as he dropped his gum wrapper into an abandoned TPF helmet.

I looked out the library window. The kids were throwing rocks and bottles at the police. I saw a woman throw a rock at the TPF. The crowd cheered. They rocked a police car until it turned over, the windows broken. A woman told them, "It's tax money property anyway. Do what you want." A teacher aide from the community knelt on the windowsill and directed the crowd outside to "get" the police. One teacher aide, who was supposed to be inside earning $2.80 an hour, was arrested.

From the high school steps City Councilwoman Louise Day Hicks addressed the mob: Let the blacks go back to Roxbury, let them out of the school. The mob refused. They took up the chant: "Bus them back to Africa." She looked scared. The crowd chanted, "Here we go, Southie," and sang patriotic songs. At the front window on the second floor I met City Council President Gerald O'Leary for the first time. I asked him, "Do you think we'll get out of here alive?"

The teachers ate with the Boston police downstairs in the cafeteria and carried milk, bologna spuckies, and cake to the students in the classrooms. Dr. Reid, attempting a smile, mingled a little with the teachers and police in the cafeteria. The angry crowd outside did not go home for lunch.

After lunch a rumor circulated that the longshoremen had left their pickets and had come over carrying chains. The crowd had already swelled to 700, later to nearly 1,700, monitored overhead by a circling helicopter, as on the first school days in September.

At the height of the riot, I saw two black boys and a girl running up to the third floor. I told them, "Come back. You'll be safer down here." The girl came down immediately; one boy came down shouting obscenities at me; the other boy, Siegfried—a well-built boy, over six feet tall and weighing about 200 pounds—came down, put his arm around me and squeezed me. I was afraid because I was alone and didn't know them.

At one o'clock the faculty convened in the auditorium to vote on whether to close the school for the rest of the week. Just as Dr. Reid arrived, the teachers got up to leave. He seemed bewildered, as if we had become part of the whirling mindlessness of the day. I told him we were going to a smaller room for privacy. The room was at the front of the building, adjoining my homeroom. A black policeman stood at the window, looking out. Girls screamed up at him, "We'll get you out of there, nigger." He defied them with snorting anger. Eventually someone pulled down the window shades.

By now the state police had arrived and formed lines on the south side of the building. I watched from my window. They started to march forward—like a liberation army. Their method is to move a crowd firmly back with their sticks crosswise in front of them. The crowd moved back. Then the Boston mounted police charged the crowd. I opened the window. A black teacher commented, "She wants the audio." Kids were at the windows and on the roofs of the houses across the street. They had shiny objects in their hands, possibly beer cans. The teacher observed, "It's like Selma, Alabama. All they need is dogs and hoses to wash the people into the ocean." Again, "This is school disintegration, not integration."

With a tremendous roar the buses, front and side windows smashed, pulled up the hill in front of the school. The state troopers marched out to the buses. A white man checked the bus, a black man got in one. Then, while everyone waited in front, the black students slipped out the side door, down the precipitous Golden Staircase on the south side of Thomas Park circle to the buses waiting under heavy guard on a street level below. The last girl down fainted.

As I went downstairs, a teacher came over and leaned against me. She said she was sick. Another told me later she had cried. A policeman offered me his cap and police jacket. He asked, "How would you like to wear that as a target?" I declined.

All was calm on the fringes of the crowd. An ambulance came for a girl hit by a flying rock. Mrs. Dazzi, the guidance counselor who rode with the girl to the hospital, said she was afraid the people would turn the ambulance over. They rocked any vehicle, they were so angry.

As I was standing outside, I heard a child run up to his mother to tell her that his father had been taken away in a paddy wagon. The mother said, "A decent, peace-loving man." The boy explained, "The policeman told him to move. He swore, and the police chucked him in the wagon." The mother said, "There goes his job. A police record. He's a night watchman."

As I got into my car, a bird flew over. I ducked. Even birds alarmed now. Jack Kennedy, "Mr. South Boston," supported himself against a car and watched.

The school is closed now. The parents have what they want. Dr. Reid was too exhausted from the activities of the day to report to the School Committee after school.

TV called the day "frightening." Eyewitness News, Channel 4, aired an interview with four of the students at Freedom House in Roxbury. Siegfried, the only one I knew because of the incident at the staircase during the riot, complained about "harassment" at the high school. Another girl from the Annex simpered shyly she was "scared" because there were only "125 of us and all those people," an attendance count not even I am aware of on any given day. A third student, struggling with a statement he could hardly read, complained about the lack of teaching. I resented the fact that they appeared to have been coached in their comments.

Thursday, December 12

Although the faculty of Roxbury High School had voted to keep their school open, all schools forming part of the South Boston–Roxbury High Paired School Complex were ordered closed by school Superintendent Leary. Instead about 300 teachers met at 9:00 at a neutral site in Dorchester. The meeting, which had been designed to be constructive, exploded over Michael's stabbing. Ruby Spriggs, a black teacher, stood and said, "He got what he deserved." Mr. Alexander, jumping up, agreed: That boy had followed him to the lavatory tormenting him. There was a roar of anger. In five minutes, I knew, the block captains in South Boston would spread Ruby's statement like wildfire.

One of the four male aides from South Boston leaped to his feet, yelling, "If Michael Faith got what he deserved, I'll see that you get what you deserve." Another black teacher from Roxbury rose. Nobody wanted to see a child hurt, black or white, she said.

I was shaking when we broke for coffee.

During the break, the teachers haggled over Ruby's remark: Ruby had said what she meant; she didn't mean what she said; she made a mistake. I exchanged nightmares with another teacher, Walter Silva: He dreamed he had been caught in a fight in the school corridor and the Ku Klux Klan wouldn't let him get away. Mary Colvario described her recurring dream — more motif than nightmare: Always she was driving her Volkswagen, filled to overflowing with students, through unlit streets in unfriendly neighborhoods. As the dream ended, she was still on her way to some undesignated place; she never arrived.

After the coffee break, Ruby addressed the teachers at the mike in front of the room: She had not meant what she said. However, chronic troublemakers should be suspended. Michael had been suspended three times before. Whites had to understand the position of the black child who feels outnumbered and cornered. Mr. James Poor, a teacher, shouted out, "Don't try to change it now. You said it."

Roxbury High teachers petitioned to reopen on Monday. No one objected. Teachers also agreed that verbal assaults should be treated as "incidents" and a record kept for reference.

When we left for lunch, some black aides remained behind, crumpled in their seats. Mr. Van Schyndel paused and held the shoulder of one of them.

Stunned, I told Joanne Leonard, teacher, as we left, "I'm picking up vibrations." She asked, "Polarization between black and white?"

While the teachers met, Dr. Reid was being interviewed by national media. His eyes hollow and black, he seemed barely able to summon the strength to talk.

> *Question:* Do you think school can continue this year?
> *Dr. Reid:* It's possible. Everything is possible. In education you live with the hope and expectation of change for the better.
> *Question:* Did you expect this would happen at the beginning of the year?
> *Dr. Reid:* No, sir.
> I had a meeting with the Student Council last week. They told me if there was a policeman for every student in the school, there would still be fights. And these were the *kids*. There is too much hate in people. Tell me how to get rid of the hate, and we're in business. I don't know where it comes from. It doesn't come from the educative process.
> The teachers are discouraged; some are disillusioned, but all are willing to try again.
> *Question:* Will you quit?
> *Dr. Reid:* No.

Dr. Reid has been made the scapegoat for everyone's sorrow and anger. Who wants to fight the crowds again; or to open for the few who will come; or to teach empty classes? We all need a rest, but he does especially.

Tom Atkins, representing the black plaintiffs, said, "The schools will be opened to all—blacks and whites—or closed down completely." It is a battle for the high school now.

Atkins blamed the riot on the white caucus pep rally and accused the white students of carrying whistles to organize fights: one whistle for the first floor, two for the second, and three for the third—a code I didn't know. Dr. Reid, holding a bag of confiscated whistles, had told us at a faculty meeting, "I personally have no objection to a young lady carrying a whistle if she feels it will help maybe."

Atkins has requested Judge Garrity to outlaw all racial epithets at the high school; to station fifty state police inside on each floor; outside to ban all gatherings of five or more people to a distance of 100 yards from the school and 50 yards from the school bus route between 7 A.M. and 5 P.M.; and to exclude all but students, school department, and city and state personnel from South Boston schools.

Friday, December 13

A more relaxed Dr. Reid opened the meeting of teachers and aides. "People say things under stress," he began. "We should understand. We should deal with our problems as a family." Applause.

Representatives of the U.S. Justice Department spoke then before leaving for the NAACP plaintiff meeting with the black teachers downtown. Mr. Martin Walsh, director of the department's Community Relations Service — "the eyes and ears of the court," reporting back to Judge Garrity — mournfully chewing gum while he talked, told us he had monitored desegregation all over the country, but this was the most difficult case the Justice Department had ever encountered. There are always those who are opposed to and those who are for desegregation, he continued, but there is always the middle ground to rely on, those who will go along with the law. In this case there was no middle ground. Support must be given to those parents willing to make the sacrifice of sending their youngsters to school despite fear of reprisals from the community.

Jim Doherty, administrator, suggested that failure to adjudicate on the thirty-eight cases in the South Boston Court and the twelve cases in Roxbury Court was the cause of the increase in violence. "Why has nothing been done?" he asked.

Captain Arthur Cadegan of station 6, South Boston, spoke next. He began by reviewing the chronology of Wednesday's riot, commenting, "You have to consider the topography of Dorchester Heights hill. The entrance is by G and 6th Street." He was notified of trouble at 9:30. It would take an hour for the state troopers to reach the high school from Walpole State Prison. They had a choice of waiting for help, or trying to get the black students out then. Some thought the students should stay all night, but then the crowds would only grow. They decided to wait for help.

The police first had to evacuate the students in the radius of the high school — first the L-Street Annex, then the Hart-Dean Annex, then the

Gavin Middle School—before the trouble spilled over, and so that the police in these schools could be released for the high school. The Boston police in the building were new to the high school. They had determined not to wear helmets in the school. When the trouble started, they couldn't go out to get them; if they went to their cars, they would be noticed and their cars demolished. They had to stand in the open with no protection.

While the Boston police waited for the state police reinforcements, the crowd grew and fed on its emotions. There were all kinds of rumors: "100 dock workers with chains had left work and were on the way over!" No way. Do you think they're crazy? "They would blow up the bridges!" Go ahead and try. No ammunition. Parents saw the ambulance stretchers coming out of the building and thought there were still people inside getting hurt. But the wounded came from the street, were treated in the school, and were brought out to ambulances.

"Try to reason with a mob," Captain Cadegan continued. "You can't play with people's emotions. If someone gets hurt, there is retaliation against the police, whether guilty or not." The police didn't like to arrest and prosecute, especially women, because they had to go back to that community afterward and work with the people. He was glad of one thing, though: Dorgan's burned-out restaurant, where the loose brick missiles had come from, was by now almost demolished.

Contrary to speculation, the buses that came up the hill to the front of the high school were not decoys. The Golden Staircase was the alternate route of escape. If the black students had been "mouse-trapped" there, Captain Cadegan said, the police might have been forced to shoot. "However, the good God was watching, because we didn't have to shoot. The next time we may not be so lucky."

The police remained late Wednesday, until after 6:00 P.M., to get rid of the damaged police cars. As soon as they left, the streets were deserted. "The uniform attracts. I don't know. Maybe television is too dull now," he said.

The community appeared quiet, but before voting to reopen school, the faculty should consider the consequences of their actions, Captain Cadegan cautioned. "Even if kids came to school in bikinis, they could still fight with furniture and chairs if they wanted to. By coincidence, only the white kids have been hurt."

The teachers voted: No school Monday. We would plan with parents to reopen.

In court Judge Garrity turned down a request by the NAACP attorney to give evidence in secret. Garrity also suggested showing a police videotape of the riot: "You can't intimidate a videotape," he commented.

Questioned by Judge Garrity, Mayor White, in court as a defendant in the case, said, "I don't think South Boston High School should open on Monday. In fact, it should be closed permanently."

Walkouts were widespread in the Boston schools today.

Saturday, December 14

There was a March Against Racism down Commonwealth Avenue to the Boston Common today. Motorcycle police waited in alert in the alleys behind the avenue. Marchers, some carrying effigies on stick of City Councilwoman Louise Day Hicks and President Ford, shouted, "Integration Yes, racism No: Hicks and Kerrigan have to go." One tattered white cloth, symbolically torn, went by with an anti-KKK chant.

The first contingent of the parade followed the approved route down Commonwealth Avenue—the parade route of General George Patton and President John Kennedy; of the Boston Marathon and the Easter Parade. Following a scuffle between the police and marchers in the vanguard, the second contingent of the march proceeded down Commonwealth Avenue. Then Senator Bill Owens tried to lead a dozen supporters down Boylston Street, although his permit had been canceled because of protests by shopowners. He was stopped bodily by a Boston police sergeant and detoured to the sidewalk.

The challenge was to the affluent, since the Progressive Labor party predominated in the march. Their literature is against the division of the black and white working classes, the poor schools of Roxbury *and* South Boston, Judge Garrity and the discriminatory busing plan; against the Supreme Court decision on Detroit that freed the suburbs from desegregation; and it is for the financing of public education by statewide taxation, rather than by local property taxes, subject to the economic barometer of the city.

Senator Bill Owens spoke last at the rally on the Boston Common. He had been attacked by the police and Mayor White that morning, and denied access to Boylston Street on the edge of his legislative district, one of the wealthiest, most affluent streets in Boston, Massachusetts, perhaps the whole United States, he said. He challenged Mayor White, saying the insurgents in the city would dictate policy and would take the leadership positions they were entitled to. They would decentralize the school system.

Senator William Bulger from South Boston addressed his contingent from the steps of the State House. He accused Atkins of making Michael Faith responsible for his own stabbing, and recommended that Atkins address himself to the problems of his community—to the violence.

Sunday, December 15

Today was the last of the rallies against forced busing. Between four and five thousand people met on the Boston Common. A member of ROAR (Restore Our Alienated Rights) said, "We don't have to go out of the city for our supporters."

Mrs. Faith—Michael's mother—spoke: "Judge Garrity does not allow us into his courtroom. I never heard of Judge Garrity until he made his fateful decision. He seems to have more power than any dictator who ever crawled the face of the earth." She continued: "When my son was stabbed, Judge Garrity's reaction was to heap more indignities on South Boston. It is now a federal offense to utter a nasty word. . . . a federal offense to breathe. We will breathe long after he is dead. . . . With our last breath, we say to you [Garrity]—Never!"

Monday, December 16

The faculty returned to South Boston High today. Fifteen state troopers were already on duty. The parking lot was almost empty, many teachers still afraid to drive to work. As I went up the lobby stairs to the office to sign in, I passed the Greek frieze along the front staircase, reminder of last Wednesday's hatred; later the bright, unfinished murals on the third floor, sign of the hopefulness of many.

Three black teachers returned: "The brave ones," a black aide said. Ruby and the teachers who testified for the NAACP did not.

The nurse asked me, "How can you guarantee to parents the safety of their kids?" Nobody feels safe now. The school may not open to students again. That is the alternative the community now faces.

At 8:00 A.M., the faculty met with Dr. Reid in the library. He told us to complete all data on student records. Then faculty divided into problem-attack groups for lobby safety, the biracial council, parent communication, or student council. I chose to work in the parent-communication group.

Later, when the English department met, we discussed whether to begin electives in January. The sophomores know their classmates and feel safe with them; they probably would not want to change teachers. Senior English classes are no problem, since there are only whites in the classes.

Josephine Murphy, teacher, talked about last Wednesday, how she had been caught in the first floor lobby when the students started out the front door to the buses. Someone panicked. The kids stampeded back, screaming, books flying everywhere. She saw blood on the floor from the kids hurt in the riot outside and, believing the crowd outside had broken through, blanked out.

When I went to get the class register from my homeroom, two teachers were there talking with an FBI agent. "But don't tell anyone you saw me talking to him," one said. "I don't want anyone to know I gave information." I didn't ask her about whom, since I didn't trust myself to keep silent.

In defiance of the court order of October 31, the School Committee refused to approve by majority vote and submit to the federal court the desegregation plan developed by the school department staff—due today. Their lawyer filed a copy with Judge Garrity to avoid contempt of court citation. School Committee members Paul Tierney and Kathleen Sullivan urged endorsement so that the board, rather than outsiders, could control the design of the final plan.

Tuesday, December 17

I called more white parents to invite them to the parent-faculty meeting at the high school the following evening. One man said he had a daughter at the high school. She had a heart condition and would never be able to work. He just wanted her to have the experience of a high school education—a prom, yearbook, graduation. "If she doesn't make it this year, I'll forget it. I'll get the money for a private school for my son next year. I worked nine years in Roxbury as a street cleaner, and I'll never let him go there." Then, "Oh, my God! My nieces and nephews!" The whole of South Boston is intertwined with relationship like the threads of a fabric. He said, "I ride in the ROAR marches every time. If they outlaw ROAR, we'll just go underground."

One mother had a daughter at Roxbury High School. She was "scared to death," she said, until the daughter came home safely last Wednesday.

Wednesday, December 18

The parents met at South Boston High in the evening. There was a brawl atmosphere in the lobby hall when I arrived, but in the classrooms small, quiet groups were discussing. The adults in the lobby demanded a general meeting in the auditorium. I insisted, "It's better to sit in small groups and talk about the problems. There will be five teachers in each group of parents and a range of views." "Just the liberals," they answered.

"Let's go to the ROAR meeting." But they stayed for the meeting. At 8:45 P.M. some left, unsatisfied. Others stayed until 9:30.

The concerns of parents in my group were that the blacks have used violent tools: lock, hammer, knife; whites haven't. The white kids have gotten hurt, not blacks. The aides are afraid; some are prejudiced. The language from some students is foul. One parent was worried about unemployment and discrimination against whites in civil service jobs. Another asked, "What's wrong with the system that my child can't go to school without being fingerprinted and wearing an ID badge?"

After the meeting I saw a teacher from South Boston with a glass of water in her hand. "I can't believe this," she said. "I'm taking a tranquilizer."

Two parents signed for the biracial council.

Thursday, December 19

I met Detective Famolare on the steps at the high school. He confirmed that there had been a "hit" list last Wednesday; that Michael was not the "hit." An aide told me that Michael had been warned that day about the list—to scare him or to put him on his guard?

The faculty met with black parents in the afternoon and evening at Roxbury High. The Roxbury community looked desolate as we rode through: burned, hollow building-shells everywhere. Yet the area has a vitality, like Roxbury High School, where we found a few students playing rock music records and dancing in the auditorium.

At the meeting with the black parents, the teachers sat in front of the room and answered questions. The mood of the black parents was subdued, not hostile, as we had thought it might be.

One woman said she could never go through that experience of Wednesday again; another, crying, said her son didn't want to go to school at all now. They complained that more blacks had been suspended than whites; another that she had been notified by a lawyer, not the school administration, that her daughter had hit someone with a lock. One woman said her son's nose had been broken as he left a classroom, yet people said it was only the whites who were getting hurt. They were worried about their children's grades and wanted to ride the buses and visit the school, but had been told that parents could visit only by permission of Judge Garrity. One man was anxious for the students to carry ID badges, since he'd heard kids at Freedom House talking about how they had gone to South Boston High at the beginning of the year in order to make trouble. Some parents asked about the evening classes at the high school, whether people from the community could get into the school and hide a weapon.

The meeting ended abruptly when a woman emotionally charged the Boston police with destroying their center at the McCormack School and desecrating their pictures of Martin Luther King; the Boston police couldn't be trusted to protect them. A black teacher from South Boston High then detailed how his desk in the auditorium had been defaced at night and smeared with spit, and feces dropped into the desk drawers. A black Youth Activities Commission (YAC) aide warned finally, "The school is dangerous."

When I returned to South Boston High, three white boys yelled from the sidewalk, "If we don't get the niggers, we'll get the teachers. We'll get the nigger lovers."

Judge Garrity decided not to hold the Boston School Committee in criminal contempt because their vote against the school department Phase 2 plan appeared to stem from honest fears for the safety of the students involved.

The U.S. Circuit Court of Appeals in Boston upheld Judge Garrity's June 21 finding of *de jure* segregation in the Boston school system by design of the School Committee, saying, "In the light of the ample factual precedents in the Supreme Court, we do not see how the court could arrive at any other conclusion."

Friday, December 20

I made out grade sheets today. It was very difficult to be fair because some students had been prevented from making up missed tests when the school was closed before the end of the marking term.

There was another meeting with South Boston parents in the morning. One parent said, "We don't want any biracial council because Judge Garrity ordered it." I urged a council on the basis that the problems we were then discussing—like "What is a weapon?"—could have been discussed three months ago; and that the biracial councils could be another way of exerting pressure on students to behave if, for instance, it were determined that suspended students had to appear before the council before returning to school. A parent deflected my appeal, however: "The issue is safety, not councils. Let's get on to safety. We should be putting our energy into changing the law."

Another woman complained, "I was all for making desegregation work until last Wednesday, when I was chased down the street by a horse." Some of us laughed. It's good they can still see the funny side, too.

Meg came in with make-up work. She seemed on the edge of nervous exhaustion. She talked of the Wednesday riot and of a TPF nicknamed Serpico, who "went crazy," climbing over a car to "get" someone and knocking another man, shirt ripped, to the ground, and beating him unconscious. The police wore no badge numbers; that scared her. She mentioned Atkins's distortion of the purpose of the whistles. She told me, "The kids feel that only our blood has been spilled." I described the faculty meeting with the black parents the day before, the parents who had cried, and the one who said her son doesn't want to go to school anymore and asked, "Why do they hate us so much?" I told her the school might close, to get the word around. She promised.

The faculty assembled for the last meeting before Christmas vacation. "Last year at this time," Dr. Reid recalled, "teachers were disgruntled about the proclamation of a 'Harry Yucker Day' celebration on Dorchester Heights"—a holiday named after a mythical, Pucklike student character who occasionally urged students to cut classes or skip school and go drinking and merrymaking. This year, we didn't need to be reminded, there was no celebration, not even a song.

Sunday, December 22

NAACP President Tom Atkins criticized the Boston police for giving $1,000 to ROAR. At best they were ambivalent about carrying out their responsibilities, he said; they could possibly be prosecuted.

Monday, December 23

Atkins declared Boston desegregation "on schedule," explaining that the process takes "from a year, and in some instances, as long as four or five or six years. In one instance ten years." South Boston High should have been opened, he said, calling its closing "poor judgment on the part of the city officials and school officials. And with respect to the first of the year, I expect that it will be opened, that it will be safe inside the school, that there will be no crowds allowed to gather outside or along the bus routes—and if any crowds do appear, they will be promptly dispersed and/or arrested." He concluded, "If the law is unenforceable, then change it. If you're not going to change it, enforce it."

Over the weekend a rumor circulated about a conspiracy by an unspecified group from South Boston planning to blow up the bridges, to make access for the school buses more difficult. Representative Ray Flynn from South Boston called the story an attempt to discredit the legitimate antibusing movement of the city. I was surprised at the credence the FBI appeared to give to the story, since Captain Cadegan had told us this was a rumor only. This kind of allegation can only make the South Boston community angrier, and the blacks more fearful.

Thursday, December 26

South Boston was peaceful and pretty. Almost all the houses were decorated with colored lights; children were coasting down Dorchester Heights behind the school. Inside the high school, the Home and School Association (an officially recognized organization of the Boston School Committee with membership limited to faculty and to parents or legal guardians of students) was meeting. Admission was restricted to parents with students enrolled or assigned to the school. I helped check parents against the lists.

Mr. Thayer Fremont-Smith, lawyer for the Boston Home and School Association, described to the parents the basis of his projected appeal in their name to Judge Garrity: There had been obvious discrimination on the part of the School Committee in changing continually the feeder pattern of the Boston schools so that some remained black. The full-scale busing of students was the "root and branch" remedy where such discrimination had been found. However, apart from the discrimination of the School Committee in keeping certain schools black, there were natural neighborhood patterns in the city: the blacks in Roxbury; the Irish in South Boston and Charlestown; the Italians in the North End and East Boston; the Chinese in the South End. "Judge Garrity is very fair and sensitive," Mr. Fremont-Smith said. "He is just interpreting the Constitution as he feels is right. I just have to show him that he could interpret it another way with my neighborhood theory."

"If he's so fair and humane, why didn't he read the desegregation plan before he approved it?" a man called out.

Mr. Fremont-Smith urged the people of South Boston to form a biracial council. If the Home and School Association wanted to have a voice for its point of view, its side of the story, its members would have to cooperate or he couldn't speak. It was especially important, since he was going to court the next day. "The alternative is a full-scale race riot. The judge is seriously considering closing the school. He would like some kind of indication from the people of South Boston that they are not flaunting the law. You know," he concluded, "he's Irish and he'll get mad."

The parents responded, going to the mike and giving their name first:

"What will it accomplish to close the school? You'll just move the problem."

"If South Boston High closes, won't Roxbury High also have to close?"

"Legally," Dr. Reid agreed, "Roxbury High is part of the South Boston–Roxbury Paired School Complex."

"If a hair pick is not illegal, can I bring a shillelagh to school?" Dr. Reid laughed.

Dr. Reid explained, "When school opens again, there will be a policewoman in the lavatories, troopers at every landing and on every floor, in addition to thirty-six aides."

"Why is the black teacher who said Michael Faith 'got what he deserved' still at the school? She doesn't deserve the name of teacher. If she was white, she would have been gone long ago. There is a double standard for whites and blacks."

One man assailed Dr. Reid, "You belong in a wheelchair. You should retire."

"What about the white woman who was burned to death in Roxbury? The murderers haven't been caught yet. How do we know they aren't right here with our kids?"

Their complaints continued: The media were slanted against them; they had no voice; they had lost their rights. They didn't mind "colored" kids coming in, but they didn't want their kids bused to Roxbury.

Mrs. Virginia Sheehy of the South Boston Information Center rose to her feet and cried, "Nobody cares." Her cry received a standing ovation.

Mr. John Duffy, president of the Home and School Association, asked, "Wouldn't you want to try the biracial council if it might possibly prevent a stabbing from happening again?"

Two hours later, when the meeting ended, thirty parents had volunteered to serve on the biracial council; the official election of the five white parents to serve remained. The progress made tonight was partly due, I felt, to the parent-teacher meetings before Christmas vacation, when all had a chance to release their fears and frustrations about the safety and education of their children.

Friday, December 27

Judge Garrity found Boston School Committee members John J. Kerrigan, John McDonough, and Paul Ellison guilty of civil contempt under a motion filed by the NAACP asking that the three men be cited, jailed, and fined $300 a day until they approved a desegregation plan. Kerrigan charged there had been more assaults on teachers by blacks than by whites;

twice as many blacks had been suspended; and a black student had stabbed a white student at South Boston High. He claimed there was a "lack of honesty in the black community, particularly in the NAACP," that they were "dealing here with a hostile, militant community."

Saturday, December 28

I met Mr. Karl Stone, a teacher from the Hart-Dean Annex to South Boston High, and mentioned that the Home and School Association had been very critical of the Annex, calling it a "zoo," and had even complained to the School Committee. He was offended. He said, "We have extortion and intimidation, but no stabbings or fights."

Sunday, December 29

Kerrigan said he would "go to jail" for his principles if he had to. Mayor White countered he wanted no histrionics.

Monday, December 30

Judge Garrity ordered the removal of all three school committee-men—Kerrigan, McDonough, and Ellison—from further desegregation decisions; a weekly fine on all commensurate with their financial statements, which should be submitted to him immediately, unless they changed their mind by January 7 and approved the Phase 2 desegregation plan; also consideration of suspension of Kerrigan and McDonough, both lawyers, from trying cases before the federal court.

Atkins left the court room smiling.

In an effort to quiet protest in the city, Mayor White promised to authorize the city to pay the costs for an appeal of Judge Garrity's desegregation order to the U.S. Supreme Court.

And school opens again Thursday!

Thursday, January 2, 1975

Faculty, but not students, returned to South Boston High today. Teachers have been asked not to park in the school yard in case of emergency; our cars were an obstruction to the police during the riot.

Police Commissioner diGrazia, afraid, has postponed opening the school to students until next Monday. He will meet with Judge Garrity today to request the closing of the high school.

As a result of the recommendations that came out of the faculty discussion groups after school closed December 11, two "cooling-off" rooms for disruptive students have been set up on either side of the front lobby entrance; the student lockers have been moved to the corridors where they will be under police surveillance. Police and "narcs" in hippie clothes combed the school for drugs and weapons.

I have removed any metal object—even my nailclip—that might delay me at the metal detectors in the lobby, which have been raised to a very sensitive pitch. Faculty and aides now must go through the scanners. It is rumored the knife that stabbed Michael Faith came through with a teacher. Or is this a ploy to impress the students? Mr. Joe Crowley, football coach, said, "They won't catch the knife. We'll be back only a few days, and the school will have to close again."

Mrs. Joanne Smith, an English teacher, exclaimed, "This is like something out of Pirandello. You turn your tie around when you come in the front door, go to your classroom and discuss *Julius Caesar* while some student is killing another down the hall. Then you go down to the cafeteria and eat with plastic spoons and knives."

Ironically the opening of the high school is the only point the Roxbury and South Boston communities have agreed on. Louise Day Hicks labeled it an indictment of the Boston police if they couldn't protect the 400 students of South Boston High, all that's left of last year's 1,700 students. Judge Garrity said the decision was the School Committee's; Superintendent Leary said the decision was the safety commission's and diGrazia's. Dr. Reid would like to keep South Boston High open.

The whole city is depressed. Attendance in all Boston schools was down to 54 percent, a record low.

Monday, January 6

On the evening TV news, Commissioner diGrazia, his eyes flashing and darting from side to side, like a secret service agent's, said, "I can't guarantee the safety of any teacher or student. When the student was stabbed at South Boston High, there was a policeman within two feet of him."

Tuesday, January 7

The executive board of the senior class at the high school met and made plans to form a biracial council. Mrs. Margaret Coughlin, mother of the South Boston High hockey team captain, collected 120 names of residents who would serve on a biracial committee.

"If South Boston High opens, I hope the right man will be there at the right time in the right place," said Charles Barry, secretary of public safety for the Commonwealth.

When school opens tomorrow, who would I *least* like to be? The first troublemaker who steps out of line.

Wednesday, January 8

The high school opened again for students with 300 state police and trepidation. Thirty-one black and 386 white students returned.

The scanner upset the students in my homeroom. They came in excited and disheveled, all pulled apart from taking off their rings, bracelets, belts, and emptying their pockets of metal. One boy even had to take the ace bandage off his foot.

My first class—senior English—lasted only twenty minutes because of the delay at the scanners. I began the play *Of Mice and Men* with the sophomores.

Today was like the old days—a light, happy feeling in the school, bright sunshine outside sparkling on the bay down the hill.

Michael Faith will have a home teacher for the rest of the year. Ruby and Mrs. Pam, the aide, will not be back.

Thursday, January 9

I realized with panic that the word "nigger" is used in *Of Mice and Men,* and wondered whether the portrayal of the crippled farmhand Crooks, his segregation, his feelings of loneliness and isolation, would offend the black students. But I had begun the play, and I didn't want to back out.

I told the class: "The word 'nigger' is used in this play. And the character Crooks is black. This play was published in 1937, a time historically of segregation in the South, when blacks had to use separate bathrooms, sit at the back of the bus, go to separate schools, but those times have changed, we hope. Can we realize that the play is about the past, and hope that better times will come, realize one another's common humanity, and accept it?" They answered, "Yes." The students enjoy the play. The exposure of how the black Crooks feels about his isolation is good for the white students.

The prediction that "hundreds" would return to school in January is not true. We have had a trickle of about ten additional white students.

Hyde Park High closed early today. There were fifteen arrests—thirteen blacks, two whites. The police, who had been stationed at the Bayside Mall for an emergency in South Boston, rushed to Hyde Park.

I used to get instant information about what was happening over the city from the Boston police, but that ended when the state police took charge. Ignorance must make for peace.

The troopers are quite friendly, more than they were. They say "hello" or open a door if my arms are full of books. Some appear gentle, others very tough, but all are watchful and disciplined. They are good role models for the boys. They are clean-cut and do their duty. In a time when people don't extend themselves, I appreciate their self-discipline, being somewhere they are supposed to be when they are supposed to be there.

Friday, January 10

During my study in the cafeteria, a no-nonsense black Boston TPF officer conducted a black student into the small teacher's room off the cafeteria. There was a rumor that the boy had a knife. I heard the beep-beep of the detector, then Dr. Reid came out. Siegfried returned to his bench, putting his belt back on. Then the girl with Siegfried was searched. The aide told me nothing had been found.

After school a voluntary faculty meeting was held in the library. Some male teachers were upset because a boy got through the detectors with a knife, hidden in a box. Another got through with a pick. As a matter of policy, the weapons brought in and the names of the students are kept confidential. Teachers generally agree they would be more unnerved if they knew.

One female teacher complained that the teacher checking at the metal detectors had gone through her pocketbook, even opening her compact; put a finger in her coffee thermos, and conducted her to the front office with an umbrella. Was it a joke? I now go to the same checker every day. It's like the airport, where one looks for the fastest customs officer.

Saturday, January 11

A group of teachers from South Boston High School met at Dunfey's Motel on Cape Cod to work with a group from the Hartford General Assistance Center, selected by the Boston School Committee, ostensibly to develop "new and dynamic teaching methods and materials." I left when I found that the group from the Hartford Center was actually intent on organizing the high school into "cluster programs," grouping students in several designated rooms set aside for them and their teachers exclusively in order to reduce student movement in the corridors. I objected to the restricting nature of clusters as opposed to the opening-up for all that is supposed to be the rationale for desegregation. There was a problem also in the special equipment required for different programs—shop, cooking, business, science, computer—located in widely separated parts of the building.

Monday, January 13

Dr. Reid seems much happier. The community attitude is positive.

South Boston High was quiet, though there were more fights and arrests at Hyde Park High. An administrator commented ironically, "They'll be looking for an alternate site for Hyde Park High shortly."

I had trouble getting my seniors away from the subject of Judge Garrity and on to *Hamlet*. I let them talk. They said, "We hate blacks," but they're only reacting to the situation. They said, "The blacks get everything." I asked, "Do you want to change places? You know they're treated like second-class citizens." They said, "We'll start trouble so the plan won't work." I told them the governor would just bring in federal troops; that they would be safer in a neighborhood and building they knew if there was trouble; that they put the odds against themselves if they moved to another strange building, and that would happen. I asked, "Can't you cool it until graduation? What about the kids who won't go to school anywhere else if this school closes? Can't you keep it open for them?" "Night school," they suggested. I answered, "You'll be too tired at night and just drop out." They wanted to know why black scores were so low in reading. I told them the white scores in reading, with a few exceptions, were just as bad in my mixed sophomore classes. They asked, "Then it's not a question of equal education?" I said, "No, it's a question of desegregation."

I grew up in the Back Bay, I told them, and loved the city. Maybe their keeping the violence at minimum would help to preserve the city. Maybe there would be sanity in the next Phase 2 plan. The city couldn't just be abandoned to lawlessness and crime.

I think I helped them.

Tuesday, January 14 — Martin Luther King holiday tomorrow

As I passed in the hall, I heard a trooper refer to the students. "Sacrificial lambs," he called them.

Lunch period was rumored to be a bean-throwing event, but troopers lined every foot of the walls of the cafeteria.

Thursday, January 16

I observed from my homeroom window the way the students enter the school. The whites wait near the corner for the buses to arrive, then they walk en masse into the building. There is a kind of holding back by both groups, as the troopers stand by with their motorcycles ready, helmets on, watching. It is a drama daily played out.

I am pleased there is no problem teaching *Of Mice and Men.* I was afraid the students might react personally to the brutality portrayed in the treatment of the black, Crooks, and take the opportunity to hurl their own slurs. But they haven't.

Teachers picked up pay checks in the office today. The two black boys in my homeroom pretended to hold me up. Is that their role image of themselves? They sit around my desk because the white students don't yet talk to them. There is a good feeling in the homeroom, though.

Friday, January 17

I mentioned to the seniors that the Chinese, who had been bused to the North End from Chinatown, were being taught Italian. I said, "It's a real mixing of cultures." They asked, "Are the Italians studying Chinese?"

The students seem to me to be relaxing a little, but other teachers say tension is building.

A knife was found on a student at the Hart-Dean Annex.

The Boston School Committee purged themselves by filing a Phase 2 desegregation plan—one that would require no forced busing.

Monday, January 20

I talked with seniors about the Mike Wallace "Sixty Minutes" segment on South Boston. They felt the program was unfair: Michael Faith was not stabbed in a "brawl," as reported, but as he was walking in a corridor; the boycotting students tutored by Jack Kennedy, assistant headmaster from South Boston, in a hall over a bar were said to be finding it "difficult to study in a barroom atmosphere." The seniors denied the bar in any way affected the study hall overhead.

I hated the close-up of the white adult woman waiting for the black student to come out of the high school and board the bus, yelling, "Come on, you black bastard." Brian answered, "We are racists. Let's face it. That's how we feel about it." I said, "Maybe if the blacks were given a chance to earn more money and improve themselves, there wouldn't be the high

crime rate." Meg said, "You don't understand, you just don't understand."
So I gave up. They were like a wall today.

The seniors held a white caucus in the evening outside the school. They
voted 144-0 against the formation of a biracial council.

Tuesday, January 21

Yesterday I called the parent of one of the white boys in my
homeroom to find out why her son wasn't in school. I assured her I felt
quite safe with two troopers in every corner and at the staircases. I was
overwhelmed when she told me her oldest boy had been stabbed to death
in South Boston on his way home from a party at Christmas. Nobody had
told me. The brother in my homeroom came back today, a gentle, respectful
boy. He stood up when I talked to him in the library.

As I was passing from class to the library, I saw a tall, handsome trooper
call to Kevin, a sophomore, "Come here, I want to talk to you. Now, I
don't like being here any more than you do." In the library Kevin told me
the trooper had accused him of bumping into him three times that day. I
asked, "Did you do it deliberately?" Kevin answered, "No." His face was
flushed. It's a good, manly way to talk to the boys. They need that.

In the evening I attended the Home and School meeting at South Boston
High. I found out, what one is not always aware of at school unless directly
involved, that fourteen blacks and one white had been suspended, the
blacks transported out in a van. Ms. Murphy theorized the black students
are "fed up" and want out. Siegfried's mother came to the high school
today to request his transfer.

The parents argued the pros and cons of a biracial council, then voted
against forming one. Judge Garrity decried the vote as "the first step down
the road toward another stabbing."

Wednesday, January 22

It was a half-day to allow time for a teachers' in-service meeting.
When polled, almost no teachers wanted to work on a "cluster program"
for the school — too punitive and limiting.

At the meeting I told Dr. Reid that the "walkers" — the white students —
had been asking when it would be their week to leave the school before
the bused students under the alternating plan. He answered, "I'm sorry I
made that statement. The black youngsters have to leave first." A teacher
turned to me and said, "They lost that right December 11." It was the
black teachers who rode down to the Bayside Mall staging area with the

buses, Mr. Gizzi said, who were holding them up. Ms. Murphy interposed, "I think what Ms. Malloy is saying is that we have to keep a good barometer on the kids' feelings, to see what's bothering them." Well, it irritates me to wait ten minutes for some teacher to get her things together and get out to the bus.

The Bay State *Banner*, Roxbury's black newspaper, reported that the blacks want the school moved from South Boston. An anonymous teacher said, "It's like a prison over there. We can't leave the school; we can't come early or on the weekends to do preparatory work. We are like prisoners. Everyday when I get up it's like getting up to go to prison."

Thursday, January 23

I dislike my duty in the cafeteria study, stopping students from leaving or trying to enter the study when they don't belong there. Students can go to the lavatories only if accompanied by an aide. The students do not study, but sit, play cards, talk, or put their heads down.

There are four state troopers in the cafeteria study now, one at each side of the room, like the arms of a crucifix, and two by the door.

One of the volunteer observers for the Justice Department, formerly an English teacher, remarked to me, "It's amazing, but there does seem to be learning going on in the classrooms."

School committeemen Tierney and Kerrigan walked around the school today. They called the school "an armed camp." Later in the day they asked for a reduction in the police force because it is a "waste" and the troopers are "discouraged."

Friday, January 24

Today I lost two white students in one sophomore class and two black sophomores in another to remedial reading. Another black girl reads with her lips and disturbs everyone. She is so conscientious, though, that I hate to unsettle her. She doesn't want to go to remedial reading.

Monday, January 27

Jeffrey, one of the two black students in my homeroom, arrived in class exclaiming about the red-haired, white-faced Irish cop downstairs who had busted him for B & E—breaking and entering. He said, "I'd like to fuck him up." The cop had "beat on" him in the police station. Martin, listening, commented, "You know, get the nigger." And he punched the air at the invisible "nigger." They live in a world of violence. They talked about selling me a joint, giving me a share of their film passes, always with an eye on the impression they make on the white students. They accept correction now about their language—swearing and grammar.

The students in my classes—an all-white senior class and racially mixed sophomore classes—are working well.

In the cafeteria study, Mr. Alexander told a girl she should not leave and roam the corridors. He asked, "Do you want to be mugged?" I don't think it's fair to talk to them like that, since that kind of language only creates anxiety. I felt sorry for her and asked, "Does he scare you?"

There were some small fights today. The mood of the school is becoming ugly. At the end of the day I saw a trooper marching a white, protesting girl down the stairs. She was angry and flushed.

Wednesday, January 29

Jasmin, a black sophomore, came to class today. I sent a cut slip for Jasmin yesterday, but she had been sent home earlier in the van. At first she wouldn't sit in her seat, just on the edge of the desk. Then she told me I was a "nice teacher," in a sense apologizing for her behavior. She sat down.

She worked on similes and metaphors. Once when I asked her a question, several other students answered out before she had a chance. She complained, "There are an awful lot of Jasmins in this class."

Jasmin seems quite intelligent, but she is a very angry girl.

Later I tested the class on *The Pearl*. Donald refuses to do vocabulary, and Jasmin had not yet read the book. I told Donald he would get one point for pronouncing the words correctly, and Jasmin that she could help Donald earn points by defining the word correctly when he failed. She was fascinated and tried to help him, quite successfully, even with words like "legerdemain."

There was a voluntary staff meeting at the end of the day. We had only two-and-a-half weeks to go until February vacation, Dr. Reid said. We had been lucky and kept the fights so far on a one-to-one basis, but constant vigilance was required. "We're just keeping the lid on—until the end of the year, we hope. That's off the record."

Thursday, January 30

Not many seniors were in today. "They're afraid," the students told me.

Friday, January 31

More Boston police—equal numbers of white officers and black officers—have been assigned to the first floor lobby at the metal detectors. The state police are now assigned to the basement and the second and third floors. The black Boston police complained about the way the state troopers handle the black students. A trooper told me, "It'll be lucky if the Boston police don't kill each other before the day is out." The hostility among them fosters fear.

Jasmin was angry when I assigned students another book to read. Just for that, she said, she would not come back from lunch.

Few seniors in. "Afraid," the kids said.

Wednesday, February 5

I was depressed and tired. It began to snow. I stayed home. School is cancelled for tomorrow: "No school in all schools all day in Boston." A snow day.

Friday, February 7

Martin was suspended while I was out. Jeffrey said, "Someone 'sucker-punched' him."

The substitute teacher had left me some poems the seniors wrote in a pattern of five lines: a noun, two adjectives, three participles, a sentence, and then a noun to redefine the first word of the poem. There was one I could sympathize with, since I had accidentally infringed on the pigeons' turf on the Boston Common recently, carrying still warm muffins from Jordan Marsh. Over 200, perhaps 300, pigeons flew at me, forcing me to run to the sidewalk, coat over my head.

> Pigeon
> Fat and ugly
> Flying, eating, shiting.
> I think these birds are useless.
> Bird turd.

Another poem by a girl stunned me:

> Nigger
> Bone head spook
> Terrorizing assaulting molesting
> This race is very obstanant.

I referred to the poem content, then warned the seniors about being discreet in what they wrote; they could be hurt if they weren't. I mentioned the recent incident at State College, Boston, where the students on flexible campus had been given a choice among three composition topics. Some students from South Boston had written on busing with their usual lack of sophistication, using words like "niggers." A professor later read their papers before an assembly with comments that left some South Boston students in tears. I told my senior class, "That's an invasion of privacy. But, on the other hand, I have a doctor friend who commented to me, 'If they write shit, throw the shit back at them. Throw the shit back at them. Let them live with it.'"

The white students in my cafeteria study were upset by the insulting racial epithets carved in the lunch tables. I told them, "Forget it." I have seen antiblack graffiti carved into the tables upstairs: "Niggers are proof that the Indians fucked buffaloes."

Judge Garrity named four masters to draw up the final Phase 2 desegregation plan for the city: retired state Supreme Judicial Court Justice Jacob J. Spiegel, who will preside at the hearings; former state Attorney General Edward J. McCormack, Jr.; former U.S. Commissioner of Education Francis Keppel; and Harvard University School of Education Professor Charles V. Willie. They will receive $200 a day, their two assistants, Robert Dentler and Marvin Scott, $200 and $100 respectively—plus expenses.

Monday, February 10

Fights are breaking out in school. A trooper's shoulder was dislocated in a fight. He went downstairs holding his hand curled up.

Wednesday, February 12

It was snowy. The parking lot was full when I arrived late. I parked downhill facing Day Boulevard, beside the variety store formerly besmeared with graffiti: "Nigger" and "Doc is a nigger lover." A man standing nearby looked down the hill where we could see the yellow buses moving along the boulevard. He commented, smiling, "I don't think you'll make it." His friendliness represented a positive change in the community. They want the school open.

Thursday, February 13

Dr. Reid passed through the cafeteria to the gym. While he was in gym, the white boys had seized Siegfried's clothes—

pants and shoes—and had flushed them down the toilet. He went in shorts to the front office to complain; he had to be driven home.

There will be revenge for Siegfried's humiliation.

Yesterday the white boys saw Siegfried's name on my study list while I was taking attendance. They told me, "Send him a cut slip." I asked what they had against Siegfried. One answered, "He's taking somebody's seat." Another boy said, "He wants to be king of the school."

The troopers have suggested it would be better if the two rivals, Siegfried and Red, put on gloves and fought for the crown.

Friday, February 14

The tension in the school was eerie and palpable. The students moved through the corridors in packs. Dr. Reid was in the corridors, alert. A trooper told me there had been two melees even before school.

My seniors wanted to leave class early to get ready for a birthday party in the library for a senior classmate. They had a huge, signed card for her with a picture of grapes: "You're the best of the bunch." I was afraid to let them go ahead.

When class ended, I waited by the lockers, telling the boys to behave. One challenged me, "Are you my mother?"

At lunchtime the class told me, "Something is going to happen. There's going to be a fight." They said no more and smiled, waiting. But nothing did happen. At lunch Siegfried remained standing, wearing black gloves while he ate. He and Red began to fight. One bottle of milk and insults were thrown. Siegfried and Red were both sent home. The school then became almost sleepy.

Sylvia tried to leave the study because she didn't want to stay there with "all those white folks."

At the end of the day, Dr. Reid, on the intercom, thanked everyone, troopers especially, for keeping the peace during the last two weeks. Then, "Bused students dismissed. . . . Walkers dismissed." Vacation begins tomorrow.

In Hyde Park today, following three successive days of violence at the high school, black students hijacked a school bus. They forced the black aide to lie on the floor, then bullied the driver to take them to a McDonald's hamburger stand and an elementary school, beat him and fled.

The National Student Conference Against Racism is convening at Boston University this weekend. NAACP President Atkins was the kick-off speaker at the general convocation. He deplored racism in South Bostom where

KILL NIGGERS was written on telephone poles and talked about the masks racism sometimes wore: the teacher carrying a book (most repulsive to me); the policeman wearing a badge (most fearful to me).

Why not include the racist in a soldier's uniform—the National Guard or federal troops?

Jonathan Kozol, educator, spoke. His sympathies were for the poor kids of Boston, including South Boston, he said. He asked whether Mayor White knew the definition of "magnet" school, and asked how, if the Stop and Shop stores had abandoned Bayside Mall, the Mall could be considered good enough for kids as an alternative learning site. Boston kids should be given the two top floors of the Prudential Tower or the City Hall itself, built by the poor people of Boston, so that, if students tired of a boring teacher, they could swing around in the swivel chairs. He suggested that land be taken from the rich by eminent domain.

James Meredith, the first black to enroll at the University of Mississippi in 1962 under protection of 500 federal marshals, spoke. People are not aware they are racists until they are confronted with the problem, he said. The people of South Boston would have deplored what happened in the South ten years ago.

Dr. Spock, baby expert, spoke. There was too much pointing the finger at South Boston, calling "shame," he said, making the "shame-on-you" finger sign. A child could never make up a lost school year. Involve the suburbs, he advised.

Finally the president of the student government at the Hart-Dean Annex was introduced as "president because the whites wouldn't vote." (They were boycotting.) In a brief speech she complained, "We aren't getting an education; there are no books, no gym. The caf is dirty." She was given the most resounding and continuous applause of the evening.

Saturday, February 15

I attended the National Student Conference Against Racism convention at Boston University again, choosing the group to be chaired by Commissioner of Correction John Boone. He wasn't there.

Discussion centered on the logistics of a march against racism. I had intended to remain silent. I didn't.

I said, "A march against racism is a march against a word. What are you marching against? You should march *for* something, for a decent desegregation plan." I continued, "South Boston was never given a fair chance. The whole junior class was sent to Roxbury. They are working-class kids; they can opt out of the system if they don't like it. All but fifteen did. Only 50 percent of the black sophomores came to South Boston. They were lost one year earlier than the juniors.

"Teaching is nurturing, directing, and counseling outside the classroom as well as inside. Some of these kids I've come to know and care for. I've protected them with my life. And next year they'll be gone. I may not see them again.

"Under the present plan, South Boston–Roxbury High students make three major school changes in three years. What suburb would tolerate their children going to three different schools in three years? Dr. Spock told you last night to stop pointing the finger at South Boston, crying 'shame,' and look to the suburbs.

"I came today because I like John Boone. He said, 'If the kids don't go back to school, they'll end up on a one-way bus ride to Walpole Prison, and it won't matter what race, color or creed they are.' We have to start caring about the kids."

I was amazed. I expected everybody to be against me. Instead, I became a weathervane for the group. When a CAR representative proposed they picket Louise Day Hicks's house, I shook my head, "No." The chairperson, a black moderator from Alabama, took his cue from me, becoming angry when the CAR representative insistently demanded a "multiracial group to take buses and circle her house." I left before NSCAR voted overwhelmingly, about 1,200 to 20, against the CAR motion.

Outside, I telephoned Louise Day Hicks, whom I'd never spoken to before, to warn her. The leaflets were all over the city, she told me. The kids knew about it and were very angry. The police had also been alerted. "It is a terrible thing to have the kids in the middle of this," she said.

Sunday, February 16

At the appointed time, South Bostonians silently left their homes with bags of rocks; but a group of about 200 CAR, having received no permit to march to South Boston, protested instead outside the home of Governor Dukakis.

Thursday, February 20

The Massachusetts House voted on Tuesday to repeal the 1965 Racial Imbalance Act outlawing racial imbalance in any school more than 50 percent black. It was a token vote, however, since Boston is now under a federal court order and would not be affected by the repeal. In an editorial the *Globe* newspaper warned that if the suburbs sided with Boston against forced busing, they might be providing an opportunity to overturn the Detroit decision and have forced busing come to them.

At the Phase 2 desegregation hearings Boston Police Superintendent Joseph Jordan testified before the masters that he could not, judging from the police information he had, guarantee the safety of the bridge (Mystic) and the TUNNELS if busing were extended to Charlestown and East Boston.

Sunday, February 23

We go back to school tomorrow.

I had a nightmare last night. I dreamed I was being attacked by two black men. I knew I couldn't win, but broke a glass Coke bottle to fight with, like Pony Boy in the teen novel we've been reading, *The Outsiders*. In the dream I was so afraid I couldn't speak, but forced myself to cry out for help, and woke. Just before vacation, Coke bottles and other glass materials were denounced on the intercom as weapons, and students put on notice that they were forbidden in the school. The nightmare spawned out of this warning, but also from a story an old black woman told me, how she had been attacked by two boys last Saturday outside her home in Mattapan. They stole her groceries including two pieces of meat, and her money, sixteen dollars, that she had put in the paper bag. They broke the strap on her purse, but she wouldn't let go because it held the key to her house.

Monday, February 24

School was peaceful—halycon—today. Most of the troublemakers are still out.

The mini-English elective programs began. I explained to the sophomores they had to make the program work by behaving, that some teachers were too nervous to attempt new classes, preferring instead to stay with students they already knew, who had learned to get along with one another. They seemed to understand.

As an introduction to my course in "Books Teenagers Like About Problems They're Interested In," I asked students to write down what they considered the biggest problems of teenagers today. Most said "drugs," one said "family," one said "school."

Red came into my cafeteria study with a hair pick. He combed his hair and howled, looking at the blacks. I ordered him out. I was surprised; he looked frightened by me.

Siegfried and Red now eat with the troopers in the North Cafeteria.

Tuesday, February 25

The Phase 2 desegregation masters and the "experts" Dentler and Scott visited the high school today and ate lunch in the cafeteria during my study. The cafeteria attendant was upset, banging closet doors and cupboards. She wasn't paid to clean up after them, she grumbled.

Wednesday, February 26

At lunchtime two somber troopers marshaled Siegfried through my classroom into the adjoining room to get his coat. He and Red had paired off in the gym to fight. They were grabbed by troopers, but not before Red got a pick scratch and went off to the Eye and Ear Infirmary.

Today photographers began taking pictures, room by room, for ID badges, seniors first. The aides sported lightweight yellow jackets with A I D E in large black letters on the back to help distinguish them in a fracas from students. Both the ID badges and jackets are ideas that came out of the faculty discussions following the December 11 riot.

At the end of the day I told my homeroom, after the black students had left for the buses: "Don't say 'nigger.'" Later, "Don't even think it." One white boy, Hal, who had enrolled late in my homeroom, frowned.

Thursday, February 27

A sympathy walkout for Red was pinpointed at one o'clock— the middle of my cafeteria study. I cautioned the students that a walkout would just cause ill will, more fights, and then the school might close; the walkout would accomplish nothing. I asked a trooper, "They say they're going to walk out. Do you think they should?" He replied, "Sure, why not?" I asked Mr. Corscadden what the school policy was. He replied, "Let them go, but take their names and send them cut slips." At one o'clock some students left. I didn't stop them, but Dr. Reid did. He met them at the front door and asked for their program schedules. They ran for the stairs then; the teachers and troopers caught them and brought them back. At the cafeteria door a hefty trooper dramatically examined a student's program, as if the student had run a stop sign and knocked down an old lady. Peter, one of my sophomores, as big as any trooper and as gentle as a lamb, just picked up a teacher, set him aside, and left the school.

The last class of the day was cancelled. We waited where we were. The trooper told me he felt bad for the kids. It was hard for them to be in a school with police everywhere. I was reminded of the senior who said, "You go out into a corridor, and, instead of kids, you see cops, cops, cops everywhere."

Monday, March 3

There were more troopers in my cafeteria study than usual, but standing around casually. One trooper was smoking in the back. A student told him to put out his cigarette.

In the corridors the troopers clustered five or six together, instead of the usual two. When I asked one trooper what they were expecting, he replied, "Nothing. We're just waiting to go home."

Outside the school on the hill there was again a massive, defensive tactic by the state police, one line of police facing down G Street, motorcycles lining the gate to the street behind the buses, and helmeted troopers in formation outside the school.

Red, like Snowball in *Animal Farm*, was rumored to be lurking at the Hill Stop Delicatessen under suspension, sending out waves of unrest.

In an after-school meeting, Dr. Reid explained: There had been a rumor that both white and black students were planning to walk out together, just what the police want to avoid. In the future there would be an emergency warning and procedure: Four bells. Everyone should stop where they were, "freeze"; they would then clear the corridors floor by floor. All unassigned personnel should go to room 300 on the third floor to escort youngsters found wandering the corridors back to their classrooms. Escorting students to their rooms was not the troopers' job.

Dr. Reid concluded, "I'm amazed there is so much unrest. I would have expected things to calm down with seniors getting ready for graduation. There is still talk of closing the school."

Tuesday, March 4

The school is quiet. Red is back in school again, but Siegfried is still out. The librarian theorized Red is a student leader because he has "enormous hands and can fight." Last Thursday, I remembered, I saw a black boy after he had been "suckered" or "sucker-punched" to the side of his head as he was going down the staircase between classes. He was being supported by two troopers. A gym teacher commented to me later, "The white boys can fight with their hands; they could kill someone with a punch."

Photo IDs continue.

Wednesday, March 5

During my lunch break, I stopped in the front office to file a student program card. Jeffrey, one of the two black boys in my homeroom, was standing there. He was on one side of the office counter; Jack Kennedy, assistant headmaster, and the Boston plainclothes police liaison, Sergeant Jim Donovan, were on the other. I asked, "What are you doing here, Jeffrey? You're not in trouble, are you?" They said, "He got spaghetti on him. Somebody threw it at him in the cafeteria." Jeffrey had his head down. I saw bits of sauce on his hair and shirt. I said, "Jeffrey is in my homeroom. Jeffrey is a good boy. What happened, Jeffrey?" I touched his arm and he started to cry. I didn't realize it immediately, since his hands hid his eyes. Sergeant Donovan said, steadily regarding Jeffrey, "I know he's a good boy." Jack Kennedy took Jeffrey into a side office to comfort him.

After school I defended Jeffrey to the homeroom. I said, "Jeffrey wouldn't do anything. I know Jeffrey and you know him. He's a good boy." I didn't tell them Jeffrey had been crying because I was afraid some might use that against him later. The kids got heavy with me; one said she'd think up a story about me and go to the office with it, though I know she wasn't serious. James yelled "nigger" out the window at the bused students.

Thursday, March 6

I stayed home today and slept. I had chest pains yesterday.

Friday, March 7

There was trouble in the front lobby before school where, besides the Boston police, only four state police are assigned. The state troopers formed a wedge, then passed the students back to the street to safety.

My homeroom was happy to see me; they didn't like the substitute. Jeffrey greeted me with a radiant smile. One of the homeroom girls, the most angry about busing, spoke to Jeffrey. I praised her later. She said, "I was just asking him a question. It didn't mean anything." I said, "It doesn't matter. You were nice to him."

Jeffrey told me that the white boy, who had been suspended, hid behind the cafeteria post, sucker-punched him, and then pushed the spaghetti in his face. A Boston policeman asked me later if I thought the incident had been "contracted," whether a boy had been paid to do it. I told him Jeffrey was a good boy. He answered, "The kids—black and white—know who the troublemakers are."

One of my seniors was wearing her sneakers, she told me, so she could run. She expected trouble. But, by noon, troublemakers—black and white—had been removed from the school.

The sophomores finished *Junkie Priest* and *Go Ask Alice*. Since drugs are still, according to my informal survey, the main problem of teenagers, I asked the class, as part of a test, to write a page from Alice's diary, as if she were at South Boston High. I thought they would write about the drug scene, but few did:

Excerpts from Alice's *Diary:* At South Boston High

Tuesday. I hate this school more and more. Every time I step through the front door. It's like walking into Police headquarters. If some of the Rich Subbean people like Garrity and Kennedy would have to get on a Bus every morning or come up this school and see all the tension, maybe they would think Better of this foolish plan and try to stop it.

A white sophomore boy

She would see a lot of Blacks and Whites fighting. She would see police excorting buses. Cafteria fights. Riots police in the corridor. She would think that Judge Garrity is crazy.

A black sophomore girl

I just passed the detector and went to my home room. Man that detector is the biggest bummer next to the fights in this hole. I just went into the bathroom and poled a couple of times with some girl freind and the day just zoomed by and I am going to the library now with Joel. See ya.

A white sophomore boy

. . . that some white and black get along and most don't and she would write that the school would be better if the students made it better by talking, laughing, sit together just like one happy family, But it could never work.

A black sophomore girl

Alice would probebly see black and white students going to class, fights, and every one on edge. She wouldn't have to worry about drugs, people hassling her because they mind there own business.

A white sophomore girl

Monday, March 10

I have an addition to my homeroom—a retired lieutenant from the fire department who will be tutoring students in math. He sits at one

of the desks and waits for classes to begin. I suggested he could look out
the window at the police activity, the biggest magnet for the students and
bone of contention with me, but he sniffed at the privilege.

I had my ID badge photo taken. Some senior classes had to be photographed twice because, intending to use the ID to buy alcohol, they lied
about their age.

The Civil Rights Commission in Washington anticipates "without positive
action" increasing segregation in cities. Although there has been substantial
school desegregation in the South, advances in the North have been minimal.
The commission wants a public hearing on the volatile Boston situation.

Tuesday, March 11

There was a knife incident in biology today. When the dissecting
knives were collected and counted, one was missing. Nothing was said.
But the class was held after the bell. There was no search, just the pressure
of sitting there beyond the bell time. Ten minutes passed. Eventually the
student turned in the knife that he had hidden in his pant leg.

Wednesday, March 12

In the cafeteria study I make a point of spending a few minutes
with the black students who segregate themselves to the side and just sit
and talk, watching me or whoever comes into the room. Sylvia, a handsome
black girl, showed me a poem she had written, called "Mean Southie . . ."
about the periodic waves of violence in the high school.

Mean Southie . . .

My first day of Southie was really a bad trip
You could not speak out or make one little slip,
They gave us a warm welcome out there in the school
They called us all NIGGERS and considered us all FOOLS.
They stoned all our buses, and hurt our friends
I thought this nightmare would never end.
The next couple of weeks were filled with tense
This whole big mess didn't make sense
The next couple of months the fighting broke out
Nobody knew what it really was about
Anne a black girl, put a white girl in bed
She hit her with a padlock right smack in the head.
Our next couple of months were peaceful and cool,
Nobody seemed to be in a fighting mood
But then more trouble becamed thy way,

> The minutes just seemed liked one long day
> The first thing you knew we had Spaghetti Day
> (And boy, we all had something to say!)
> Everyone had Spaghetti all over their clothes!
> But luckily no one got hurt though.
> Then there was bickering here and arguing there
> But it was something we all had to bear
> The kids started getting suspended left and right
> The majority was black but there were a few whites
> Then things got quiet for a while
> Again trouble is starting to pile
> It seems like the white kids have a contract out on us
> I can't wait till two, to get on my bus
> The white youths all gather in the halls in mobs
> Why don't the cops do their jobs?

I asked Sylvia, "What does it mean, 'It seems like the white kids have a contract out on us'?" She answered, "If one of us does anything wrong, they gang up on us." Referring to the poem, I asked, "The police don't let the kids gang up in the corridors, do they?" She answered, "They're so busy looking at the girls' bottoms, they don't have any energy to stop the fights. A white girl went by and said 'Hello' to a trooper, and he answered 'Hello.' Then I said 'Hello' to him, and he didn't answer. I told him, 'Fuck you.'" I praised the poem, and told her I would like to have a trooper read it. She agreed. I asked Trooper Jennings to read the poem and give it back to her. He said, "I can't." I was disappointed. I asked him if he would read the poem and return it to me where she could observe. He said he would, and did.

Friday, March 14

I went to school early. Trouble was expected: a drinking bout on Dorchester Heights, then anything. Two passing postmen guffawed at the bus positioned horizontally as a barricade across the end of the street in front of the school.

My homeroom students came in, complaining of the cold. Jeffrey came in, a little breathless. He expected trouble.

There were only seven students in my senior English class, among them the president of the class—a good indicator of the student thinking, I reflected. In celebration of St. Patrick's Day the seniors were preparing a dramatization and choral reading of *Finnegans Wake*. While looking for a clear space on the recording tape, the seniors came across a dramatic skit created by Michael Faith when he was a sophomore. I had kept it because it was good. The faces of the seniors radiated as they recognized the voices of Michael, his sister, and other members of the senior class, then two years younger and more innocent. Mike has become part of their pain, I think.

Dr. Reid stopped in and said "hello."

In my study the four black students asked me about the Irish green I was wearing, and wondered why I was wearing orange also. I told them, "Orange, white and green are the colors of the Irish flag, and symbolize the hope one day of a united Ireland." I was surprised at their interest, since generally the word "Irish" now is enough to make them twist their faces, like lemons.

It was a quiet day. Many students stayed home.

Saturday, March 15

I went to a ROAR meeting—my first—at the Officers' Club in South Boston with Ms. Murphy. Nobody objected; they were even a little pleased at our presence. All the South Boston politicians were there. Among the prizes awarded at the festivities were a pair of tennis shoes to Congressman Joe Moakley so he could catch up with the antibusing movement, and to Ed McCormack, a graduate of South Boston High and one of the four desegregation masters, a blank check for his efforts.

There was such tremendous community there—singing, dancing, camaraderie—that I don't believe their spirit will be broken.

Four ROAR buses will leave South Boston for Washington, D.C., on Tuesday, forty from the city. They plan to march Wednesday, and hope to talk with congressional leaders.

In South Boston the St. Patrick's Day shamrocks are now on sale—to subsidize an alternative private school in the community. Formerly, shamrock money was donated to the high school for the paperback library.

Sunday, March 16

I watched the St. Patrick's Day Parade in South Boston with Ms. Murphy and a South Boston family—raw with tension. The mother has four children in four different schools: Roxbury High, South Boston High, Columbia Point, and an elementary school in South Boston. She sits at home by the phone and waits for the schools to "blow." She said, "Some families have already moved out, promising to be back when the trouble is over. Who needs them?" She believes the busing movement is a big-business maneuver to take over the area and put up high-rise apartments after the families have left.

Mayor White marched part of the parade route, Senator Bill Bulger all the way. He is the daaarlin of South Boston. One of my seniors, "the best of the bunch," was the queen—a lovely colleen.

Tuesday, March 18

Many white students were absent today, boycotting, in sympathy with the ROAR delegation that left for Washington, D.C., today.

The troopers took Red to the Framingham barracks over the weekend, I heard. They think he is a good kid. Red now wants to be a trooper.

Wednesday, March 19

No one from the Massachusetts congressional delegation met the Boston busing protesters at the Capitol building in Washington. The rain poured down; the city was shrouded in mist. The people sludged through the rain and mud, drenched. I thought, "It probably is the only pair of shoes some of them have." Many of them had paid for the trip on time payments, and will be paying for months to come.

The students are no longer afraid in the corridors, possibly because most of the roughest kids have dropped out. The seniors will be leaving soon. They have daily senior class day practice.

Meg told me she flirts with the "staties."

Thursday, March 20

There was a student council meeting. Kathryn, the homeroom delegate, reported back that the students voted: one, to have Michael Faith at graduation, state troopers if necessary; two, to leave school at the same time as black students, or alternate with them every other week; three, to be marked tardy at a definite time, not just after the buses have arrived.

"Can you give a tardy slip to a bus?" Ms. Murphy had asked.

Friday, March 21

When I reported to the front office to sign in before school, I found my name circled with a notation to speak with the administration. After I had left school early yesterday—with official permission—the teacher next door reported my homeroom for misbehaving in my absence. With all our troubles, why do teachers have to hassle one another? We have been silently angry with one another since the beginning of the year when she said, referring to the boycotters, "Who cares about them? Let them stay out. That's their problem." Dr. Reid stood by and listened to my explanation that another teacher had promised to supervise the class for me. He said nothing.

Martin was back in homeroom again. The card returned to me by the truant officer read, "Suspend as usual process." The truant officer just didn't bother going into the Columbia Point project to investigate. I should have used the personal contact at the project a social worker had given me. I gave Martin a pep talk about finishing the year.

During homeroom I made out the list required by Judge Garrity of assigned students who did not return to school this year. Most of them are now over sixteen years of age, and could not be obliged by law to attend.

In the library I asked an aide what he thought of the masters' Phase 2 desegregation plan. He answered, "I do not believe in forcing people to do anything." His voice was so loud I felt anxiously he was making a statement not to me, but to the South Boston boys in the library.

After the aide had left, one of the boys threw a white rolled paper snowball in the direction of a black girl sitting near them. The boys sat there — grinning — big, tough, and one of them toothless, smiling. I frowned. I gave the girl an *Ebony* magazine and talked about the hair styles on the front cover. I found the latest *Mad* magazine and gave it to the boys. Then, while straightening up the books on the tables, I picked up the spare paper ammunition. The aide's speech had, I suppose, sanctioned their feelings against blacks.

It was a beautiful day. In the study, when I went to take the attendance of the black students, sitting apart in the back, one asked me, "Why don't you take the attendance from over there? You know our names." I replied, "I came to say 'hello.'" They mentioned it was the first day of spring. I replied, "That's good news."

Saturday, March 22

I asked the South Boston branch librarian her opinion on the masters' Phase 2 desegregation plan, what the people of South Boston thought about it. She asked me, "Have you heard Representative Ray Flynn from South Boston? He hadn't yet studied the plan in full, but liked the college involvement and was glad busing had been cut down [17,000 to 14,000], especially of first graders. One had to be careful of educational jargon, though. For instance, he noted, a child now can go to school in his school district, but 'district' is not 'community.' Mission Hill, for example, is not the Brighton 'community.'"

However, the masters have diffused emotion from the busing plan and broken the antibusing alliance of Irish and Italian—ROAR's Italian flag with the shamrock—by postponing busing out of East Boston until a year from now, when the East Boston community high school is scheduled to be phased out and a citywide exam technical school, linked with MIT, substituted. Why fight if you don't have to? This has been a year of delicate balance.

Two MIT students were picked up in Kenmore Square, stabbed viciously, then dropped from the car near the D Street project. As they fled, one was hit on the back of the head with a tire iron. He died shortly after at Boston City Hospital. The suspects are from South Boston.

Monday, March 24

My homeroom students were talking about the knifing, very upset. "We get blamed for everything," one said. Someone mentioned that the house of one of their classmates, absent today, had been splattered with the murder victim's blood from his half-severed head. Debbie, a white girl, got up and went to the window for air. James said, "They're animals. Animals."

Jeffrey was sullen for the first time, sitting on the edge of his desk. When I asked him to close the closet, where he stores his books, and pick up the dust pan that his book bag had knocked out, he didn't move.

During my study in the cafeteria I talked with a trooper and a federal observer, now referred to by some teachers as "federal spies." The trooper gave the observer the police figures: 100 MDC police and 150 troopers in the school; 300 in the area. The trooper was pessimistic. He saw "no difference between September and now. The troopers are the wedge between fights and bodies on the floor. You cannot force people."

Tuesday, March 25

The girl whose house had been splattered with blood came back today. Her face looked disturbed. I thought she might have been in a fight, and expressed my concern. The murder suspect was her cousin, she told me. She had seen the half-severed head outside her house when she arrived home five minutes after the police. Then she cautioned, "Shhh!" But the kids were already looking up at her, stunned.

The teachers have always known that there was an element of the student body that needed socializing, humanizing, and worked hard to achieve that goal. Reaching them, I felt, was a major justification of the community school. But, if they are not in school, we can never reach them. A federal observer commented that students who have come to school this year have learned tremendous lessons: in adjustment, physical courage, and moral courage to attend school despite social pressure. I said, "What about the thousands who have not come to school?" He replied, "They will be paying for the rest of their lives." I added, "Society will be paying for the rest of their lives."

Today the second sophomore assembly was held, a science lesson on snakes by a lecturer from the Museum of Science. The assembly had been kept a surprise to avert student-planned disruptions. Fifty troopers stood along the walls of the assembly hall and in the balcony, some with walkie-talkies sputtering, while others waited outside.

As the classes filed into the hall, a fight broke out in the first few rows under the speaker's nose. According to a federal observer, who witnessed and wrote up the report of the fight, a white administrator asked a black boy to remove his hat, and the boy refused. A black teacher intervened his physical presence passively between the two, but the boy went around the intermediary to take a poke at the administrator. The administrator punched back. The boy was apprehended by police and taken to court.

The lecturer began on schedule, repeatedly clearing his throat. Three out of five troopers on the front left, I counted, were vigorously chewing gum. I felt relieved when I heard the students laugh. The lecturer was holding their attention. But there was so much fear, it seemed impossible the students would remember anything. When the lecturer stretched the skin of a thirty-foot python across the stage, Debbie almost fainted. Later she did throw up. If the classrooms were as fearful, students would learn nothing.

Thursday, March 27

A group of teachers assembled in the library with Dr. William Kantar, the school psychiatrist, for a fifteen-week course in Crisis Prevention, meeting after school for one-and-a-half hours. The course is voluntary, open to the first fourteen teachers to enroll.

We talked about the way the students have segregated themselves by color in the classrooms. A supervisor participating in the course seemed interested in the possibility of assigning blacks and whites alphabetically so they would have to mix racially. I commented, "They're afraid. What is the point of that?"

Friday, March 28

A few of the girls—blacks and whites—occasionally wear skirts now. They look like spring flowers, despite their aggressive "Attica" or "Stop Forced Busing" or "Never" pins.

I was late. The buses rolled up at 7:50, just as I arrived at the hilltop. As I reached homeroom, my coffee bag broke, spilling over the floor. Four troopers stood at the door, watching. While I put my books down, a trooper came bearing the mop. He called me by my first name, though I don't know his. I said, "I'll clean it up," but was touched by his thoughtfulness. A student finished mopping for me while I went off to get my papers.

I have been very, very tired, too tired to look at the troopers' faces lately.

During my break, I went to the cafeteria for coffee. As I approached the front lobby landing, I heard loud, animal-like wails, and a terrific smashing sound coming from the holding room for blacks. Two Boston policemen ran to the door: "Who's hurt, the girl or the police?" They listened, ears near the door. A trooper stood poised on the edge of the stairs, ready to move down, watching the door. I said, "My God! What's the point of all this madness?" He ignored me. I passed on.

The girl was an emotionally disturbed student, one of those students with special disabilities—physical, mental, or emotional—who had been mainstreamed to the high school under a recent act of the Massachusetts legislature, Chapter 766. She had kicked out the door panel of the sewing room, nails and splintered wood shooting out into the corridor. The petite sewing teacher, Sara Elbery, reluctant to have the girl led off by troopers, tried to calm her and called the front office for "nice Miss Weston. You like Miss Weston." The class waited. Seconds later metal chairs and waste baskets were flying around the room.

Later I tried to remember the Boston police outside the holding room door, but couldn't, nor whether they were black officers or white or both.

Easter holiday begins. The buses arrived and the black students boarded them, while the white students waited inside until they left. If they are religious, they go off to celebrate the passion of Christ. The troopers leave for their double duty. Male teachers turn neckties around to the front again, and we go off for a jolly-up faculty party, sparsely attended, no black teachers. Mothers breathe a sigh of relief that their children will be home, and for a few days they won't have to sit by the phone and wait for a riot call. Weep, Madonna, for your child!

Monday, March 31

A Boston policeman told me two twenty-year-old youths had been killed near the high school over the weekend: Southie is getting tougher, and busing doesn't help.

Tuesday, April 1

A new group of troopers is in the cafeteria study now. They feel useless and helpless to do anything constructive. They call themselves "rent-a-cop." I quoted Milton: "They also serve who only stand and wait."

Thursday, April 3

In my Teen Lit course, the sophomores have been reading *The Outsiders* and the sequel, *That Was Then, This Is Now*, stories about gang warfare, sometimes involving the police. We talked about Boston and state police, comparing them, but when I asked them to write a composition, the boys balked about putting their names on paper: "We already talked about it; what do we have to write about it for?" The consensus was that the Boston police are older, have earned their stripes, and don't have to "bust" kids to make their own records look good, but give them a chance. The staties are younger, better organized, at their assigned places, and don't mess around. Gretchen, who didn't mind signing her name, wrote the best summary:

My Opinion of the Policemen at So. Boston High

To me all policemen seem like nice guys. When I go through the hall every morning, they greet me nicely. I can't really give an opinion about how they handle different situations because whenever there is a fight, I scram. However, I do know that some are prejudiced. They may accuse kids of crimes without proof just out of their own heads. This prejudice may be due to kids' races or environments. Others are really understanding individuals and care and feel sorry for others.

A trooper who had once student-taught in New Hampshire came to my door today as I was going to lunch. He asked me why I bothered to teach in South Boston: The kids didn't care about studying and learning; their books were dirty; they lay across their desks; half of them had records with the police; they were using the busing as an excuse to raise hell. He made me angry.

I asked, "Then what is to be accomplished by busing them over the city? We know what we have. Why not leave them alone so we can work with them? They can be challenged, but it takes a little more time. Dr. Reid is aware that 'the roar of the street corner in Southie is much stronger than the appeal of books.'" I missed lunch.

The NAACP will appeal the constitutionality of the racial percentages of schools in West Roxbury, East Boston, Charlestown, and South Boston, assigned in the masters' Phase 2 desegregation plan. The masters' plan allows variation from 95 percent white schools in East Boston, 80 percent white in West Roxbury to 70 percent black in parts of Dorchester. Full-scale desegregation, Atkins recalled, had been the goal of the black plaintiffs since they first filed suit in 1972.

Sunday, April 6

Antibusing demonstrators mobbed Senator Kennedy in suburban Quincy, forcing him to walk four blocks to the underground subway. They flattened the tires of his car and put their children under the wheels of his aide's car.

Tuesday, April 8

I have always felt secure in my classes, that the "war" was out there. Never more. There are violent emotions in some students, black and white, and they can explode anytime.

I was taking attendance, my head in my book, while Ted set up the projector for the film version of *Phoebe*, one of the novels in my sophomore elective dealing with teen problems. Suddenly Anne was screaming abusively at Ted to pick up her pocketbook that he'd knocked over with the projector. I asked Ted to pick up the bag. He did. That should have been the end of the confrontation, but Anne continued her verbal attack. Ted's face turned white and strained. I went back to them. Later Ted told me that Anne was jabbing the table with her pen, and that I was holding her. I don't remember. I was watching Ted's face, his lips whitening and his face contorting with anger, wondering if he would, or if I could, help him control himself. When he lifted—slightly—the cover of the projector, I said, "You're not going to touch her," and put my hand on his arm. Anne warned him, "If you touch me, you'd better kill me, because Michael Faith isn't the only one who's going to get stabbed around here."

The class just sat and watched in stunned and humiliated silence.

I scolded Ted for being thoughtless in his actions, even with me sometimes; he had to be more thoughtful of people. I told Anne, "Your language is not entirely polite either." I was not harsher with her because I wanted to prevent trouble, rather than create it. They would have to behave, or leave, I ordered. The screaming had lasted so loud and long I thought the police might come, but they didn't. Perhaps the sound was muffled by the fire-wall barrier.

I was afraid to turn out the lights for the film. But, since the class had read the book, they were interested in the film visualization. I was glad, because I was so nervous I wasn't sure I could talk. At the end of the film screening, Anne's face, when I looked at her, was sorrowful. I sent Ted off to return the projector to the audio-visual room while the rest of the class worked on a value questionnaire on the film.

Anne and Ted were two students I never expected would fight. Anne had talked to me earlier in the year about transferring out of South Boston High School, and I had asked her not to. Ted can be fresh, but I have never seen him overtly antiblack. But the teacher doesn't know what problems the students have already encountered outside the classroom and are bringing in with them, and what feelings or animosities they have developed toward others in the room.

After class I talked to Gretchen. She was afraid because the girl kept up her verbal abuse. Louis, when I asked him, said, "Well, I wouldn't have let them fight."

Wednesday, April 9

Anne was out. I complimented the rest of the class on their behavior yesterday. The incident demonstrated to me, I said, that they are capable of, wanted to, and did exercise control over the situation.

After school, faculty met again with the school psychiatrist for the Crisis Prevention seminar. When the other teachers talked about their nice classrooms, their "control," I mentioned the incident in my classroom. The psychiatrist suggested, "Maybe you should have told the class, 'I feel afraid about turning out the lights and turning on the projector. What do you think?'"

We discussed the alienation of some white students, who feel so deserted by the teachers that they can't talk to them as they once did because of the liberal attitudes of some teachers toward busing.

I asked about sorrow, if sorrow didn't follow anger. Dr. Kantar seemed reluctant to answer. When I insisted, he said then, "Yes, but sometimes the anger lasts a long time."

Thursday, April 10

When I reached class, Anne was outside the door with her friend. "I'm not going to class. I want to do research in the library," she said. I told her she had to come, then left. In a few minutes, Anne came in. "I'm not going to talk about Tuesday," she announced. She pushed away her *Catcher in the Rye*. "I'm not going to read that. I don't like it." Just then the gym teacher came by to borrow some chairs. I asked three boys, blacks and whites, to help carry them, mindful of our discussion at the Crisis Prevention seminar yesterday, that the students are very conscious of the teachers' actions, and the delicate balance of white and black. Anne called over boldly to the gym teacher, "What are you doing in here? Why aren't you in your own room?" The class looked up with pained expressions. The gym teacher didn't react. When she had gone, though, I asked Anne, "Do you like the gym teacher?" She answered, "Yes." I continued, "It would be very difficult to tell by what you said that you like her. When we talk to people, we send out signals. Unless we are very clear in the signals we send out, they can be misinterpreted, so that we are not communicating what we want to communicate to others. We are now in a very sensitive situation in this school, and you have to be extra alert to the kinds of signals you send out to others so that you won't be misinterpreted. That misinterpretation is what happened in this room the other day." My speech seemed to clear the air for all the students, and they relaxed. Anne also relaxed and reached for her copy of *The Catcher in the Rye*.

Friday, April 11

While I was in the front office copying some material, I heard an administrator talking with two lawyers. He said, "Of course I want a criminal charge! He came in school with a scalpel knife. What are we using the detectors for? Is it all a charade? There are signs up as you come in listing the weapons. They've been told repeatedly." The other administrator agreed. Though I am curious, I prefer not to know who brings in what weapon and don't ask; knowing would only make me afraid.

One week until vacation.

Monday, April 14

I was tired this morning. I had to park on the hill, facing down toward the bay. A trooper standing there asked me when school got out, if school would close early because of the shortage of funds. I asked, "Who cares?" I had trouble with my car keys. "Damn!" I said.

Tuesday, April 15

Anne did not come to class. I passed by her afterward in a little room off the corridor, guarded by a policeman. She apologized for missing class, "I didn't cut." The policeman affirmed her statement. Some white girls came by, like angry hornets. Anne disappeared behind the door. She looked exhilarated. I think she enjoys fighting.

Wednesday, April 16

The South Boston–Roxbury High School connection has been severed. There will be no joint prom; no joint yearbook; no joint graduation. The divorce is an admission that the desegregation plan was a failure.

The Crisis Prevention group met again after school. We discussed our feelings about the past year. Almost everyone had the depressed feeling: "This is the last. The end of an era."

Mr. Van Schyndel enthusiastically said, though, "This is the beginning of a new and better time."

I learned that the Anne of my English class is the one who hit the senior on the head with a padlock at the beginning of the year. I was stunned. I was glad I hadn't known.

Thursday, April 17

During my cafeteria study, the white girls hassled me for twenty-five minutes to get Jasmin out of the study, probably because I wouldn't let one of them leave to make a phone call. I knew Jasmin was not assigned there, but another teacher had left her behind, promising to return for her. My attention meanwhile was diverted by a large influx of white boys, some from the van outside that was "too cold," some from the library that had closed for National Honor Society induction ceremonies.

Toward the end of the study, a black boy passed by to the water bubbler, perhaps intending to direct my attention to the back of the room. Almost immediately a silence fell over the study. One of the boys talking to me, without looking around, said, "Listen how quiet it is. There's going to be a riot in a few minutes." I thought that was amusing, reminding me of the sign in the front office, "School used to have its laughs. Now it's a riot."

The bell rang and I looked back. A trooper was standing with the white girls and Jasmin, who had moved over to their bench. He was telling them, "You girls should try to get along and talk nicely to each other." I went back to thank him.

The white girls had been giving the black girls the finger behind the post, whispering "nigger," he said. He thought the two black girls walked by, maybe deliberately, heard an insult, then sat down on the bench with the white girls to try to figure out who had made the remark. That's when he moved over. "You can see it coming," he said.

As we talked, I noticed Jasmin, a pick in her hand, run out the cafeteria door, a pack of black students with her, and up the stairs after Jane. Catching up with them on the second floor landing, I ordered Jasmin to go along to class. After the crowd cleared the stairs, I walked with Jane to her class. I told her, "You girls provoked that. I told you to keep your mouth shut." I was angry and went to the office to ask the administration to talk with the girls. The students were there ahead of me, reporting me for neglect of duty.

Friday, April 18

I interrupted my first class, at Dr. Reid's request, in order to finish my report on the cafeteria incident. As I left the front office, Jane's mother, who was waiting to talk with Dr. Reid, warned me, "Don't you ever tell my daughter to keep her mouth shut when someone insults her." Dr. Reid broke in, telling me, "Go to your class."

Friday, May 2

Jasmin came in again to my cafeteria study and sat down. I asked her to leave, gave her a few minutes, then asked the gym teacher to get her to class. Jasmin left then, but yelled at me as she went, "Big mouth!" I laughed. The troopers looked at me, astounded at my reaction.

One trooper remarked on how much time and trouble is spent protecting the school when the troopers and teachers outnumber the students.

Saturday, May 3

Militant members of the Progressive Labor party marched without permit to Louise Day Hicks's house at 8:00 in the morning. According to the police chief, a "strike team" wearing ski caps, white T-shirts, and leather belts attacked the neighborhood kids, charging them and running a distance of 50 to 100 feet. They karate-kicked and hit them with sticks. The kids withdrew but returned 1,000 strong with stones and baseball bats. The party members tried to hoist a red flag at the Kosciuszko Traffic Circle in South Boston, but the kids tore it down. Over 300 police battled to keep the peace. The PLP then marched on to Franklin Park, where they promised to "be back all summer."

How can there be peace at the high school after this?

Monday, May 5

Siegfried took part in the Saturday PLP march, I heard. The kids are after him.

Wednesday, May 7

Siegfried wore a red PLP flag to class. Dr. Reid went to his homeroom and asked Siegfried to put the flag in his locker.

I was a little late leaving the classroom. Mr. John Power, who follows me, had already come in along with his senior boys. Suddenly we heard the roar of a fight. Boston police, blacks and whites, were running down the corridor with jellyfish-fear faces. Mr. Power left. I stayed at the door, blocking it. One boy pleaded to leave. "We've been told to turn in names of any students who don't obey directions when a fight breaks out," I told him. "I don't care if I get a court record," he answered. Just then a boy reported back to the room: Siegfried had been hit with a chair. A crowd of white boys marched by, chanting, "Roh, roh, roh. . . ." Four emergency bells sounded. Troopers hurtled up the stairs from their staging area in the North Cafeteria. Mr. Power returned. I went on to my assignment in the library, calling to boys by name to go to class. They tend to respond to their names.

As I passed a trooper in the corridor, he said, "Things are picking up. One boy was arrested already today, brought down to court, and booked. That'll keep him out of trouble for a while."

Dr. Reid was in the corridors throughout the day, walking them. His face looked strained, but he smiled. Just yesterday, at the faculty meeting, he was talking hopefully about "a few more days and a successful year."

By dismissal time, a crowd had gathered at the hilltop corner. I hurried back to my homeroom, mindful of what the psychiatrist said, that the black students are very much afraid of crowds gathering on the street, that their tough act covered up fear. I chased the students away from the window so Jeffrey would not become alarmed.

After Jeffrey had left for the buses, the Southie "walkers" talked about their fears. Some of the black kids said they would beat them up after the seniors left; there would be another stabbing.

When the trooper bus and squad cars left, the crowd outside booed. A Boston police officer commented, "It doesn't take much to set them off, does it? Just anything could explode them now."

Thursday, May 8

Trooper Jennings, in riot helmet for the first time, was standing at the main entrance steps when I arrived. "This is a very special day," he smiled. South Boston had been leafleted overnight with unsigned notices urging the residents to keep the Communists out of the school, to meet at the school at 7:00 A.M. A crowd of 300 adults and youths had already gathered.

Almost all troopers were on duty outside the high school, their numbers augmented by 400 Boston police and TPF. A double line of troopers faced down G Street.

Jeffrey, the only black attending in my homeroom, was too nervous to be diverted by the morning newspaper. He asked, "Will you call me a taxi and I'll slip out the back door?" Debbie became sick from the boys' talk of the possibility of violence in the school and outside.

There were no troopers stationed in my cafeteria study. A group of white boys tried to force their way in. One challenged, "All you white teachers are afraid of the niggers," and began calling "nigger" over my head at the black students inside. I replied, "I'm just doing my job, and you know it."

After the boys left, the white girls demanded, "Are you going to write up an incident report about the black girls who have been yelling 'honky' at us?" I argued, "I can't report what goes on behind me. If every teacher picked up every student on every little thing he did wrong, there would be a steady stream to the office." One girl showed me her knuckles she had bruised banging them on the wooden bench in order to keep her anger under control. She couldn't go to typing next period, she said.

Helping to release anxiety is one good effect the troopers have when they stand and talk to the students during the studies.

At dismissal time I joshed Jeffrey to make him relax. "Are you a Communist, Jeffrey?" He grinned. "Be sure not to wear any red tomorrow."

He would determine whether to come to school the next day, he said, by watching the school buses; if they were full enough, he would be in.

The school buses left without incident. When the state police left, the crowd cheered them. I asked Mr. Gizzi, who meets the buses every day, "Do they like the troopers or not? Yesterday they booed, today they cheer." He answered, "They half do and half don't."

Friday, May 9

It was Class Day for the seniors, with early dismissal for all. The streets around the high school were deserted.

When I was free, I talked with a trooper, who told me he feels so frustrated by what he sees in the school and his inability to do anything that he sometimes punches the walls.

As we talked, a sophomore came by to return his books; he was moving to suburban Braintree. "How long have you lived in South Boston?" "Seventeen years."

Siegfried will not be back, the trooper said. I believe the boys will kill him if he does return.

All students ate early lunch, then the school buses slipped in and away at 11:30, the troopers immediately after. Only a few Boston police remained on duty. The seniors had invited the troopers to stay for the Class Day exercises, but an outraged mother interviewed in the *Herald* declared she had never heard of such a thing.

The Class Day show, an all-white cast, was good. I discovered a Mae West, a Charlie Chaplin, and a few romances I didn't know about from my English class. There was a party afterwards in the cafeteria. The senior who tried to break into my study yesterday threw a duffle bag to his friend over my head, so low I had to duck. It was the only bad note of the day.

Outside eight TPF on motorcycles blocked off the street. They basked in the peaceful sunshine, the metal hardware of their bikes glinting in the sun. They didn't even protest when we passed them going the wrong way on the one-way circle outside.

Such a bad week—with a happy ending. Dr. Reid was very pleased.

Saturday evening at a press conference Robert Dentler, the court's chief desegregation "expert," unveiled Garrity's final Phase 2 desegregation order. The new plan, devised by Dentler and Scott, keeps the direction of the earlier masters' plan—the university-business alliance as well as the division of the school system into one citywide or "magnet school" district and eight community districts—but has adjusted the district boundary lines drawn by the masters to make them conform to more uniform racial percentages. The experts' plan will honor student assignment preferences according to a more racially balanced quota system than the ratios stipulated in the masters' proposal and will double the number of students involved in mandatory busing that had been projected in the masters' figures—up to 24,000 in grades 1 to 12—leaving East Boston, however, almost untouched.

Mayor White declared angrily, "By this order, Judge Garrity has virtually guaranteed a continuation of the present level of tension and hostility throughout the city."

Monday, May 12

It was a beautiful day today. Few students were in school and almost no one was on the streets.

The two ROAR leaders, Mrs. Virginia Sheehy and Mrs. Rita Graul, accompanied by Mrs. Louise Day Hicks, were in court on NAACP deposition to answer questions about the crowds that gathered last week in front of South Boston High. Judge Garrity warned there was a point where the First Amendment did *not* allow freedom of speech. He compared South Boston High and Hyde Park High to "powder kegs ready to explode at any minute," and threatened to close them if there was violence. He mentioned the potential for violence in the city, that the police should be prepared. A policeman had told me: "South Boston is a trigger for the city; the city will go as it goes."

Mrs. Hicks left the courthouse, promising, "If Judge Garrity wants to make Boston the battlefield, so be it."

The U.S. Supreme Court refused to hear appeals filed by the Boston School Committee and Mayor White on Judge Garrity's desegregation order of June 21, 1974.

Tuesday, May 13

As I walked in the corridor, I noticed a senior girl writing on the windows of the third-floor auditorium doors: "Niggers beware May 15." I asked her to erase it. She denied she wrote it. A trooper told me, "Forget about it. Let things stay cool until the seniors go." His captain came by then and told him to rub it off.

At the end of the day, I overheard two troopers telling a small boy in a peaked cap, "Take off your hat. You have it on backward, or maybe your head is turned around." Their hostility surprised me. I told my fifteen-year-old nephew, curious about his comments. I thought he would be sympathetic to the boy. He said, "I don't blame the police. They want to be out chasing burglars, not standing around in the school."

In homeroom James watched the buses leave under double police escort. He exclaimed, "It looks like it's the President leaving!"

Wednesday, May 14

Today was the seniors' last day. The police anticipated trouble. The seniors have been threatening, "It's revenge time now. Who cares if the school closes?"

It was a foggy day. Most cars had turned on their headlights. I wondered what would come out of the mists around South Boston High as I passed the state police car waiting, as always, at the rear horseshoe entrance to the circle around the Dorchester Heights Monument.

The number of troopers on duty had been doubled. If they knew me, they called me by name.

Outside my senior class two young troopers stood, one on either side of the door, as if with invisible raised swords for a wedding. It was impressive, dramatic, and unnecessary. When I closed the door, they moved away.

We had a good last class together. I collected books or money, signed their papers, gave each a carved ivory pin from the thousand I bought in India several years ago when I was planning to start a mail-order business. The class president showed slides he had taken of South Boston with an NDEA-grant camera, giving us a short, nostalgic trip through the community and year; then the bell rang. The card I gave them with the elephant pin read, "I'm glad you came."

At lunchtime the cafeteria snarled, snapped, and roared. Benches and bodies bumped, but with troopers lining the walls, there was no chance to fight. The administration tried to schedule the seniors for lunch, but finally abandoned the attempt. The seniors left before noon.

Thursday, May 15

A white girl came down late to the cafeteria study shaking—from fear or anger, I don't know. She wouldn't talk to me. There had been a fight on the third floor. Mild and gentle Hal, one of the white boys in my homeroom, had provoked the incident. I had difficulty believing the report. Hal was suspended.

Saturday, May 17

While ROAR held seminars at the Hynes Memorial Auditorium in the Back Bay, the National Student Coalition Against Racism marched peacefully down Commonwealth Avenue holding aloft effigies of Hicks and Kerrigan. Contingents from the NAACP—which had sponsored the march—Sinn Fein, Gays, Bryn Mawr, the Universalist Church, and a few clergy—a priest and an Anglican minister—also marched. Parade marshals linked hands together blocking off the access streets to the ROAR rally nearby. There was no violent defection from the well-organized march.

Some Progressive Labor party members did infiltrate the ROAR meeting. Channel 7 TV interviewed them with the lead-in, "ROAR is just a hum."

Sunday, May 18

Michael Faith, jogging on doctor's orders along Carson Beach, rescued a man from drowning. Michael reached over the dock, pulled out the man's false teeth that were choking him, and lifted the man out of the water to safety.

Monday, May 19

Hal came back from suspension. He said with some wonder, "The troopers really pulled my hair." I don't think he'll forget that. He asked, "The other boy wasn't suspended, huh?"

Tuesday, May 20

A woman representative from the U.S. Civil Rights Commission sat down beside me in the study cafeteria. She wanted to know why the students were afraid. I asked, "When did they tell you that?" She said, "At the beginning of the year." I answered, "They weren't after maybe February. Before that they were afraid of who might be coming up behind them, and walked looking back over their shoulder." I gave her the reasons for the change:

1. Increased police numbers.
2. Metal detectors.
3. Introduction of a cooling-off room where students could stay until they were taken out, instead of being left in the library all day, the only option at the beginning of the year.
4. Identification of the core troublemakers, most of whom had gone by

now, either by suspension or choice, as dropouts or transfers to other public
or private schools.

5. The van. Dr. Reid, on the Thursday before the stabbing, announced
we had made a big advance by the acquisition of a professional van service
with driver, which could move the black troublemakers out of the school
after a fight. The police had been unwilling to drive them, and, in any
case, it was unsafe to drive a car of blacks through South Boston. The school
day could calm down once the troublemakers — black or white — were out
of the building.

In response to my question, the lawyer told me she had become interested
in civil rights while she was working on an Indian reservation, but that
problem would go on for years. The busing problem was immediate and
very exciting. And, she said, she didn't have a chance to march in Selma,
Alabama. South Boston was her Selma.

I told her, "A great injustice has been done to the people of South Boston
by forcing on them a desegregation plan that didn't consider the needs of
the students or the working-class background of the community." I continued, "But I don't think the courts are alone guilty. The Massachusetts Board
of Education is also responsible. They should know better." She replied,
"The Boston School Committee had ten years to act."

She talked about the constitutionality of forced busing, based on the
Brown vs. Board of Education decision. "There cannot be separate but
equal education," she said. "Of course, the Constitution doesn't say anything
about numbers. More liberal judges will have to be appointed to the Supreme
Court before the law can be changed to include the suburbs in busing."

As we talked, she glanced down at the table where Siegfried used to eat
standing, in brooding silence, wearing black gloves. "Ooh," she exclaimed,
and she rubbed at the graffiti cut into the table top: "Zigfried, have you
pissed your pants today."

After school I asked Hal about his brother, a junior dropout. "Will he
return next year?" Hal answered, "No, he's making six dollars an hour in
a meatpacking house." I thought of the civil rights worker with her college
degrees, her social and working mobility. Is Hal's brother expendable?

Wednesday, May 21

At the Crisis Prevention seminar after school, Mr. Milton Bornstein,
a supervisor, suggested for consideration an actual crisis situation: A Boston
teacher was pushed down a flight of stairs by a student. The teacher is still

out of work. What would you do when faced with such a situation? I replied, "Quit."

TV news reported that a gang of black teenagers—fourteen, sixteen, and eighteen years old—stabbed a white cab driver to death in Roxbury. I wonder what school, if any, they attend.

Thursday, May 22

These are halcyon days, though there is a lump of sadness at my heart. So many teachers and police, but no students. So many youngsters are at Carson Beach, there is some fear of attacks on the school buses.

The troopers' morale is low. They are tired from overtime work; their overtime pay is late. Sometimes they sail airplanes out the windows; sometimes they roll coins or stones down the corridor to pass the time.

Friday, May 23

Michael Faith was at school reenacting the stabbing scene for detectives. He had been stabbed in the corridor outside the library and had walked about eight steps to where I saw him lying on the floor outside the auditorium door.

Going home I passed long lines in front of the U.S. Unemployment Office in suburban Newton. If there was any one best time for court-ordered busing in Boston, it is now, when people don't have the money to move away. Boston may hold together.

Wednesday, May 28

Participating teachers in the Crisis Prevention seminar voted to continue next year, since the meetings acted as a safety valve for tension, helped us to see students in perspective with other teachers, and allowed us to know our fellow teachers better.

I mentioned how much it bothers me to show a white film or pass out white books all the time. What is it like for blacks to live in a white world and cry when the white man cries, while the white man won't cry for him?

Thursday, May 29

These are peaceful days. The police are slipping away to their summer jobs. Their numbers are noticeably decreased. Some remaining continue to compete, sailing paper airplanes out the third-floor windows.

Friday, May 30

For the first time in the study I saw white students sitting at the same table the blacks have used winter-long. Although the white students didn't talk to them, they had the option of sitting anywhere in the cafeteria, and sat there.

In the library the students asked me my feelings about busing: "We want to know whether you're for it or against it." I said, "It doesn't matter what I think or feel; it's a court order." They insisted on an answer, but I repeated the statement. One girl used the word "nigger." I frowned. Later, when I saw her again, she used "nigger," then corrected herself to "black." She said, "I know you don't like the word." I answered, "First of all, to use 'nigger' isn't cool or sophisticated. Besides, it isn't kind, and I know you're a kind girl." Those weren't my priorities of reasoning, but, if they were good enough for the suburbs, they were good enough for them. She accepted the criticism with a smile of good will.

Tuesday, June 3

I was late today. The buses had already arrived. The ugliness of the scene—the goggled motorcycle police waiting while the buses emptied, the metal detector search and hand-scanning in the lobby—depressed me.

Most of the white sophomore girls in my cafeteria study told me they would be attending parochial school next year; they had been on the waiting list for a year. When I asked about Cardinal Medeiros's statement that he would not allow a white flight to parochial schools, one replied, "Money talks."

Gretchen was concerned that I would lose my job because of declining enrollment. I was touched by her concern, that, besides their own safety, the students have to worry about the welfare of their teachers. I suggested that it would be better to save her $500 tuition for college, but she had already made a down payment of $50. It would be too much of a hassle to make up school work if there were more problems at the opening of school next year, she said. Students know the direction of community thinking, and I have found we have to listen to them.

At a meeting for aides in the library, one South Boston male aide announced as he arrived, "I don't want to listen to any more shit from the federal judge."

Wednesday, June 4

At the last meeting of the Crisis Prevention seminar, the psychiatrist talked about the "threat" that an Irish-Catholic community like South Boston feels when kids with different cultural attitudes and values come into their community. Before discussion we determined, at my insistence, that the community was not identifiably Irish except in its elected politicians, but rather Catholic, since the numbers of Italians, Poles, and Lithuanians were also large.

Thursday, June 5

A lacrosse demonstration was held in the boys' gym today. White students sat on a mat on the gym floor, while most of the blacks stood. About thirty troopers, bristling with restrained force, mixed with the students or watched, standing along the walls with the teachers. Dr. Reid hailed the mixed assembly as "a beginning for next year."

Friday, June 6

There were 75 state troopers, 20 Boston police, 30 aides, 100 teachers, and 220 students in school today.

I talked with a trooper in the study cafeteria. The United States started to decline, he claimed, with the failure to salute the flag. I said, "It was before that, when a national anthem was adopted that nobody can sing because the notes are either too high or too low."

Monday, June 9

In my sophomore "Humor" course we watched *The Golden Age of Comedy*, a historical review. The only blacks in the film were shining shoes. Blacks have come a long way. Still, I was mortified.

Tension is picking up. The white boys are shaving their hair to close whiffles and talking about "getting a nigger."

During my cafeteria study, Sylvia got up, went over to the white girls, and asked them, "Why do you always act like asses?"

Tuesday, June 10

Today was the last day of my "Humor" mini-course. Final exams take up the rest of the week.

A mid-morning assembly for sophomores was held—a science lecture on gases—air, helium, carbon dioxide—elementary and excellent. Some students wouldn't be quiet: The lecture was "boring." One of the troopers, standing in horseshoe formation at the back of the hall, was disgusted with what he called the students' "show-me" attitude toward education. I commented, "You have to stand on your head to interest these kids." "Naked," a colleague added.

Wednesday, June 11

A student film festival followed exams. The highlight was a student film on busing, *They're Watching Us*, with scenes of the December 11 riot and a voiceover of students' comments on busing, the year, and the government that had made "puppets" out of them. The student body responded positively. They felt the film was fair, though some white students were disgruntled by the black boy's boast that he had "wasted a dude" with a chair. The white students did not like being portrayed as the losers in a fight.

At the faculty meeting at the end of the day, Dr. Reid called the screening "a calculated risk, an experiment." He said, "I felt it worked." I felt so also. The film only reproduced what the kids think and say to one another all the time. The riot crowd of December 11 had ballooned in my memory to fill all the crevices of my mind; seeing the film brought the crowd and day down into proportion and perspective—I'm sure for the students also. But Mrs. Folkart and some others did not agree. There had been a fight in the girls' lavatory at the end of the day; a policewoman was hit with bookbags when she went in to break it up. Some teachers felt the film was responsible for the fight.

In the evening the class of 1975 at South Boston High School was graduated in ceremonies at the Hynes Auditorium. Dr. Reid thanked the teachers and parents for making the graduation possible. Applause. There had been a tentative list last June of a possible 340 seniors, and about 292 had made the graduation. Applause.

School Committeewoman Kathleen Sullivan spoke, calling the "beloved" Dr. Reid, along with Mrs. Coughlin, the mother of the hockey team captain, "the two people most responsible for the reopening of the school in January." "Beloved" Dr. Reid. Like Mr. Chips, I thought, Dr. Reid has arrived at the third stage: obeyed, honored—now loved.

Michael Faith was among the graduates.

Thursday, June 12

Sylvia left school in the van before school. She had refused to submit to the routine search by teachers at the metal detectors and sassed a trooper.

I was assigned to the South Cafeteria study for the first two hours of the morning exams. At nine o'clock students poured down from the assembly hall for brunch. A trooper exclaimed, "There are too many kids!" Then he submerged behind a sea of moving bodies. "Move along and sit down," I told the students. They did, squeezing into benches, black girls and boys dividing into quadrangles, facing their white counterparts like squares on a checkerboard. Dr. Reid came along then, moving through the group still blocking the passageway. He said loudly, looking at me, "Everything's all right." "Brunch" settled down then into fifteen minutes of silent watching and waiting. When the students left to view cartoons made in Mrs. Smith's film class, they went peacefully. Gretchen, her face worried, came last, ready to "scram" if she had to.

As I walked down the stairs to my homeroom almost at the 11:00 dismissal time, I saw a black boy slug a white boy. Within seconds the stair landing was wedged with boys and troopers—two of them wrestling with boys on the floor—a mass of hitting, swirling violence.

I started to run, then checked myself. I stood there repeating, "Stay out of it. Go along."

One of my black sophomore girls walked up the stairs without a backward look. Earlier in the year she had said, "Wait until we get them next year at Roxbury High." The plan had been abandoned; there would be no revenge.

I hardly recognized the knotted, angry faces of whiffled boys from the happy faces of my "Humor" mini-course, as troopers marched them to the cooling-off room.

My homeroom students were angry. They said, "Wait until tomorrow." I was amazed, as I always am, at how detailed their knowledge of the fights is, when and where they took place, who was involved, who got hurt. James stuck out his tongue at Martin's back. They stood angry at the windows as the buses left.

Friday, June 13

Before school, a trooper told me he was getting too old to wrestle kids on the floor; it was bad for his heart. Outside, troopers would just break a guy's arm or handcuff him, but they didn't want to hurt the kids. They were just babies. But he was concerned that if a youngster got pushed or thrown down the stairs, he could be killed. In a situation such as yesterday, he said, the troopers ordinarily block the entrances to contain the crowd. Otherwise, when one or the other side is losing, the friends jump in to help. Sometimes the best thing to do in a riot, he advised me, was to run. He asked how the day would be. I answered, "It all depends on the organization. If it's tight, no trouble. They want revenge."

But everything was superorganized today. After exams, students returned to homerooms, rather than massing together in the cafeteria.

My homeroom students threatened to walk out. James said, "We have no rights." But within minutes Dr. Reid was at the door, dismissing the white students room by room throughout the building, like an evacuation. "Revenge" evaporated in the joy of freedom. When the "bused students" announcement came, my two black students, Jeffrey and Martin, both survivors, said, "Good-by. We won't be back."

At 11:00 A.M. the troopers assembled outside. Dr. Reid presented them with a Certificate of Appreciation. At their own party later, the group awarded their police captain a plaque with a gold brick and a pair of dice, symbol of the wheel of fortune that had involved them in the destiny of South Boston High.

Monday, June 16

The U.S. Commission on Civil Rights began hearings on Boston school desegregation.

Wednesday, June 18

The Civil Rights hearings continue. Cardinal Medeiros testified yesterday that Phase 2 school desegregation in Boston is "morally right and good."

Next year the Hart-Dean Annex will be closed and all permanent black teachers moved to the L-Street Annex of the high school. Eleven white permanent teachers have been declared "excess" and will be dropped into a teacher pool in order to comply with the federal court order racially balancing faculty with 30 percent blacks. One of those is Alice Kerman, who alone in the December 11 riot, of all the teachers, police, and aides, carried a fainting girl in her arms down the Golden Staircase to the yellow school buses waiting below. Dr. Reid praised her courage.

With almost no students left in the school, there were two incidents today. In one, a black girl hit a white girl in the face, as she sat across from a trooper at a cafeteria table. I saw the police reports. I was surprised to see that the troopers, in their write-ups, use qualifying phrases like "John Doe, a sensitive boy."

Thursday, June 19

The Civil Rights hearings continue.

The newly elected school superintendent, Marion Fahey, who officially begins her three-year term next September, testified she had "every confidence" that parents, teachers, and students would make Phase 2 desegregation successful.

Friday, June 20

The Civil Rights hearings ended. Commissioner diGrazia told the commission that the police wouldn't be needed if the teachers were doing their job disciplining.

At the high school the assembled state troopers posed for a picture in front of the building, their officer muttering to them, "Don't smile." They left after the last school bus at 9:30 A.M. today.

I compiled the year's cumulative attendance for my homeroom. Of my original homeroom list, three boys never came, and one came for a day; four girls never came, two girls came for fewer than thirty days, and one completed the school year with a home teacher upon recommendation of a psychiatrist.

The highest attendance of 145 days out of a possible 163 total was for Kathryn, who came the first day and spent the last two months on a flexible-campus program at Thompson's Island. The attendance read as follows:

Students	Number of Days		
	Present	Absent	Tardy
Boy (white)	116	36	11
Boy (black)	89	74	0
Boy (white)	64	53	5
Boy (white)	1	91	1
Boy (white)	77	71	13
Boy (black)	103	52	1
Boy (white)	52	106	15
Girl (white)	24	35	3
Girl (white)	90	41	0
Girl (white)	48	80	5
Girl (white)	141	22	1
Girl (white)	145	14	0
Girl (white)	74	53	10
Girl (white)	100	9	0
Girl (white)	28	46	0

Both black boys and more than half the white students were living with only one parent, the mother, either because of divorce or death in the family. The number of children in a family ranged from one to seven.

The *Globe* remarked that a "universal sigh of relief" would accompany the final day of Boston's most "volatile" school year. For me, there is only a tremendous feeling of sadness for the kids who never came to school or who gave up; for the black kids I like who won't be coming back and the white kids who will leave for private schools or the suburbs; for the weakening of the high school by excessing of faculty; for the waste of local, state, and federal money, and the sham with which it is sometimes allocated; for the talk of revenge in Phase 2 desegregation and intervention by tanks, National Guard, or federal troops.

Dr. Reid told the faculty everything looks fine and hopeful for next year. But then, didn't the teachers, including me, think everything would be all right after the seniors left? The hatred among the sophomores will carry over to next year. If the students have had a good experience in another school, the hatred here will absorb them like a sponge. After all, the only light at the end of the tunnel of the long Vietnam War was Ho Chi Minh City.

I pick up my books and go home to chronicle the year.

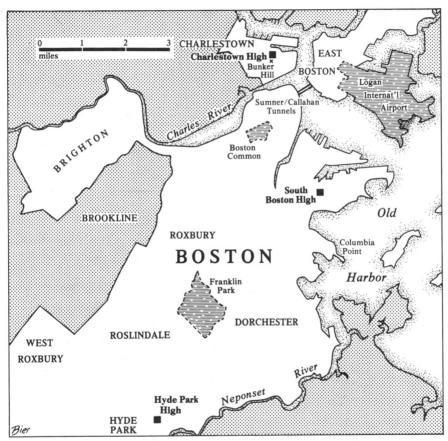

Boston's potential trouble spots. Based on a map from *Time* magazine.

Graffiti on a South Boston housing project. Massachusetts State Police.

Aerial view of South Boston High School and the Dorchester Heights Monument. *Boston Globe.*

September 12, 1974. Phase 1 desegregation begins. The buses get through. *Boston Herald.*

September 13, 1974. Dr. William J. Reid, headmaster of South Boston High School, directs students to buses at the end of the school day. AP/Wide World.

September 13, 1974. View from Dorchester Heights. School buses are now escorted by police in and out of South Boston. *The Pilot.*

October 16, 1974. Members of the Boston Vigil for Peace and Education demonstrate on City Hall Plaza for peaceful desegregation of the Boston public schools. *Boston Globe.*

October 28, 1974. City councilwoman and ROAR leader Louise Day Hicks addresses an antibusing crowd in excess of 5,000 at rally in South Boston. *Boston Herald.*

December 11, 1974. The Massachusetts State Police prepare to force an exit for the black students trapped inside South Boston High School after the stabbing of Michael Faith. *Boston Globe.*

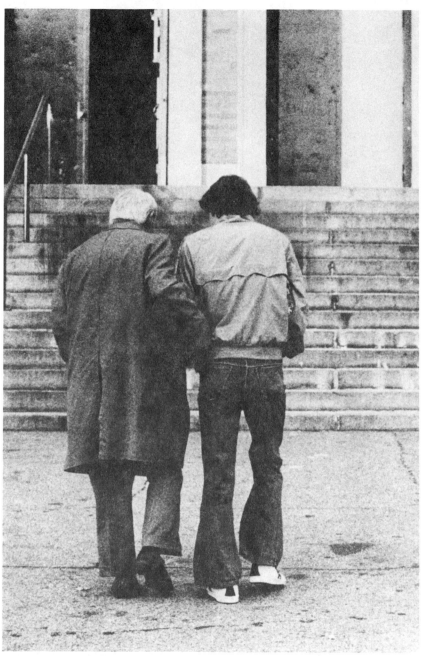

December 12, 1974. Dr. William J. Reid with student as Southie High is closed. *Boston Globe.*

January 8, 1975. South Boston High School reopens for students with 300 Massachusetts State Police. UPI/Bettmann Archive.

January 8, 1975. State police fan out to guard the streets along the bus approach to the high school.

Makeshift command headquarters of the Massachusetts State Police in the basement of South Boston High School. Massachusetts State Police.

January 9, 1975. Dr. William J. Reid inspects the metal detectors in the entrance lobby of South Boston High School. *Boston Globe.*

Phase 2 Desegregation, 1975–76

Four months after the opening of school, South Boston High School would be in federal court receivership; Dr. Reid and his administrators would be removed from their positions; and the demoralized faculty would be demanding reassignment to other Boston schools. But in early September, at the preschool faculty meeting, Dr. Reid spoke with great expectations. He anticipated that conditions at South Boston High would be better for several reasons: The court order of December 13, 1974, requiring crowds to keep back from the school a distance of 100 yards, was still in effect in the whole city; no more than three people would be allowed to group around a school's premises; and the juniors would be back in the high school building. He had, moreover, received many assurances over the summer from private citizens in South Boston that they would cooperate in maintaining calm in the community. Finally, there were fewer personnel changes than at any other school opening he remembered; the stability of the faculty was one of the high school's greatest assets.

What Dr. Reid did not take into account was the student body, many of whom — including two-thirds of the black student population — were new to the school under the revised Phase 2 desegregation plan, with no loyalty to faculty or administration, and little time to develop any, since already in September a citywide teachers' strike was imminent.

Dr. Reid had hoped for improved educational facilities in the building, but four classrooms, including my old room on the second floor front, had been set aside for Chapter 766 students with special disabilities. In addition, two rooms on the first floor had been set aside for Mongoloid youngsters, some of them twenty-one years old, mainstreamed into the high school. I had been given three sophomore classes and one senior class, with an assignment in the library after lunch, but no homeroom.

The building had been painted, Dutch doors installed in the holding rooms in the main lobby entrance, and the gym windows had been replaced, only to be broken again two days later—the grill protecting the windows pried up and the glass shattered.

Of the 1,100 students assigned to South Boston High and contacted by teachers, about 50 percent planned to attend—an anticipated enrollment of about 600 students. Some South Boston parents had asked to have their youngsters assigned to the high school, Dr. Reid said, but assignment of students was not in his power. Under the Phase 2 plan, 43 percent of South Boston students had to find seats in the citywide thematic "magnet" schools.

The commencement of the school day was advanced fifteen minutes earlier than last year, to 7:30 A.M., as an economy measure to allow fuller use of the school buses through a staggered starting time at different grade levels throughout the city. The buses were to come up East 6th Street and line up in front of the school in a pattern of nine buses, five more than last year.

This September, for the first time, Charlestown was also to be involved in busing. Fearful of snipers, the FBI cleared the rooftops—even of a woman hanging out her laundry.

There have been rumors that the Southie kids plan to "take their school back." Virginia Sheehy of the South Boston Information Center told the media she had a "feeling" things would be bad.

Monday, September 8

Last evening about 70 antibusing protesters from South Boston and Charlestown demonstrated outside the Navy's Fargo Building in South Boston where 600 riot-trained military police, members of the National Guard, had been quartered at Mayor White's request. The guardsmen had been called to fill in the ranks—if necessary—of several hundred Boston police who had missed duty call in an unofficial labor dispute "sick-out." After skirmishing with the police, the demonstrators then moved on to the high school, their numbers increasing as they marched. The police finally dispersed a rock-throwing crowd of over 300 from the area around the high school. By 7:00 A.M. this morning, the first teachers had arrived.

The opening of school was a peaceful media event for the 50 cameramen awaiting the arrival of the buses outside the high school gates and for the four helicopters hovering just over the flagpole. The state troopers marched out through the school gates, breaking off in groups of three to guard the ends of the streets that empty into the Thompson Park circle around the school, permitting students to pass through their lines only to enter the building.

Attendance for the day was higher than last year: 76 blacks, 216 whites— three times as many whites as last year on the first day.

Driving home through South Boston after school, I passed the state police lined up along D Street beside the housing project, while the buses filled with small black heads pulled away from the Condon Elementary School, escorted by motorcycle cops. Mothers crowded the sidewalk, distressed and silent.

Tuesday, September 9

Today was another quiet day. There were 147 blacks and 306 whites in the high school—still two-thirds of the anticipated attendance.

In South Boston a few trash barrels were set on fire. In suburban Brookline last night, two men fire-bombed the kitchen of the JFK birthplace. On the sidewalk in front of the JFK home they spray-painted in black: BUS TEDDY.

Thursday, September 11

More trash barrels were burned in the vicinity of the high school last night, and oil was poured on East Sixth Street between H and G streets so that the seventeen motorcycle police escort would slide out of control, but the buses and escort were simply rerouted. When the teachers arrived, the community was again calm.

Dr. Reid met with the faculty after school. He seemed very optimistic. We were ahead of last year, he said. The only problem was the "uptight" teachers; they should relax. "A few of you are pushing a little too hard," he commented. Some teachers complained about "the sullen black kids," and tempers flared about the causes and means of handling them.

Friday, September 12

The day appeared normal until lunch. I was eating in the teachers' room off the cafeteria, when I heard loud voices getting louder. The atmosphere was ugly, barely controlled by teachers and troopers. Assistant headmaster Captain John Hurley, now reassigned back to South Boston High, hustled the students out, breaking them into groups, although it was still a few minutes before the bell. Trooper Greg strode on the benches as the cafeteria emptied. The cafeteria was like a tinder box that didn't go off. Someone used the word "riot."

National television commentators noted the end of the first week of Boston school desegregation and suggested three reasons for its success: plenty of police, federal presence as watchdogs, and the good will of many people opposed to forced busing.

Since busing began, Boston has become a minority school system in a majority white city; 53 percent of the students in Boston's schools are now nonwhite, although the percentage of minorities in the city is still about 25 percent.

Monday, September 15

The cafeteria at lunchtime was again blanketed with blue trooper uniforms. I asked Trooper Greg if he was afraid during last Friday's lunchroom incident, or if he went on "automatic."

"These kids, phew," he replied, disgusted.

"Child's play," said an older trooper, annoyed, standing next to him.

In the afternoon, I saw two troopers, followed by aides, marching a black student, his arm twisted behind his back, to the office. The troopers move fast and with determination; otherwise they relax and watch in the corridors. One trooper demonstrated how the corridors were a perfect place to practice throwing his stick between the imaginary fugitive's legs, to turn him around and off balance. Some of the troopers, following a vote, are now carrying loaded guns. Last year no guns above the basement level were loaded.

At the end of the day, some of the 100 federal marshals now posted in Boston were testing the metal detectors in the school lobby. The marshals wear business suits and combat boots with metal toes, rumored to have knives that pop out when they click their heels together.

Buses carrying black students in East Boston and white students from Columbia Point were stoned.

In Charlestown, the police are relaxing with the community, giving horseback rides to preschoolers. There are daily prayer walks, the women carrying rosary beads and reciting the "Hail Mary" with Louise Day Hicks.

Jimmy Breslin, the columnist who has been attacking the hypocrisy of probusing liberals, willing to do everything to support Roxbury but send their own children there, has left his Charlestown haunts and returned to New York. There are only so many ways to say the same thing: "Everybody knows busing is a private school idea for the use of public school people. Nobody wants to know that even so, busing can save blacks and it is immoral to oppose it. All they know is that there are so many ways to beat busing, to keep children from having to go into schools in black neighborhoods, that the ones who do wind up as part of a busing plan are only those at the bottom. In Southie, in Charlestown."°

Wednesday, September 17

Before school, two troopers were laughing at School Superintendent Marion Fahey's reports to the media that everything is wonderful at the high school. But they predicted a worse year than last. A black boy had received a broken jaw and internal injuries in the shop yesterday, they said. He was carried out a back exit on a stretcher.

The shop instructor elaborated: At the end of class, a shop tool was discovered missing. No one, the instructors said, could leave until the tool, a potential weapon, was located. Then a terrified black student picked up a hacksaw. If anyone tried to keep him, he would cut his throat, he said. It was the boy's first day in the isolated shop, and he was as yet an unknown quantity. Saying nothing, a white boy hit him in the mouth. The two boys were locked in struggle when the police separated them. They were in such hot blood, the injured boy must not have realized his jaw was broken. At first, before it was determined that the blood came from the jaw, it was feared he had internal injuries because there was blood in his lungs. The doctor who examined the black youngster conjectured the other boy must have had a piece of steel in his hand to have done so much damage. No metal was found in the shop. "In the past the shop boys have always kidded each other good humoredly about what they would do to each other, but it was always pretend," the shop teacher said. "Now there is real enmity between some of the blacks and whites; they mean their threats."

The information made me nervous, and I snapped at my first class. But they were calm. A black girl, who sits up front sucking her thumb, scored 85 percent in the spelling test. When I consulted the psychiatrist about her after school, he said, "The thumb-sucking is a release of tension. Maybe, as she learns to trust you, she won't suck her thumb."

At the end of the day when the bused students were called, I went down to the lobby to observe. The dismissal was wild and ugly, with frantic screams and pushes to claim checked objects before the buses left—hair picks or umbrellas—that had been stored in the lobby. One girl shrieked and smashed her books to the floor, refusing to leave without her sister,

° *Boston Globe,* Sept. 8, 1975.

who was writing out an incident report. The troopers moved toward her, drawn by the noise, but were ordered back to their posts. Afterward a teacher, Jerry Ball, asked the psychiatrist standing by why he hadn't jumped into the situation. He answered, "I was afraid."

Voting for the faculty senate was held today. With one exception, all women were voted out.

Thursday, September 18

I woke up with a headache. Two aspirins failed to rid me of it. After my first class, the headache was worse. Sandra, one of the black girls, loud-mouthed about my "throwing" the spelling papers at her. I distributed tests for *Of Mice and Men*. Lillian put hers back on my desk. "Idiot," she called me. She had not finished the play, and would do no more. "That is a decision you'll have to make," I replied, but decided to hold back on a conduct slip for her. Two new white girls enrolled in the class. The girls had not attended school last year, but their records would be arriving soon, they told me. Then one of them asked to go to the lavatory; she had stomach pains. Her face was so flushed, I thought she would be sick then. I was sorry the class, which is usually good, had upset her. After school Ms. Murphy told me she had found a blonde girl crying uncontrollably in the lobby before school. This could have been the same one.

Today was the most depressing for me yet. I felt barely able to finish the day. Interviews with black parents published in the *Globe* are full of despair, reflecting the mood of the school. We have only 48 percent of our projected enrollment; at Charlestown High, the boycott is 85 percent effective. But the students will be back in school on Friday: absent Friday, no football game Saturday—and the game is Charlestown versus Southie.

Friday, September 19

All classes were good. The black girl, Sandra, was still bold, talking out when she shouldn't, but she appeared to be taking a wait-and-see attitude.

When I asked the class to describe their "dream" for the future, like Lennie and George in *Of Mice and Men*, James, from Southie, wrote:

I want to grow up and become a cop. I also want to get married and have a lot of kids, around 10 or so. I also want to live in the suburbs with a house of my own. I also want a couple of dogs. I know this may be impossible, but I'm going to try . . . heck if it don't come true I can always be a bum.

After lunch, shortly before one o'clock, the roar of a police motorcycle outside surprised us. "Are the buses here already?" a surprised YAC asked. From the library windows I could see the motorcycle police positioned in a line outside the school, just standing beside their bikes drinking soda pop. Beyond them police faced the streets running down the hill, watching and waiting.

About 200 South Boston mothers had asked City Hall for a marching permit. The permit had been granted, then cancelled. An alternative block party was substituted instead. The women bought sandwiches at shops along Broadway and ate them standing on the sidewalks around G Street and Fifth, and G and Seventh, two blocks from the high school and beyond the 100-yard limit set by the court, now marked by a white line painted across the street and the words: FREEDOM ENDS HERE.

"Where are the mothers?" a trooper asked, coming to the window to observe. "Why don't they just get some machine guns and mow them down?"

At the end of the day, school personnel, as required, signed a superintendent's circular calling to our attention a federal mandate cautioning against aid to alternative private schools like South Boston Academy through donations of used school equipment or books.

A bus was stoned in South Boston today; in the evening the Summer Street Bridge to South Boston was set afire with gasoline, blocking it off for two hours; at night police kept a flashlight vigil parade of 250, mostly women and children, from approaching the high school; afterward, police cars around the high school were stoned in the dark.

Saturday, September 20

Siegfried, I heard, is being prosecuted for a murderous assault last summer. According to Ms. Murphy, who was his English teacher, Siegfried was a decent boy the first two months at Southie. Now he is in line for a possible jail term. Was Siegfried a monster, or was he made a monster by busing? In full-scale desegregation, it's the kids in the front line, like the boy in shop, that get hurt.

Monday, September 22

A citywide strike of Boston teachers has been called, just eight days after the opening of school. Besides salary, grievances at issue are the loss of jobs because of desegregation and consequent drop in enrollment, loss of reading specialists, and failure to limit class size. All Boston police not on vacation have been ordered to report to work at 6:00 A.M.

At the union hall meeting, one teacher motioned the Boston Teachers Union to take a stand against forced busing. Hissing and booing were the response. Then Henry Robinson, union president, declared that the union stood for quality integrated education. His own son went by bus to a school in a formerly black district school, and was very happy there. The union members applauded.

Black leaders met meanwhile at Freedom House, then ordered black teachers back to work. They didn't want to deprive black students of a single day at school.

Tuesday, September 23

Ten percent of Boston school children attended school in Boston today; 91.2 percent of the teachers stayed out. Dr. Reid sent 142 students home when only four temporary teachers showed up. He told a TV interviewer, "It isn't order so much as education. We have the police here, we maintain order. But temporary teachers don't have the experience."

In general, the teachers felt the "Old Man"—Dr. Reid—had supported them, though one male teacher grumbled, "If he were really with us, he'd be out here picketing."

Ms. Murphy replied, "That's like asking Captain Ahab to abandon the white whale."

Wednesday, September 24

The teachers set up a picket line outside the entrance to Thomas Park behind the high school, where a trooper car waits daily. At 7:00 A.M. the troopers moved the pickets the mandatory 100 yards away from the building. The students must regard the police as the strikers do: the friendly enemy.

After breakfast teachers again gathered at Florian Hall. The union leadership was introduced. Then there was a question-and-answer period. Teachers went to the mike set up among the membership and addressed the union executive board officers sitting before a table opposite them:

"What about the Commissioner of Police in Boston whose wife is going in during the strike as a substitute teacher? Name? His first name is Bob, and he wears funny buttons on his suit, and he has big pig signs over his breast pocket."

"What can be done about the principals who let subs go early or keep them late to avoid the picket lines?"

"Why aren't the school bus contracts unionized?"

Before the meeting ended, a spokesperson for the Black Caucus and the black union membership announced their support of the Boston Teachers Union–AFL-CIO strike, reversing their previously held position.

Monday, September 29

The strike was settled about noon. Those who signed in at their respective schools were promised a full day's pay. I saw Dr. Reid when I went to his office to use the copy machine. He didn't raise his head. I said, "It's good to see you again."

He answered, "The feeling is mutual."

Tuesday, September 30

This morning I took the homeroom attendance for an absent teacher. Two white girls sniggered and giggled in front of me. Finally I said, "You're awfully hard to take so early in the morning." The students carry such burdens of feeling when they come to school, they burden one another.

Two black boys arrived smelling of alcohol.

I saw Sam today. I was surprised he was back at South Boston High this year after being hassled last year for fraternizing with black students. I had thought he would be at Roxbury High. "Things are worse this year," he said. I asked why. "Some boy keeps telling me he'll get me," he replied.

"Black or white?" I asked.

"Black," he said, but he didn't know the boy.

After school, at the faculty meeting, Dr. Reid suggested that we all keep our voices down. Loud voices, he said, tend to exacerbate a situation.

Wednesday, October 1

I was outside the front office when little Billy, the Southie aide, came out, hand extended authoritatively to hold back nearby students twice his size, and called for trooper assistance. Several troopers rushed into the office; the sound of furniture knocking followed while troopers struggled with a black boy whom a white teacher identified to me as "a three-and-a-half-minute boiled egg," so disturbed he required instruction on a one-to-one basis, but assigned to the school under Chapter 766. The boy was handcuffed and taken to court, where he was charged with alleged assault on an administrator. It is rumored he had been circulating a petition claiming that blacks are being treated unfairly. During the incident, which must have confirmed her worst fears, a white parent waited for records to transfer her daughter to South Boston Academy, opening next week. She was concerned first with the safety, then with the education of her children. "Busing for quality education," she scoffed. "Nobody's said *what* quality."

The Massachusetts legislature voted today, 117 to 106, to include white students in the METCO program busing black students to suburban schools. Mrs. Jean McGuire, black coordinator for METCO, and Mel King, black representative from the South End, objected to the inclusion of white students on the basis that METCO had been instituted to integrate the suburbs. Commissioner of Education Anrig commented that the METCO program had been already opened to white students under a ruling from the state attorney general in April 1974, but whites would be allowed to leave Boston for suburban schools only if their departure would not disturb the racial balance.

Thursday, October 2

Customarily I talk with the black students in my study, but today, when I took attendance, Keith ignored me and the male black teacher when we spoke to him. He then left the study.

Keith later stopped by my class near his locker to tell me, "Don't say nothing to me in any of my classes or study, because you ain't going to get through to me."

Keith became one of the silent leaders at demonstrations calling for the closing of South Boston High School. As Student Number Five, he filed an affidavit against Ms. Murphy at the evidentiary hearings in the Federal Court House that terminated in the receivership of South Boston High.

Razor blades and a knife were picked up from black students today, a trooper told me.

Friday, October 3

A white student walk-out was planned for 10:00 A.M. I passed one of my seniors going down the stairs, past the two helmeted troopers stationed at each landing. "You are going the wrong way to class," I said. Then I heard the roars of the boys as they met the troopers lined up at the front lobby doors, blocking them. Eventually they trickled in late to class, angry: They had a right to walk out; no one had a right to stop them.

"At 10:00," Ms. Murphy told me later, "I planted myself in front of my door and told the kids, 'If anyone wants to walk out, he has to leave his footprints on my face.'"

Dr. Reid was in the library anteroom when I went there to work. He was checking records of students waiting in line for ID photos. Once a homogeneous student body, the students in line resembled a mini League of Nations: blacks with tiny pigtails, white girls in washed-out slacks, a girl—Spanish or Indian—wearing a blanket and unable to speak English, some Chapter 766 special needs students.

A trooper told me that more razor blades and a knife were confiscated this morning at the metal detectors.

Monday, October 6

There were many fights in the school today, though I saw none. I stopped to talk to one of my sophomore students peering over the Dutch door in the lobby. He got into a fight with a "white boy," he told me—that's all he knew—"a white boy" in gym.

Sixty-six white ninth-grade students staged a walk-out of the L-Street Annex to South Boston High, protesting inadequate protection: just four MDC police and no troopers. They marched up the hill to the high school, but the state police chased them. The kids easily outdistanced the big and awkward troopers.

During the football game at White Stadium—Jamaica Plain versus South Boston High—after school on Friday, the Southie team's lockers were rifled, their lockers and wallets cleaned out. Two black students later flaunted stolen articles belonging to Southie football players. Ms. Murphy commented, "The blacks are making a statement about the all-white football team." One team member had told her, "We'll let the blacks on the team when we're ready."

Tuesday, October 7

A stink bomb was dropped in the main front lobby. The first floor down to the cafeteria smelt vile, like urine and vomit.

The students are beginning to move in packs again. Some tried to walk out after lunch, but Dr. Reid intimidated them with loud demands to see their classroom programs. "The parents are transmitting fear to the students," one teacher suggested.

The school librarian asked me, when I went there to work, to pull the catalogue cards of lost or vanished books. I felt, as I sat there, like Melville's Bartleby the Scrivener: All seemed an exercise in futility. We seem to be going to a dead end.

Dr. Reid looked distressed today. On TV he said, "We have soccer and cheerleading teams racially mixed, but not the football." Of walkouts he said, "We have enough staff, so we will be in control, and any youngsters who walk out automatically suspend themselves."

There were 384 whites, 166 blacks, and 63 others at South Boston High today; 91 whites, 116 blacks, 11 others at the L-Street Annex. The number of troopers at the high school has been reduced to 90 compared with 200 last week and more than 300 at the opening of school. An average of eight troopers are stationed in the cafeteria at lunch time.

At a luncheon of the NAACP Legal Defense and Education Fund today in Boston, Congresswoman Yvonne Burke, a Democrat from California, called Boston the "center" of the civil rights fight.

Wednesday, October 8

As I sat reading by the window in the library before school, I heard the buses roar up the hill, then I heard shouting. I went to the window. The blacks in the buses chanted, "Let's go, Southie"; then "Here we go, Southie." The police, who had been idly polishing their motorcycles, came to attention. They moved into a wedge on either side of the approach to the buses. The troopers who had been standing, one at every corner of G Street, moved over. Some black students came back out of the school building and entered the buses.

A liaison aide and a black YAC worker went into the buses, one by one, then came out again. The doors closed. A cheer went up from the buses. Dr. Reid waved the buses on. Troopers on street duty climbed into the green teacher van in order to follow the buses to the Bayside Mall. A group of about twenty white boys now walked, without reacting, past the buses, past shouts inaudible to me on the second floor, and into the school.

Troopers on duty watching from the window were appalled. "You can't force people to do anything," one said. I was glad the buses had gone because most of the police were on duty at the airport for the arrival of the victorious Red Sox team, returning to Boston with the American League pennant.

A walkout of white students had been planned to take place during the middle of my cafeteria study, though I wasn't aware of it. There was a roar of voices from the lobby upstairs as the white students tried to leave. Four emergency freeze bells sounded. I pursued a small boy who left the study and held him by the arm. A trooper came by and asked kindly, "Where are you going, son?" I liked that. When Dr. Reid came through the cafeteria on the way upstairs, the girls were running along the benches to the windows and I was yelling at them to sit down. The white students argued, "If they walk out, why can't we?"

There was a faculty meeting at the end of the day. Mr. Harold Goorvich, assistant headmaster, moderated the faculty meeting since Dr. Reid was still at the Lena Park Center meeting with representatives of the black community about suspension of the black students who had refused to leave the buses. Dr. Reid felt they should be suspended, just as the seventy students who walked out of L-Street on Monday had been suspended. Mr. Joseph McDonough, area superintendent, agreed with him, but Superintendent Marion Fahey did not. The teachers angrily opposed a double standard, and wrote a letter supporting Dr. Reid. There were no dissenters, although the black teachers had already left with the buses and didn't have a chance to vote.

A group of radical blacks, Mr. Goorvich recounted, had tried to break up the Lena Park meeting.

Mr. Goorvich asked the teachers to remain after school to call parents and verify the attendance of students on the buses, since some aides had told the black students not to give their names to the authorities. But the president of the faculty senate advised the teachers not to work overtime without pay, reminding them that the School Committee during the recent strike had quibbled about work hours; teachers should receive overtime pay, the same as police.

The nurse, who sat beside me, reported that about 50 students had been down to her office—all wanting to get out of school. "Nerves," she explained. Ms. Murphy told me she was so nervous and upset about her students that she didn't sleep last night. She wrote up four incident reports yesterday about her black students.

Demands by the Ad Hoc Black Student Caucus, published in the newspapers, are: First, black and white balance on the student council. Black students complained they were not represented because they were outnumbered in the voting. Second, more fairness in handling of incidents of violence. The police pretended that they couldn't catch up with the white offenders at the high school, and the blacks were getting the worst deal. Third, more black teachers. There are now six black teachers in the high school. Fourth, an equal number of blacks to match the whites in the school's population. Interviewed on the school bus for evening TV, Robert, a black student, said, "If there are 1,000 white males at South Boston High, there should be 1,000 blacks. It should be equal right down the line."

Dr. Reid announced on a late TV news broadcast that the students who refused to leave the buses were suspended, but they could have the suspension lifted as early as tomorrow if their parents came to school with them: regular procedure.

Thursday, October 9

As the buses emptied this morning, a high piercing scream heralded the troubled day ahead. A white boy, knocked unconscious at the metal detectors by a black youth, had an apparent seizure and was taken, unconscious, to Carney Hospital.

My study in the cafeteria was empty when I went there, except for two troopers. In the teachers' room just off the cafeteria, Major Charles Gilligan of the state police was meeting with members of the Ad Hoc Black Student Caucus and with adults from the black community: Mrs. Ellen Jackson of Freedom House, nicknamed the "Pentagon" of the black community by the Boston *Globe;* Ruth Batson, associate professor of psychology at Boston University and organizer there of Crisis Intervention Teams for black students; Lyda Peters, coordinator of the Crisis Teams program at Boston University; and Percy Wilson, director of the Roxbury Multi-Service Center. Other black surrogate "parents" for suspended students included Maceo Dixon, a national officer of the Young Socialist Alliance, and Mac Warren, former SCAR (Student Coalition Against Racism) leader. Dr. Reid was also present at the meeting.

Slowly a few black students assigned to my study straggled in late, followed by some white girls, and sat down. Then a pack of about thirty-five black students, boys and girls, swept through the cafeteria to the rear, where they stood, angrily shouting and gesturing to a black adult. The white girls wanted to leave. Why couldn't they walk out and have their own assembly? Nobody listened to them, they said. I sat with them, reminding them that they were all L-Street or Hart-Dean Annex grads, and veterans, and tough. I talked trivia to divert them. Then the black girls at the rear of the cafeteria came forward and encircled the white girls, sitting on the lunch tables, pushing in beside me and at the end of the benches. Nobody reacted. One, with a tuft of yellow hair and front teeth missing, hissed at my back, "Fuck whitey." Two male teachers came down to the cafeteria and looked in. I asked them to stay.

A black girl said to me, "I know you dig him."

I answered, "I dig everyone unless I have a reason not to like him."

She said, "I didn't mean that kind of dig. You know what I mean." I ignored her.

One trooper stood at the cafeteria door with a walkie-talkie, an alarmed expression on his face; another trooper stood beside me, both of us facing the students and about ten silent, well-dressed adult representatives of the black community, sitting on the cafeteria benches. "I wouldn't want to be an unarmed teacher in this school," the trooper commented. "There aren't enough troopers if a riot did break out."

Everyone waited. At 10:09, the white girls announced they would leave. I asked them not to. I said, "This is the most interesting place in Boston right now. You don't have to read what happens in the newspapers. All you have to do is keep your eyes open." I was surprised. The black girls seemed to want to listen, to see that I wasn't excluding them. They sat contentedly and peacefully on the tables around the white girls.

Suddenly a small white girl jumped up, threw her books on the floor, and ran out of the room. A girl had been pulling her hair, she later told me. Neither I nor the trooper had noticed.

The bell finally rang. As I climbed the stairs to my senior English class, my heart seemed to flip. "Slow down," I told myself.

Since my class of eleven seniors is not integrated—there are only three blacks in the entire senior class—the students speak freely about what's bothering them. If Judge Garrity closed the school, as he was threatening to do, the boys said, they would have to close the rest of the high schools in the city. They would go out and kill people themselves. They complained about the language, the burned-out or poorly kept houses of blacks, and the fact that blacks were getting "everything." If they couldn't afford to live in the suburbs, why should the blacks? They mentioned the fight earlier in the day when a paring knife had been taken from a black student's pocket. The student had been suspended, but the knife, which rumor had magnified considerably by the time I heard of it, could not technically be classified as a lethal weapon.

At dismissal time, I went down to the lobby. About ten white boys looked out over the Dutch doors of the holding room, one of them with an eye already swollen half-closed. There had been dozens of students in there all day, I heard.

A loud moan bellowed from the black holding room, curdling the air. The girl with the tuft of yellow dyed hair was terrified the buses would leave without her. She left the school crying. Two white boys mocked her tears; as they left, "Nigger!" they yelled into the face of a black gym teacher, Earl Garrett. Barbara Faith, Michael's sister—now an aide—went to the gym teacher then and stood talking with him.

After school the faculty assembled in the auditorium.

Major Gilligan of the state police spoke first on the operation of the police in the building. He praised his men. A policeman's was a good job. His men were used to being free and on the open highway. The school situation was a new one. The role of the police was to safeguard the faculty and students. They had to remind themselves they were not in Walpole State Prison.

The police would not be in the high school forever. The city could not pay for them, and they were needed in the rest of the state. "You have to resolve this problem without wall-to-wall police."

Teachers had to control the students. They were not to let their power erode, to give an inch. People were always trying to erode the authority of the police. "What you give up today, you will never get back. You have to decide if there is a learning process going on here, or a reform school. We ask you to be stronger than you are. Be watching situations. You have got to keep people moving. Otherwise someone gets a sucker punch, and then there is a brawl.

"Everyone who comes into this school is under some kind of pressure. Today there were adults here without IDs."

Major Gilligan concluded, "You have a great staff and principal. Many people tried to advise Dr. Reid to close the school, but he refused. It was the right decision.

"We will make mistakes because we are human. But my men are not going to get hurt here. This is not a game. We are policemen."

After Major Gilligan left, Dr. Reid talked. It was the first time the faculty had met with him since the black student demonstration in the buses. "I was the most relaxed last Thursday since a year ago last September. I went home very optimistic. Friday was touch-and-go. Something seemed to go wrong last Friday, and things went downhill," he said, and reviewed the crises of the past few days.

Of the black student demands he said, "I and other administrators discussed grievances with the youngsters for two-and-a-half hours at the Lena Park Center. Some of their requests were legitimate. The fact that the youngsters think they are grievances makes them important."

About the black community representatives in the cafeteria that morning, acting as surrogate parents for the suspended black students, Dr. Reid noted that, according to the student handbook, a responsible adult can represent the pupil if the parent is unable to come to the school. "In the past, sometimes the clergy represented students. The major point is: Does the adult understand his obligations to the student and school?"

Teachers were concerned about the number of unidentified outsiders in the building. I was surprised at the hostility to the Citywide Coordinating Council, apparently among the faculty generally. Teachers did not want them in their classrooms or in the teachers' rooms.

If they didn't want to answer their questions, Dr. Reid responded, teachers were not obligated to. "Tomorrow only those two CCC, who are assigned here, will be allowed in," he promised.

"The fact that the youngsters went off after school today to football is a tremendous asset to the school," he concluded.

It was on this day, in this atmosphere, according to affidavits filed by students for the evidentiary hearings culminating in the receivership of South Boston High School, that teacher Jim Scalese allegedly stood in his doorway "making monkey gestures at black students in an insolent manner."

Friday, October 10

From the library window I watched the white students walk past the school gates away from the high school. Inside, some black students went to homerooms; others refused, instead roaming the corridors in packs, or screaming over the bannisters. As I passed a trooper with a walkie-talkie, I heard a call for Dr. Reid to go to the cafeteria. Since I had no homeroom, I went downstairs also.

About forty troopers stood around the cafeteria and clustered in the corridors leading to the cafeteria, listening, upset and angry because the black students were claiming they got no protection. A white female teacher tried to reason with the students; a black woman aide yelled "Liar!" at one boy. Finally Dr. Reid gave them a choice: Go to class or leave. Thirty-three black students walked out and were suspended. As they left, passing a line of troopers, they chanted, "Southie ain't fit, Southie ain't fit."

Two hundred white students, one of them carrying an American flag, then moved up the hill, ostensibly to go to school. They pledged allegiance, chanted "Equal justice for all," and presented a list of demands to Major Gilligan. The troopers then moved out in a line, and the white students retreated quickly back down the hill.

Three of the white student demands concerned the American flag: that it be displayed in a place of prominence in every classroom at the high school; that time be allotted every morning for pledging allegiance; that the flag be raised every morning on the flagpole outside the school. Earlier this week, when a white student came to my class checking to see whether the room had a flagpole, I mistakenly assumed she was looking for potential "weapons," like the window poles confiscated last year.

Another part of the list read: "We are aware of the conscious effort of the black community and the black students to create incidents to provoke the closing of South Boston High. Under no circumstances will the South Boston community tolerate the closing of the high school."

Teachers also feel unanimously that there is an effort by the blacks to close the school; they are urging the faculty senate to make a statement that the school is to remain open.

The rest of the day moved slowly. Classes were small. Total attendance for the day was 93 blacks, 103 whites. In one sophomore class I had just one black student, who told me he would have preferred to be at the Burke High School in Dorchester, where he had been accepted on the football team. He said, "I've broke an ankle, two ribs, and a finger playing football. I love the game." But, he said, because of the size of the boys on Southie's team—perhaps he meant "color"—he hadn't tried out. Later I sent him down to the gym to apply for the team, but he returned saying football would interfere with his Saturday religious activities; it would just make him start cursing again. Roy is a Jehovah's Witness.

We looked out the window. The Boston TPF were holding the Dorchester Heights—sitting on the monument hill, lying asleep on the tops of cruisers, police horses pawing the side of the hill.

Roy said, "I like animals."

I replied, "I was watching our cat yesterday. He is so naturally refined; he's so much classier than some of our students."

There was one fight today in the health class, provoked by a white girl's complaint that she wished everyone would be quiet so she could learn something. A girl behind her then grabbed her by the hair and held on. Another jumped her and clawed her face. When the teacher tried to break up the fight, she was knocked down.

A CCC monitor commented to me in study, "I wonder how the teachers get any teaching done." I replied, "The classrooms are the only place where the students feel safe." I might have added, "Some classrooms, some times."

In the evening, Ms. Murphy and I went, as a kind of sensitivity training, to the meeting of the National Student Coalition Against Racism in the Cabot Auditorium of Northeastern University to hear the scheduled participants—Dr. Spock, Jonathan Kozol, and Luis Fuentes, a Puerto Rican educator who had fought for community control of the New York public schools. We bought tickets and signed the register at the door, then sat down on the bleacher seats at the side of the auditorium between the exit staircase to Huntington Avenue and the platform on the other end. I noticed Keith facing the platform, and saw that he was watching us. Other black South Boston High students must be there, too, I guessed.

Mrs. Malcolm Peabody, mother of former Governor Endicott Peabody, was introduced from the audience and received a sprinkled applause. Then Maceo Dixon, who had been at South Boston High on Thursday as a surrogate parent representing the suspended students, talked, describing the bus ride to the high school: They boarded the buses at the Bayside Mall. Then one student told him to watch a certain corner when the buses turned. He did, and saw an old woman in her nightdress giving them the finger. They turned a corner and there was another woman giving them the finger. They are there, fair and foul weather, waiting to give the finger as the buses pass. He described the arrival of the buses at the school and the three metal detectors in a lobby where a huge sign listed forbidden weapons: picks, nail files, knives, Coke bottles, guns. Right near him, he alleged, a white boy spat in the face of a black boy, and the black boy laid him out. There were cheers from the audience.

After Maceo Dixon, black students at South Boston High spoke. I couldn't distinguish their faces from where we sat, but they had obviously noticed us. I would have been anxious if I had realized that one was the student with the tuft of yellow dyed hair and missing front teeth. Ms. Murphy did recognize several of them from her class. They had suddenly turned surly, she said, and she had written up four incident reports about them on Wednesday. *Their charges that evening became substantially the basis of their affidavits that precipitated the evidentiary hearings and receivership of South Boston High.*

The first student alleged that the police had stood and laughed at them in the cafeteria demonstration (Wednesday, October 8); then, after they had been returned in the buses to the Bayside Mall, pushed them with their sticks. The police are friendly to the white girls, say, "Hi, good to see you," but tell the black girls to move along or they'll be suspended. Black students couldn't go outside the building for a practice fire drill, and were in danger of being burned to a crisp in a fire. She concluded, "We want what the white students have, a right to equal education."

The next student, radiating charm, told how she had been grabbed by a trooper, all 200 pounds of him, and held tight around the neck until her "black face turned red"; how her arm was twisted behind her back; how she beat up a white girl because the white girl had insulted her, and how she wanted to get the white girl before the white girl got her. Again there were cheers from the audience.

Stopping periodically to consult with the other students for the names of the offender-teachers, she singled out two teachers: the health teacher because she had criticized their homes, she alleged, without knowing what their homes were like, and Mr. Scalese, who allegedly had jumped up on his desk and acted like an ape, mocking them. The nurse, she alleged, charges a dime for dirty bandaids and won't take their temperature with a thermometer, just feels their forehead and tells them they're all right— but takes the temperature of the white kids. The student concluded, "They'll give us our demands or we'll close the school."

The audience stood and applauded; we sat. In the meantime a group of black youths moved screaming into the open area on the floor below us, pointing at Ms. Murphy. When the girls on the stage had finished speaking, they left by a back exit and joined the circle of young people below us. I continued to ignore them and face the platform, but Ms. Murphy said, "Those are my students," and went down to them, telling them, "If you have guts enough to take the bus to South Boston every day, why shouldn't I have guts enough to come here?" Lita answered, "You mother-fucker."

Lita's affidavit, later filed at the evidentiary hearings in the federal district court, would be numbered Student 20.

The students then surrounded Ms. Murphy and jostled her, but a black delegate intervened and escorted her back to the bleachers, then sat down beside us. He was delighted to meet two teachers from South Boston High, he said.

A small boy moved behind Ms. Murphy, pushing his knee into her back, and smiled when I looked at him. Then a white marshal came over. "We can't guarantee your safety," he warned. "You'd better leave." A black marshal repeated the statement.

Ms. Murphy protested, "What about my civil rights?"

"I'm taking your advice," I decided, and asked the black marshal to accompany us to the door. The girl with the yellow tuft of hair danced after Ms. Murphy like a puppet dangling crazily on a string, trying to poke her, but held off by the marshals. Most of the other black South Boston students remained behind, while youngsters we had never seen before ran smiling down the stairs behind. One shouted at Ms. Murphy, "I'll cut you with a razor." Afraid to wait on the avenue or to walk to the subway alone,

I asked the marshal to wait with us on Huntington Avenue until we hailed a taxi. When it came—almost immediately—he hopped in beside us.

Minutes afterward, we were still shaking. The marshal commented, "You're not used to violence. Blacks are. You were very courageous to go to the NSCAR meeting, since you represent the establishment. This is a powder-keg situation."

Referring to the incident at the NSCAR meeting, Ms. Murphy explained that she was there, a witness to the students' lie, and they knew it. For instance, the black aide who the students alleged had been pushed by a trooper into a locker, beaten, and then released had in actuality been accidentally kicked by a white boy as he was running away from a fight; Ms. Murphy had helped the aide write up the incident report.

"I'd like to go to South Boston," the marshal suggested.

I cautioned, "Don't. You're a black face. The kids would smash the car windshield. On the other hand, we're not safe in Roxbury."

"It's a very polarized city," Ms. Murphy concluded.

Publicly Dr. Reid commented today, "I am very disturbed about rumors that the high school would be closed. I don't know where this talk is coming from, but it disturbs me very much. It is obvious from newspaper accounts that some prominent persons have made statements along this line. . . . There are forces trying to close this school down, forces unknown to me, forces the United States Justice Department should look into. How else can you account for the events of this week? It's imperative that this school remain open."

Sunday, October 12

Statements made by black South Boston High students at the NSCAR meeting Friday at Northeastern University were repeated by them again on Channel 7's evening "Black News."

Tuesday, October 14

There was a black student protest again today. Twenty-two students were suspended and sent home in mini-buses.

Dr. Reid met with groups of black and white students separately; he had forms printed with their "demands" and his responses to them.

There were 140 state police at the school. Forty sat all day in the North Cafeteria; not wanting to be any more visible than necessary, they waited in the buses during the lunch period.

Ms. Murphy was absent today.

Wednesday, October 15

Midmorning, Dr. Reid announced on the intercom that a new assistant football coach had been added to the staff, providing opportunity for more boys to try out for football. Three white boys left my class to report. I encouraged Roy again to sign up, and told the black gym teacher about him, how much he liked to play.

During the study a trooper told me he thought Dr. Reid "looks bad"; he had been under a terrific strain, but had made good decisions from their viewpoint, and had stood by them. He was fair to both blacks and whites. Even their Major Gilligan showed the effect of the pressure every day from the governor's office on down. The Major didn't curse and hadn't taken a drink for twenty years, but now he was beginning to swear. Today it was quiet, the trooper said, so their captain was "picking, picking" — their shoes, ties, haircuts. When they were involved, on the alert, there was "no time to pick."

After school Dr. Reid met with the staff and reviewed the white and black student demands. He also informed us that the school had been offered the aid of a mediation panel of five to negotiate disputes between black and white students. After discussion, before deciding, the faculty agreed first to meet all five mediators together and hear their views.

Thursday, October 16

Black students arrived and sat quietly in the buses. White students drifted past the school gates to the Hill Stop Delicatessen, an occasional student carrying his "demands"; few came to school.

I was anxious about my first class. It was small—only four black sophomores and one white. They seemed upset, but not at me, although Sandra's cousin was one of the speakers at Northeastern University last Friday night.

Later, while I was in the front office to get some papers, Dr. Reid took me by the arm. He asked me, "Did you see the notebook from Ms. Murphy's class that Keith brought down here?" I hadn't. "It plays right into their hands," he said.

I saw Jim Scalese in the library, and asked him what he could have done to make the students allege he had acted like an ape. He replied, "I don't want to say anything. I have a lawyer."

After school the white students met in the school auditorium to discuss their "demands" with Dr. Reid. They opposed the newly appointed black football coach so vehemently that Adrienne Weston, the black teacher-administrator, left the auditorium shaking. She went outside and smoked a cigarette on the front steps where the troopers stood in formation to prevent parents from entering the school with the students. She said, ironically, "I'll stay here and let the troopers earn their money." Before desegregation she had commuted daily to the high school by public transportation.

Friday, October 17

Before school I was in the library reviewing my lesson plans for the day and watching from the window. When the white students walked past the school gates down toward the Hill Stop Delicatessen, I decided it would be an easy day. Then a trooper announced, "The white kids are coming." They followed the football team into the building, "exchanging racial slurs and obscene gestures with blacks," according to reporters. Some tried to sit down in the lobby, but a roar from Dr. Reid dispersed them; they left and went back down the hill, yelling "scabs" at those who entered.

The remaining white students, more than 100 boys and girls, then gathered in the auditorium. I tried to contain them there, but the pack swept past my outstretched arms and up to the third floor.

Ms. Murphy later told me she had gone up to the students and done her "number": She was wearing a blue skirt, a white turtleneck jersey, and a red and white flowered blouse. She told the students, "Look at me. I'm wearing red, white, and blue. Why don't you salute?" No laugh, no response. She felt helpless then, she said.

Four emergency bells sounded. Billy, the aide, and troopers sealed off the third-floor doors, cornering the students by the lockers. Teachers and aides then escorted them to their homerooms, one by one.

At the front office, Assistant Headmaster Goorvich ordered Lita out of the school. "You're suspended," he yelled, and asked a trooper to escort her downstairs.

Then Dr. Reid came on the intercom: "Good morning. When your parents sent you to school today, they intended you should act like ladies and gentlemen. I expect you will do that."

After the announcement that the first class would last an hour, I substituted "Humor" for my lesson. The students read, laughed, made cartoons of idioms, and left peacefully an hour later. "Have a good day," I wished. There were two white girls and one black girl; five black boys and no white boys. The black students sat up front; if the white students had been there, the blacks would have sat in the back.

In my second class I had one black student. She worked diligently, at first sucking a lollipop; I did not tell her to put it away. Later I saw her in the corridor hustled along to class by a teacher. She was swinging her body around in an exaggerated gesture, mocking, an angry edge in her voice, "You have to look from side to side, and all around you, when you walk in these corridors."

After lunch, four emergency bells again sounded. The faces of the troopers in the lobby were clouded. In the black holding room I saw one of the students from my humor class, his face angry and as twisted as the little braids on his head. On the evening news, I saw another, Chuck, being taken out of the school to a police wagon. He hadn't worked in class, but had put his head down most of the time.

There were four arrests today—two blacks and two whites; eleven students were suspended. One white student was hit over the head with a chair by a black student and received seven stitches at Carney Hospital— the most serious incident of the day. Another, Jane, had been jumped by a pack of black students. "More hair was pulled from her head than I *have*," the aide Billy told me, "more than I could hold in my hand."

After school a bus of white football players followed by a bus with four black players rode off with police escort to the field for practice. The white students invited the blacks to ride with them, according to the newspaper reports, but they were escorted to the other bus by the police.

Monday, October 20

About two hundred people demonstrated at the high school last night. From 8:30 P.M. to 10:00 P.M., the Boston Tactical Patrol Force fought roving bands of youths. And it was a rainy night.

But today was a quiet day. There are 80 state police at the high school. Trooper Souza said the school will be kept open if the violence can be contained with that number, going up to 250 troopers as needed.

There was a meeting after school with Ms. Jane Cass from Superintendent Fahey's office to discuss the possible assignment of a five-person Instructional Task Force from the School Committee's headquarters as ombudsman trouble-shooters in South Boston High School. The teachers did not respond. A reading teacher, Mr. Fred Murphy, commented, "What we need to teach is a discipline force. We had a great tutor program here, but tutors have been absent for the past two weeks because they are afraid."

This rejection of the Instructional Task Force Judge Garrity cited as evidence of obstructionism among the faculty, although Dr. Reid, in his testimony, had explained: Miss Cass proposed that there be an emphasis on the reading program. There were already seven certified teachers in the reading program at the high school who felt that, if they got the proper equipment and materials, they could handle the situation themselves; and second, Miss Cass's Instructional Task Force would conflict with and duplicate the programs already developed through the summer with the University of Massachusetts under the court order.

Tuesday, October 21

I quake when I see the girl with the tuft of yellow hair running hollering down the halls, especially in the vicinity of Ms. Murphy, but I try to warn the police. Ms. Murphy has no idea who the girl is.

In English class I asked the two white senior football players, Tony and Bill, about the blacks on the football team. My question seemed irrelevant. "We're in trouble," Tony said, changing the subject. The team was "getting a bad name." A handout being passed around accused them of leading the white students back into the school and breaking the boycott.

I told them angrily, "If you don't come to school, they'll close it. You have to decide what you want, what is best for *you*."

The students are under tremendous peer and community pressure, and "outside" adults—those not familiar with the community, including many of the teachers—don't always realize this, Dr. Reid commented.

Wednesday, October 22

The "Up With People" middle-America choral group performed for South Boston High, among other concerts they gave in the city. The police presence was minimal: eight troopers in the hall, and two federal marshals. State police remained behind the doors at the front of the auditorium visible only when the doors opened. I had overheard Dr. Reid a few days earlier say that he couldn't see what it would accomplish to have an assembly with wall-to-wall police. Silke Hanson and Martin Walsh from the Justice Department stood at the back, observing.

Only one song, "What Color Is God's Skin?" provoked a negative response. Some twenty students, choosing to ignore the song's message, yelled out, "White!" and guffawed. I stood in the aisle behind the last row of tough white boys and two black boys. The black boys half-stood, leaning against the edge of their upturned seats—one with a pencil at ready in his hand—to see better, I thought at first. But when they relaxed, they sat down. There was great fear. In the first assembly for the seniors and juniors, there was one mixed couple among the dancers; in the second assembly for the lower grades, none. For the grand finale, Dr. Reid was coaxed to the stage with other teachers, and stood there clapping in time to the music. The students were delighted.

As the students left the auditorium to return to their classes, the singers stood in the aisles, greeting them. There were no fights. It was the most positive event yet, "a calculated risk," Dr. Reid commented.

"The fact that we had the assembly is perhaps a major achievement," Dr. Reid later testified at the evidentiary hearings. Judge Garrity cited this remark as one of five "findings of fact" about Dr. Reid for placing the school under federal court receivership.

I had hoped for great rapport to emanate from the concert, but in a fight between the regular antagonists, a teacher, Ms. Jackie Wynne, was knocked down; she hit her head, hurt her back, and had to go home. Her class was in an ugly mood when I went there to stand in for her. One boy sat at the back of the room, snapping his book open and shut, glaring at the two blacks in front who had just opened a newspaper with the announcement, "Let's see what happened in South Boston today."

At the end of the day, there was a voluntary faculty meeting in the library with the Citywide Coordinating Council Mediating Board for the purpose of deciding whether the biracial team would be of benefit to work with the students. I waited for a cue from Dr. Reid, who was sitting at one of the library tables in the front. He said, "I need all the help I can get." I decided to vote for the Mediating Board, and left the meeting early at 2:45, an hour after the close of school.

Thursday, October 23

It was a very quiet day. Almost half the students were out.

There was a football game today. Blacks went off in a separate bus with one motorcycle cop.

In his "rationale" for the receivership of South Boston High, Judge Garrity wrote: "On October 23, the proposal to accept the mediating board's services was rejected at a meeting attended by from 70 to 75 faculty members."

Judge Garrity cited this veto as an instance that the "faculty has, in Dr. Reid's phrase, felt 'put upon' by desegregation, and this has impeded integration in the school."

According to court testimony by John Cunningham, faculty senate president, the meeting began at 1:50 P.M. and lasted three minutes.

Friday, October 24

I was reading in the library, waiting for the buses to arrive. Suddenly I heard a tremendous racket—screams, bumping and banging in the lobby entrance below. The signal was a dropped lid, then "jump any black in sight." I went downstairs. The lobby doors were already shut. Some of the troopers, sinister-looking in their black gloves, were wrestling violent students, resisting, to holding rooms. Trooper Norman Bernard, with whom I have discussed his hobby of ceramics, was moving a white boy to the holding room, his arm hooked around the boy's neck.

Outside Boston TPF lined the front fences and blocked the streets. Double lines of police held the white students at a distance until the three unloaded buses returned to the Bayside Mall.

A male teacher reflected, "I knew it would be a bad day after what happened yesterday at the South Boston–Dorchester High football game at White Stadium. The white cheerleaders had water spat at them during the half-time break. During the game, more and more blacks came over to the South Boston side. After the game, the stonings began. Eighty Boston TPF were brought in to quell the riot. The cheerleaders were taken home in two police wagons."

While black students were en route to the mall, teachers and aides escorted white students, one by one, to homerooms. Then the buses were signaled to return from the Bayside Mall, and the procedure was again repeated with black students. I was happy to see students I knew: Sean, a senior, who had tears in his eyes; Bill, football and hockey star, grouchy and grumpy, back after a week in Florida; Roy, the Jehovah's Witness, so depressed he could hardly whisper answers to my questions.

I wondered anxiously how I could interest students in my lesson on D. H. Lawrence's short story, "The Rocking Horse Winner." But my worry was wasted. My first class, a study in the cafeteria, lasted until early dismissal at 12:30, interrupted once briefly when the bell rang to change classes, then was countermanded on the intercom.

There were a few uneasy moments at first when one boy tried to get to a rumble in the adjacent gym, explaining, "I have to go to my brother." I dodged with him, obstructing his way until a trooper grabbed him. Then another black boy, the cooks after him, sped through the kitchen and out to the cafeteria, snatching up a heavy utensil with a sharp lifting edge. "Get him. He has a knife," a worker yelled. The boy and I wrestled with a wooden slat in the gym door until, at about the same time, we both realized that the slat was bolted to the door. We looked up just in time to dodge a shoe hurtling violently out the gym door, narrowly missing a paraplegic on crutches. Still refusing to yield the utensil to a trooper, the boy was wrestled to the holding room.

About 100 parents had gathered outside; two came to the study looking for their youngsters. One was a woman crying, who asked in broken Italian for her daughter; another was a father, who must have been impressed by the calm in the study—thirteen students, blacks and whites, sitting separately and talking, presided over by angry kitchen workers, troopers, and three teachers. Dr. Reid came by once with teachers checking student programs.

After the students left—blacks escorted to their lockers and leaving directly to the buses—the teachers sat at the lunch tables and talked. One teacher, Joanne Leonard, assigned to the morning search of students' pocketbooks and books and baggage at the metal detectors, had been in the lobby melee. She was hit in the back and pulled by her hair backward by a black girl. Ms. Leonard told us, tears in her eyes, about a white girl who had been beaten up in the front office by six blacks, boys and girls. She was kicked in the groin, and, according to her parents, her shirt was ripped off. She was taken bleeding to the hospital.

A black student was on evening TV interviewed at the Roxbury Multi-Service Center: "Well, this white girl started calling us 'nigger' so a bunch of us got after her. The white boys in the 220 area hassled us all day."

There were fifteen arrests; eight students were charged with disorderly conduct, and seven with assault and battery. Eleven were black, four were white. The football game at White Stadium was singled out as the cause.

Dr. Reid called a faculty meeting after school. He asked for our opinion whether to close the school or not. There were no raised hands.

Mr. Wendel English, a black music teacher, asked for more black personnel, from the administration to the kitchen help down, as ordered by Judge Garrity. Mr. Andrew Vaccari, guidance counselor, said there was a question of tenure and qualification; it was not a question of race. Loud applause followed. Kevin Weeks, an aide, asked at the microphone, "If you want more blacks—administrators, police, and aides—where are the aides now? Why didn't they stay for the meeting?" Ms. Leonard said, "That isn't fair. They had to go with the buses."

Dr. Reid answered Mr. English: He was supposed to get a black administrator; he had asked for one last year, and had one name to interview that day, but he now had to go to school headquarters to talk with Superintendent Fahey. Replying to the allegation that the police had used undue force, Dr. Reid said that the police do not touch a student unless he refuses to do something; and if the student responds immediately, they remove the hand or restraint. Troopers grab hold of students four at a time, one on each limb, so they won't hurt him. They would much prefer to handle a boy than a girl.

When Dr. Reid asked for suggestions, Mrs. Smith suggested asking the mediating team from the Citywide Coordinating Council to get the students together to talk. Another teacher said that, as much as she hated being badgered by some of them, we should meet again with the parents.

In his rationale for the receivership of South Boston High School, Judge Garrity cited an affidavit submitted by Kenneth Brociner as a "credible white substitute teacher, who attended the meeting":

> *I reported to the office and was told that I should attend the faculty meeting at 1:00 P.M. I went to the faculty lunch at 12:30 P.M. In the lunchroom I observed that white teachers were laughing and engaging in mock fights among themselves while the black teachers present appeared subdued. We all went to the auditorium for the faculty meeting. Dr. Reid stated that he was to meet that day with Supt. Marion J. Fahey and he was sure that he would be asked for the faculty's opinion on closing the school. A discussion of the problems at the school ensued. I was surprised that there was no discussion of the racial nature of the incidents of the day. A black teacher stood up and suggested that there should be more black teachers, administrators and aides in the school. His demeanor was non-belligerent. After he spoke a white teacher spoke against his position stating that "qualified people should be hired." At least half of the white teachers began to cheer loudly at this point in apparent response to the position taken by the white teacher. Another black teacher (or aide) stated that he had witnessed what he considered police brutality against black girls. A white teacher stood up to dispute this, stating that there were no such incidents. Again there was a great response from the white teachers, who cheered the white teacher's position. The only times that there were loud or vehement responses during the meeting came after black teachers offered their suggestions and were contradicted by white teachers. The whole tone of the meeting was whites against blacks.*

Judge Garrity accepted Mr. Brociner as a "credible" witness of the day's events although Mr. Brociner arrived at the school at 9:00 (one and a half hours late) and reported to a classroom, where he stayed until 11:45, when his students were dismissed. During that time he had two students, and then another two, when the bell rang for change of period. In addition, Mr. Brociner admitted in court he did not know the names of any of the teachers (except Mr. English, who was identified for him at the meeting) and he had no idea whether the speakers at the microphone were teachers or aides, nor could he, in fact, tell whether the applause came from teachers, as his affidavit alleged, or from aides.

On this date, according to court testimony by faculty senate president John Cunningham, the faculty again rejected the mediating services of the Citywide Coordinating Council on a voice vote of 26 to 24—a negative vote by one quarter of the faculty. I heard no announcement of either today's meeting or yesterday's, did not attend, and did not vote. Mr. Cunningham, who would have been in charge of today's meeting, was absent.

The possibility of closing South Boston High is now being debated openly. Mr. J. Stanley Pottinger, assistant attorney general and chief of the U.S. Justice Department's Civil Rights Division, said: "Federal policy is ordinarily not to allow schools to close because of normal problems associated with desegregation, but if events reach a point where physical safety cannot be guaranteed, we will not hesitate to make that recommendation rather than pursue a principle." Superintendent Marion Fahey was adamant: The school would remain open. At the community level, Mr. Kelly of the South Boston Information Center charged: "The black students are being used as pawns to incite turmoil within the school to give the appearance that the situation at the school is uncontrollable. The black leaders' intention is to punish the white students and residents of South Boston because of our strong resistance to the insanity of forced busing and refusal to appease the blacks at all costs."

Percy Wilson, black director of the Roxbury Multi-Service Center, responded, "The conspiracy theory is absolute paranoia. . . . If there is no learning going on, the place should be closed."

Saturday, October 25

A funeral procession was staged in Charlestown, halting for taps at Charlestown High. Then an effigy of Judge Garrity, carried in a coffin draped with an American flag, was dumped into the water; his effigy was pounded into submersion.

Monday, October 27

It was a quiet day: National Boycott Day. Six white students, in addition to forty Chapter 766 special needs students, attended school. The antibusing crowd of over 7,000 marched down Broadway to Marine Park, where State Senator William Bulger and City Councilwoman Louise Day Hicks then addressed them.

Louise warned: "Don't tread on us, George," alluding to labor president

George Meany's statement about the "discredited dissidents from the Boston area" who oppose busing, endorsed three times by the AFL-CIO. Senator Bulger challenged the absent Commissioner of Education Anrig, desegregation adviser Dentler, and Judge Garrity to put their own children under the disposition of a federal court as an example for others; then he would believe them. Bill Bulger is a great favorite in South Boston because he speaks from a conviction of innocence, not, as I suspect Louise does, from political opportunism.

Tuesday, October 28

The white students are now admitted to the school by groups of ten through police lines.

Students, black and white, are moving in packs. If I know them, I call them by name and order them to their homerooms. The state police in such a situation are helpless, because their duty is to stop fights once they have begun. They are wearing their black gloves.

At a voluntary faculty meeting after school, Dr. Reid reported that the number of white students had dropped by 50 to 498, but not many fewer black students. Will there be fear and rejection now?

A paring knife and a razor were taken away from one student coming through the metal detector today.

Wednesday, October 29

During my free period, I was in the front office using the copy machine. I overheard Mr. Goorvich, whose desk is in the same room with Dr. Reid, talking to a black girl about a knife she had brought in.

"How did you get it through the detectors?" he asked.

"It was in my locker."

"Did you threaten a boy with this?"

"He threatened me first with a pen."

"Did you write out an incident report?"

"No."

"Go and write it out then at that table."

I was surprised later that I hadn't even turned around to look at the girl or the knife.

Thursday, October 30

It was a rainy day.

Before school, about 30 black students roamed through the corridors, the black aides marching along behind, trying to get them to homerooms. The police captain remonstrated with his helmeted troopers because they had allowed the students to pass by them. The few I tried to stop ignored me.

The sound of a girl screaming came from the sewing room next door to my senior English class. Through the door window we could see a trooper move down the corridor in that direction.

Bill spoke, "You know who it is."

The girl with the tuft of yellow hair misbehaves because she likes to go to the office. The sewing teacher is afraid, since her students work with scissors.

Later in the day, I myself bumped into the girl. I nearly fainted from fear, and apologized, but she only smiled. I heard her yelling a few minutes later, and saw her pass Ms. Murphy with no sign of recognition. Either she was deliberately set on Ms. Murphy at Northeastern University, or she was reacting spontaneously to the negative vibrations of the other students.

Three black students in the holding room barricaded the door and ripped off part of the paneling. Mrs. Smith commented, "They told you they didn't like it there." They were arrested for being disorderly persons.

Friday, October 31

The last two buses with the student protest leaders were emptied first—for the first time; these students were directed to their homerooms. Then the quiet four lead buses unloaded.

Monday, November 3

Mrs. Smith wrote a report on Keith. She told Dr. Reid she didn't know whether she herself was the problem, but she didn't want him in her room; he had called her a "bastard."

Dr. Reid replied, "There are silent leaders who don't make much noise. They are being well coached."

At the end of the day I passed Lita going up the stairs accompanied by an aide. She turned to me and asked, "Are you Ms. Murphy's friend?"

"Yes," I answered.

"Where will she be next period?"

"I don't know."

"It's a good thing you won't be with her."

Mr. Corscadden and Sergeant Donovan of the Boston police went to Ms. Murphy's room and watched by her door.

Tuesday, November 4

Today was a quiet day. I heard that two black football players had been dropped from the team after the football incident at White Stadium; another two were dropped because of smoking in the bus and on the field; one hit the cheerleaders with his football bag at White Stadium.

Wednesday, November 5

The first class lasted an hour, from 8:30 to 9:30. We read "No News from Auschwitz." I talked about man's inhumanity to man. The sophomores looked at me, said nothing.

There had been a fight on the second floor. Mrs. Rosalie Packard put a hand on the corridor wall, held another teacher's hand, and formed a human chain to keep the kids from pushing into the fight. Miss Jackie Wynne, standing outside her door, was again knocked to the floor. There was blood on the floor from noses and knuckles. There were seven arrests — four whites, three blacks.

A white girl, who is bused in from Roxbury, was caught in the melee; she dropped out of school.

Later I mentioned to Mr. Jerry Ball, a teacher, how "high" the students in the study seemed. He explained, "They smell blood."

Even Mr. Van Schyndel, who stopped by the cafeteria, cautioned a boy at the water fountain with a scraped arm from gym, "You'd better wash that arm off. The blood will attract the sharks."

During my senior English class, I was alarmed by the sounds of screaming downstairs. The seniors were reading and listening to the record of *Antigone*. Finally they looked up and asked about the noise. I'm constantly amazed at how much more sensitive and anxious I am than they are.

The school quieted down after 10:30, according to the police and Dr. Reid, who detailed for the media how the staff secure the building after a fight. Behind him scrawled on the school building was graffiti: "S. B. PRISON."

Friday, November 7

There was a football game today. Members of the team came down to my cafeteria study today — ostensibly to have their legs bandaged for the game. They moved into the tables across from the four black students, studying them. The fear became palpable. Chester and the other black students began moving from seat to seat. Chester took out his black plastic pick and jabbed at the air. Three black girls went upstairs to the office, complaining. "They're bigger than we are."

Coach Perdigao came by then and told the team to leave; they didn't belong there. They left.

There was a one-to-one fight in the library, but the fight didn't spread, the librarian said.

Monday, November 10

The students were good today, but a little "high" in study. Melissa called the other study teacher a "cross-eyed dog." The teacher, who couldn't quite hear her, asked, "Did she call me a racial epithet?"

"No, she just changed your species."

Matthew passed in an extra-credit composition on *Animal Farm,* George Orwell's satire on the totalitarian state. Matthew wrote:

> You could compare Animal Farm with the busing in Boston. Napoleon could be the judge, where he runs everything, whereas before busing he was almost a nobody. Old Major could be the people who thought up deseregation, but not by busing. The ravan could be the media. They tell how good busing is going. The pigs could be city officials knowing everything, but not saying a word. The students going to school could be Boxer—always trying harder to get an education. Mollie the cat could be the school committee purring, and everybody thinks it is nice. Mr. Jones could be the old school system. Squealer could be the superintendent of schools.
>
> In the story there is a part when the hens find out that Napoleon was selling their eggs and they go on a kind of strike sitting in the rafter laying their eggs so they would break. This lasted a while, but was put to a stop by Napoleon. So the hens could be the boycotting students.
>
> Another part is whenever anything was said the sheep didn't like, they yelled them down, so the Sheep could be the anti-busing.
>
> The dogs were the police and stand for the police.
>
> All changes in this story are mine, all have the words *could be,* which do not represent *are.* I do not agree with force busing. I wouldn't go if I had enough money to be educated elsewhere.
>
> I think parents should be able to send the children anywhere they want. It is marked as public and just like in the south, black and white signs were hung over water fountains and they were public, but were they? Not if they are forced. Neither is our school system.

Of the administrators, Mr. Gizzi is out for a stomach operation. Mr. Doherty was out with pains in his arm for about two weeks after the teachers' strike. Mr. DiMaggio is now on medication for chest pains. Captain Hurley will be gone until January for an eye operation. Mr. Goorvich was out today. Only Dr. Reid survives, and he is showing the strain.

Wednesday, November 12

It was a quiet day.

In the library I asked Joyce, a South Boston girl whose attendance has been regular, to talk to one of my sophomore girls who has been staying away from school because of the fights. I introduced Joyce as a survivor of two years of busing, who would be graduated tough enough to meet the problems of the world, and asked her to tell Alice how she did it.

Joyce outlined, "You answer them back if they say anything to you. If you don't, they hit you. If you say something, they hit you anyway. You don't let them get away with anything."

That was not the advice I anticipated. I had advised, "Just keep your head down and mind your own business."

Thursday, November 13

After the early dismissal of students at 12:15, the faculty from South Boston High and the L-Street Annex met with representatives from the University of Massachusetts to discuss proposals developed over the summer for in-service training in the subject areas of reading and math. Seventy teachers signed up to participate.

Friday, November 14

I called in sick. Mr. Goorvich told me I was the twentieth teacher to call in that morning. He asked, "Is there a convention or something somewhere?" I felt sorry I had called, but ended up with a two-day headache and sick stomach.

Saturday, November 15

Tom Atkins, president of the Boston branch of the NAACP, told the annual NAACP banqueters that he would request the closing of South Boston High.

Police Commissioner diGrazia attended the banquet. U.S. Magistrate Willie Davis, the master of ceremonies, bantered diGrazia about his "Afro" hairstyle.

Monday, November 17

Mr. Atkins, back-pedaling now, wants South Boston High investigated, not necessarily closed.

The South Boston High faculty issued a statement to the media, criticizing Tom Atkins's call for the closing of the school:

> The faculty of South Boston High School deplores the remarks of Thomas Atkins, President of the Boston Branch of NAACP, calling for the closing of South Boston High School. We feel that even though there are problems within the school, these problems can be overcome. We also feel that his remarks about "the atmosphere not being conducive to education" are false. There is education for any student who desires it. Our problem lies with disruptive students that are causing most of these problems.
>
> Closing the school or moving to a neutral site is not the answer. To relocate would be detrimental to the continuity of the educational process for the students. A more feasible solution would be to remove constantly disruptive students out of South Boston High School and the tensions can be lessened.
>
> There are today and there have been in the past other schools with the same kind of problems that exist at S.B.H.S. The situation is not unique and yet he has not called for the closing of other schools. Therefore, the faculty of S.B.H.S. demands that the school be kept open and that responsible citizens on both sides of the issue refrain from making inflammatory statements that would be detrimental to the educational atmosphere at South Boston High School.

Dr. Reid on TV warned: The closing of South Boston High would create a domino effect in the city. Dr. Reid called Tom Atkins "a politician."

It's a struggle for the ultimate control of the school now.

Tuesday, November 18

"I can't believe the rumor I just heard—the NAACP has accused Perdigao and Scalese of racism and asked for their dismissal," Paul Moran, a teacher, said, coming into the English office, shaking his head.

At the faculty meeting in the library after school, the rumor was confirmed. With sworn affidavits from fifteen black students, the NAACP had petitioned Judge Garrity to close South Boston High, calling its atmosphere "unconstitutional," and to dismiss three racist faculty members—teachers Jim Scalese, Arthur Perdigao, and aide Donald Bilotas, referred to only as "Big Red." Mr. Scalese allegedly had jumped up onto a desk and mimicked a monkey to demonstrate that blacks were descendants of apes. Coach

Perdigao allegedly ousted blacks from the football team—for smoking, though one doesn't smoke; he made the team ride in segregated buses; and he told the white players to "get them" after the game at White Stadium. Ms. Murphy was also accused: Her students had to fill in blanks of "racist" sentences made up by students, and she gave out a lot of conduct cards to black students as opposed to whites "for things like asking questions in class."

In addition, the NAACP asked for punishment of boycott-advocating groups.

Judge Garrity had agreed to an evidentiary hearing in the federal court.

At the faculty meeting, teachers spontaneously rose and gave character testimonials for the accused teachers. The state police captain, who also attended the faculty meeting, denied the allegations against them: The police had documentation for every incident. No trooper had used his stick or raised a fist against any student. His men had reacted splendidly in a difficult situation.

Dr. Reid was not at the meeting. He was giving depositions at court and wanted to be there with the incident reports so they would not be tampered with.

Ms. Ellen Nikas, the health teacher, raised her hand and asked why she hadn't been named for court appearance, since she had been accused on Channel 7 TV "Black News" on October 12.

Mr. Doherty, member of the Boston Teachers' Union executive board and assistant headmaster, replied, "Because you're a woman. The greatest victims of racism are racists. If they charged a woman, they would lose sympathy. It has to be a white male."

Someone yelled, "You're too pretty."

Wednesday, November 19

The biracial council election results came in: The students selected represented almost the entire list of the most polarized students in the school.

At a staff meeting at the end of the day, the faculty unanimously adopted a resolution to file a class action suit in behalf of Scalese and Perdigao against the NAACP. The aides had already met and voted to support "Big Red"—Donald Bilotas—by letters to Dr. Reid, the NAACP, and Judge Garrity.

Dr. Reid arrived at the meeting with Superintendent Marion Fahey, who declared her full support of the faculty. Jack Cunningham, faculty senate president, expostulated angrily to her that Major Charles Gilligan of the state police had responded immediately to the media, and denied the charges made against his men. Why hadn't she come similarly to the defense of the teachers? Why had her reply to the media been, "No comment"?

Superintendent Fahey explained: She had not made public statements supporting the teachers because she had been at a meeting and it wasn't the right time.

In Washington, an antibusing resolution was tabled in Congress. Rita Graul of ROAR said, "We'll let Charlestown take care of [Speaker] Tip O'Neill."

Thursday, November 20

There was a boycott today by white students protesting the NAACP suit to close the high school, and also the allegedly "premeditated" attack yesterday on Jane.

I had seen Jane, wearing her perennial costume of long pants and pigtails, sitting in the front office before school yesterday, frozen with fear. I saw her with her parents again at the end of the day, a long scratch down her right cheek and a clawed corner of her eye, the tear duct. Although accompanied to her class by an aide and trooper, she had been jumped in the classroom while the teacher was still standing at the door talking to the aide.

"Jane, can't you stay out of fights?" I asked.

"No," she answered.

I showed Part II of the *Animal Farm* film in my sophomore classes. The attendance in the first class was three black girls. Sandra was delighted and explained the story to her neighbor who had not read the book. Celia screamed when the donkey was hurt, and she held her cheeks during the Battle of the Windmill. A total of only six students, five black and one white, saw the second part of the film; and of those six, only two saw the entire film—because of shortened periods, or the reading test, which the 400 boycotting students missed and had to make up during class time.

Dr. Reid held an "emergency" meeting after school so that faculty at the high school "as of November 19"—the day the NAACP filed its disposition—could fill out a form for the federal court: name, address, race, subject taught, date first assigned to South Boston High.

One teacher protested, "It is unconstitutional to ask a person's race."

"I have observed that civil liberties don't mean much to civil libertarians in all cases," Dr. Reid replied. He concluded the meeting by informing us that he would be at court in the morning with Mr. Goorvich to represent us.

Later in the afternoon, faculty met with parents as part of the Home and School program held throughout the city. Two different parents told me that their youngsters start out for school, then return home and tell them, "There was trouble at the school." The parents don't know how to discipline them because the other kids will harass them, they claim, if they go to school.

One father, despairing, said his son was good, conscientious, and intelligent, but he was slipping further and further.

The *Globe* newspaper carried a series of black student affidavits. The most alarming for me was of Paul, who came to school on crutches with his foot wrapped in a bandage. During homeroom he allegedly unwound it and said, "This is my new nigger beater. I am going to use this crutch on the first nigger that says anything to me."

At the Crisis Prevention seminar, the school psychiatrist asked, "Did he ever use the crutch as a weapon?" He did not.

On WGBH public television, Channel 2, Representative Ray Flynn from South Boston accused NAACP president Tom Atkins of polarizing the black and white communities, setting community against community. He accused Atkins of pushing the city to the brink of disaster with the Carson Beach episode last August, when Atkins, with members of the NAACP, the Progressive Labor party, and the Coalition Against Racism, had joined with residents of the Columbia Point housing project in an attempt to desegregate Carson Beach; the demonstration had ended in a violent confrontation with police and Southie residents. Flynn declared that Atkins's request to have South Boston High investigated was "more of the same," making communities restless waiting for statements from both sides.

Representative Flynn declared that education was taking place in a situation where students were being forced—black and white—to go somewhere they didn't necessarily want to go. The problem would be the same at an alternate site. He mentioned that Charlestown had been sympathy-boycotting with South Boston for the past two days.

Teachers had to be on target in these matters, he concluded, noting that both black and white aides and teachers would testify with Dr. Reid the following day in federal court.

I telephoned the WGBH TV newsdesk and asked why their newscasters had slandered teachers by name on that evening's news broadcast and not given the identity of the accusers, pointing out that a statement had validity only if the accuser had validity. Who were the accusers?

Some of the teachers didn't know they had been ordered to appear in court until they read their names in the morning newspaper.

Friday, November 21

Evidentiary hearings, presided over by Judge W. Arthur Garrity, began today at the federal court house to determine "whether the Court's desegregation plan is being implemented down at the South Boston High School and its L-Street Annex," not to determine "anybody's liability." *

THE COURT (Judge W. Arthur Garrity): That is the issue here today before me; that is, whether they [the defendants] and others are working against implementation of the court order at South Boston High and L-Street Annex or not. . . . With respect to the coach, Mr. Perdigao, the question is what affirmative action has he taken, if any, to carry out the provision of the plan.

MR. BARRY M. PORTNOY (counsel for the high school staff): Your Honor, with regard to the proposed testimony today, in my clients' interest, may I respectfully request that we be given an opportunity to prepare to represent them in this case? I was retained last evening at seven p.m.

THE COURT: We will see how it goes. . . . I consider this a matter of very great urgency.

MR. PORTNOY: Your Honor, may I respectfully state that I am not prepared for effective cross-examination or presentation of evidence on behalf of my clients.

THE COURT: Do your best.

At this point, ten minutes after the court hearing opened, a clash broke out between would-be spectators and security officers in the corridor outside the courtroom, drowning out the proceedings. Recess was called. One witness raced out the door crying, "That's my mother." Five blacks were arrested outside the courtroom. Representative Ray Flynn, who was also too late to be admitted to the courtroom, became a state witness to the assault on the court officer. One of those in the corridors was Leon Rock, SDS activist of the 1960s, now Boston NAACP Youth Council director, who protested his courtroom exclusion on the evening TV news.

When court reconvened, lawyer James J. Sullivan, defense counsel for

---

* *Tallulah Morgan et al., Plaintiffs, v. John J. Kerrigan et al., Defendants,* Civil Action No. 72-911-G. Transcripts of hearings before Judge W. Arthur Garrity, November 21-28, 1975, U.S. District Court, District of Massachusetts.

the Boston School Committee, renewed his written objection filed the day before: that one working day was not enough "to rebut the allegations contained in anonymous affidavits."

THE COURT: *Don't you see that the very turmoil that is out in the corridor moves this court to act in this matter expeditiously? This matter was brought to the attention of the Court of Appeals yesterday. This matter should be heard and decided promptly, in my view.*

Mr. Sullivan again protested the "absence of procedural due process" by the failure to allow the defense lawyers as much preparation time as the plaintiffs. His motion was set aside.

A motion by John F. McMahon, counsel for the Boston Teachers Union, to impound a list of names and addresses of South Boston High teachers and administrators was allowed as a precaution against harassment.

The Court then revealed that, of the fifteen affidavits filed by black students, only the twelve "whom the plaintiffs' lawyers designated" would be called as witnesses: numbers 1 to 4, 6, 7, 9 to 14. Those names, said Judge Garrity, had been disclosed yesterday "to counsel for at least the Home and School Association."

Again defense lawyers Kevin F. Moloney (Assistant Corporation Counsel assigned for non–School Committee city defendants), John F. McMahon, and Thayer Fremont-Smith for the Boston Home and School Association objected to "the proceeding and type of notice that was given to counsel."

MR. FREMONT-SMITH: *I think it is almost inconceivable how I can conduct any intelligent cross-examination today.*

THE COURT: *Well, we will see. . . . I am not interested in finding out who hit whom on some particular dates. I am trying to get a picture of the situation: to what extent is it characterized as being in turmoil, with all sorts of incidents.*

Major Gilligan also entered a protest that the state police had never received an official copy of the affidavits, although several officers under his command were mentioned in them.

MR. FREMONT-SMITH: *We are apprehensive, however, that there is a move to close down this school of long standing as part of a political strategy, and to that we cannot subscribe. We feel the only way to see what the true state of the facts are at this school is for us to have the full information with respect to specific allegations. There is no other way to defend or to set the record straight with regard to this type of broad, shotgun allegation except to examine the specifics and to do that we need to have access to the particular school and police reports to see if there is any substance to them.*

THE COURT: I want to get some evidence of the — I am just not going to keep repeating myself — of whether this plan is being implemented in South Boston High School and L-Street Annex.

So let's get the first witness here. We will hear from them one at a time. Here it is 11:15 and we have not even started.

According to procedure set by the Court, students were to read affidavits, give direct testimony confined to the affidavit, and then be cross-examined on subjects covered by the direct.

Dr. Reid sat and listened to the testimony "with averted face and doleful expression," a reporter noted.

Student Number One, a sophomore, was sworn in and read his affidavit:

STUDENT NUMBER ONE: During the first or second week of school this year, before my schedule was changed, one of my teachers was Mr. Scalese. One day, in Mr. Scalese's class, a white student asked Mr. Scalese where does niggers come from. . . . Mr. Scalese answered they are an extension of apes. The white students laughed at that answer. . . . A few weeks later, . . . as I was going past his room, Room 218, a black girl said to me, 'Come look at this fool.' I walked into the door of Mr. Scalese's room and saw Mr. Scalese standing on top of the desk at the front of the class, about twelve feet from where I was standing in the doorway. He was scratching himself on his ribs and making gestures and noise like a monkey. I watched him doing this for what seemed like a minute, a full minute, put it that way. The white students were laughing and enjoying the show. One of the black students then called a state trooper to come and see what was going on in the room, so Mr. Scalese got down off the desk.

When the teachers act like this, it is no wonder that the white students make all kind of racist slangs at us.

THE COURT: That is the end.

Mr. Sullivan was first cross-examiner.

MR. SULLIVAN: And this thing that you have been reading, this affidavit, did you write it out yourself?

STUDENT NUMBER ONE: Huh? No. I said word by word and I had somebody dictating it.

MR. SULLIVAN: Did you dictate it?

STUDENT NUMBER ONE: Huh?

MR. SULLIVAN: Did you dictate it to somebody?

STUDENT NUMBER ONE: Break it down for me.

MR. SULLIVAN: Well, are these your words?

STUDENT NUMBER ONE: Exactly?

MR. SULLIVAN: Exactly your words?

STUDENT NUMBER ONE: Yes.

Mr. Portnoy examined the witness next.

MR. PORTNOY: Do you know what Mr. Scalese looks like?

STUDENT NUMBER ONE: Yes.

MR. PORTNOY: Can you point him out in this courtroom?

The student scanned the room.

STUDENT NUMBER ONE: No.

THE COURT: Is he in the courtroom?

MR. PORTNOY: He is in the courtroom, your Honor. . . . You cannot point out Mr. Scalese, is that correct?

THE COURT: Stand up and see if you can see this man.

The witness stood up as directed.

STUDENT NUMBER ONE: Ain't that him over there?

THE COURT: If you can, point out or describe whereabouts.

MR. PORTNOY: What row is he in, please?

STUDENT NUMBER ONE: Second.

MR. PORTNOY: And could you count the number of people from one end or the other?

STUDENT NUMBER ONE: Three.

MR. PORTNOY: He is the third person from the end?

STUDENT NUMBER ONE: Yes.

MR. PORTNOY: The third person from the end of the second row, will you please stand?

A young man with blond hair rose to his feet.

MR. PORTNOY: Is that Mr. Scalese?

STUDENT NUMBER ONE: That looks like him.

MR. PORTNOY: What is your name, sir?

THE MAN: Mr. Hammond. °

THE COURT: Excuse me. I direct Mr. Scalese to stand up.

MR. PORTNOY: Mr. Scalese, would you please —

THE COURT: And Mr. Hammond to stay with him.

A grey-haired man stood up, fifteen pounds heavier and fifteen years older than Mr. Hamann.

° The transcript incorrectly spells William Hamann's name as "Hammond."

THE COURT: All right. One is Mr. Hammond and the other is Mr. Scalese. All right. Please be seated.

MR. PORTNOY: Let's take the second sentence of paragraph two of your affidavit. It says, "One day in Mr. Scalese's class, a white student asked Mr. Scalese where did niggers come from." . . . Did he hear this white student when she asked where did niggers come from?

STUDENT NUMBER ONE: She didn't say it then. You know, like she waited until class started, right? And she asked him how did niggers come into the world, so then he said they are from a family of extension apes.

MR. PORTNOY: I see. That was the first thing that happened in the class that day?

STUDENT NUMBER ONE: No. Attendance was tooken first.

MR. PORTNOY: Now let's look at the next sentence, which is the most serious charge you have made in this affidavit, all right? . . . Let's read it very slowly together. "I walked to the door of Mr. Scalese's room, and I saw Mr. Scalese standing on top of his desk at the front of his class about twelve feet from where I stood in the doorway." Is that what happened?

STUDENT NUMBER ONE: On the desk acting like a monkey.

MR. PORTNOY: Yes.

STUDENT NUMBER ONE: Exactly what happened.

MR. PORTNOY: But are you sure it was Mr. Scalese?

STUDENT NUMBER ONE: Am I sure it was him? No. She [a black girl] said it was his room, but I ain't seen no face, I seen the back.

MR. PORTNOY: You did not see the teacher's face?

STUDENT NUMBER ONE: No.

MR. PORTNOY: Let's go on to the next sentence there. It says, "He was scratching himself in his ribs, and making gestures and noises like a monkey."

STUDENT NUMBER ONE: You know, "Oo, oo," a noise like that.

MR. PORTNOY: You are absolutely sure that is what was going on?

STUDENT NUMBER ONE: The monkey bit? Yes. I'm positive.

MR. PORTNOY: How do you know it was a teacher?

STUDENT NUMBER ONE: Who got hair all in their face? Do you ever see a student — You seen a student like that in school?

In his affidavit, Student Number One also alleged he had been clubbed on the head by a state trooper, and three troopers had worked on him "all together." When he asked the nurse for a bandaid for his scratched arm, she told him it would cost him a dime apiece; she swabbed his arm with a "dirty" cotton pad.

Student Number Two, a junior, who like Student Number One had attended the Jeremiah Burke High School last year, next read from her affidavit. Like the other affiants, she had dictated her affidavit to plaintiff lawyers at the Multi-Service Center in Roxbury several weeks after their allegations at Northeastern University. One of the lawyers then present was Roger Rice from the Center for Law and Education at Harvard University.

> *STUDENT NUMBER TWO: On Wednesday morning, October 8, 1975, my bus 208 arrived at South Boston High School. . . . As I was standing beside the door of bus 209, a police officer said to me, "Get your ass on that bus or get your goddamn ass inside the school. . . ."*
>
> *The following day, Thursday, October 9, 1975, I went to the office to fill out a complaint form about this incident. No one has ever been in touch with me about it. I don't have any reason to believe that anything was done.*
>
> *On the morning of Friday, October 23, 1975, there was some fights between black kids and white kids. We were around the front door of the school waiting to go through the metal detectors. This was the day after the school football game at White Stadium. After a morning of fights lots of white kids went outside the building and stayed in the yard around the school.*
>
> *I went to my homeroom 208, where my teacher is Mr. Hammond. I heard white kids outside the school making noise, and went over to look out the window. The kids were standing outside chanting, "Two four six eight, assassinate nigger apes." Later in the period, some of the white kids came back in the school. When they came to my homeroom, some of the white kids still said, "Two four six eight, assassinate nigger apes." Mr. Hammond told the students to be quiet, but most of them continued. He did not tell them that they were suspended or anything, and I don't think that there was any disciplinary action has ever been taken against them.*

Mr. Sullivan's cross-examination picked up on an incident in the cafeteria, where, on November 17, Student Number Two reportedly "jazzed" through a line of white girls, and sat at Table 14, where white girls were sitting.

> *MR. SULLIVAN (reading): This was considered by the observer as a provocative act. Student Number Two admitted that her action was deliberate, and said that she can sit where she wants to.*
>
> *STUDENT NUMBER TWO: That's right. I can, sir.*
>
> *MR. SULLIVAN: And you told some supervisory person in the school that on that day, didn't you?*
>
> *STUDENT NUMBER TWO: Dr. Reid. That's right.*

After lunch recess, Mr. Robert Pressman, plaintiff lawyer, redirected examination of Student Number Two.

MR. PRESSMAN: *Now, there was an incident about the cafeteria. Would you state in your words what happened?*

STUDENT NUMBER TWO: *We came from typing. And we went to the lunchroom, and we went up to get our lunch, and some of my friends, they had already got there, and they went and sat down, and some of the black boys were in the room and they came and sat down with them, and I was coming back. I only had milk, so — and then I went to sit at the end of the table, because it was kind of crowded. I tried to squeeze in, but it wasn't enough room, so I got up and I moved to the next seat, which some white girls happened to be sitting at the time, and so I just sat there, and after lunch was over, I went upstairs to my sixth period class, and Dr. Reid came up and he said, "You know what I am here for," and I said, "I don't know what you're talking about," so he said, "Well, we can discuss it here or we can go up to the office," and I told him I don't know what he was talking about, so we went upstairs to the office, and then he said that that was a very provocative move, and I asked him what's he talking about.*

He said going to sit with the white girls, that was a very provocative move. I asked him is he telling me that I cannot sit where I want to sit, and he kept saying, you know, it was a very provocative move. He said, "You could see that you weren't wanted there," and you know, I was kind of mad with him, so I didn't really want to reply, so he just filled out his incident report and he let me read it, and he said, "Do you agree with this?" and I told him no. He said, "All right. You can go back to your class," and I went.

MR. PRESSMAN: *Was this a situation where there were two tables next to each other?*

STUDENT NUMBER TWO: *Yes.*

MR. PRESSMAN: *And at the table where your friends were sitting, there wasn't any space left?*

STUDENT NUMBER TWO: *Right.*

MR. PRESSMAN: *And you moved to the next seat available?*

STUDENT NUMBER TWO: *Yes.*

MR. PRESSMAN: *And there were some white girls sitting there?*

STUDENT NUMBER TWO: *Yes, that's right.*

MR. PRESSMAN: *No further questions.*

In his recross examination of the witness, Mr. Fremont-Smith again returned to the cafeteria incident.

MR. FREMONT-SMITH: *Now you mentioned an incident in the cafeteria. Was that an incident in which the white girls had been sitting in the seats and you took one of their seats?*

STUDENT NUMBER TWO: *No, it isn't.*

MR. FREMONT-SMITH: *Then why did Dr. Reid consider it to be a provocative act?*

STUDENT NUMBER TWO: *I do not know. Ask him.*

Student Number Three, a junior, the final witness of the day, testified that a black aide had been clubbed on the head by a state trooper who mistakenly thought the aide was reaching for his gun. Student Number Three alleged she had found the aide crying in the front office, and the aide recounted the incident to her.

Mr. McMahon cross-examined Student Number Three.

MR. MCMAHON: *Now directing your attention to October 10th, did you refuse to report to class on October 10th?*

STUDENT NUMBER THREE: *Yes.*

MR. MCMAHON: *You were in the cafeteria.*

STUDENT NUMBER THREE: *Yes.*

MR. MCMAHON: *Do you recall saying to Dr. Reid, "We are going to close this school"?*

STUDENT NUMBER THREE: *No.*

MR. MCMAHON: *Did you ever make that statement to any teacher?*

STUDENT NUMBER THREE: *No.*

Under cross-examination next by Mr. Fremont-Smith, Student Number Three again denied saying, "We are going to close this school."

MR. FREMONT-SMITH: *When did you first discuss the possibility of closing the school?*

STUDENT NUMBER THREE: *When —*

THE COURT: *Excuse me?*

MR. RUDOLPH S. PIERCE (Plaintiff lawyer): *Your Honor, I am going to object.*

THE COURT: *Sustained. The Court is interested in what is going on inside the school. This objection is sustained. We are not seeking to investigate the Multi-Service Center or Lena Park or Mr. Wilson or anyone else. We are investigating this plan and whether it is being implemented or not being implemented at South Boston High School, so the ruling stands.*

MR. FREMONT-SMITH: But, your Honor, the purpose of my inter-rogation was to investigate the credibility of the allegations. I don't have before me any of the incident reports, because they are not here. I do think it is relevant, because Dr. Reid will testify that he was told that they intended to close down the school on October 10, and I think it is —

THE COURT: Well, we will hear that from Dr. Reid when his turn comes. . . . I sustain the objection, and would ask that you put another question.

MR. FREMONT-SMITH: Did you tell Dr. Reid on or about October 10 that you intended to close down the school?

STUDENT NUMBER THREE: No, I didn't. It's not my right to close the school down.

MR. FREMONT-SMITH: Did you tell him that you would close down the school?

STUDENT NUMBER THREE: No.

MR. FREMONT-SMITH: All right. I have no further questions.

Mr. Michael J. Haroz, counsel for El Comite de Padres, pursued the question of seating.

MR. HAROZ: Would you refer for a minute to the October 8th list of demands of the Black Student Caucus. And Item Number 12, segregated patterns in classrooms, could you explain about that?

STUDENT NUMBER THREE: Well, the white —

THE COURT: Excuse me. You have got to — You are starting to back off. Come a little closer to the microphone.

STUDENT NUMBER THREE: The white students would sit on one side of the room and the black students would sit on the other side of the room, and the teachers, when they were talking, they have to keep looking back and forth, or either the blacks will sit in the front and the whites will sit in the back, and that is how the racial slurs started up. Somebody will start up a slur, and things start like that, instead of just mixing us in our seats, you know, and everybody would — well, I'm not going to say anything to somebody sitting in back of me, somebody sitting on this side of me, but having us all separate, blacks on one side and whites on one side, they feel it's just like having gang fights. You feel like you can take all the whites in the school and take all the blacks in the school.

MR. HAROZ: And this is the — does this segregation occur —

MR. PHILIP TIERNEY (Counsel for the School Committee of Boston): Objection.

THE COURT: Wait, please. Here it says on page 2, "There shall be no

segregation within schools, classrooms, or programs in the school system."
This is the first I have heard of that.

Is this separation of the whites and blacks on different sides?
STUDENT NUMBER THREE: *Yes, yes.*
THE COURT: *Are seats assigned in the cafeteria?*
STUDENT NUMBER THREE: *No. No, they are not.*
THE COURT: *Are seats assigned in the classroom?*
STUDENT NUMBER THREE: *No.*
MR. HAROZ: *If the seats are not assigned in the classrooms, how do the blacks and whites end up sitting on different sides?*
STUDENT NUMBER THREE: *When they walk into the room, whites automatically go to one side and blacks automatically go to the other side.*
MR. HAROZ: *Have you ever observed any attempt by a faculty member to change that situation in the classroom?*
STUDENT NUMBER THREE: *Yes. Yes, I have.*
MR. HAROZ: *Has it worked?*
STUDENT NUMBER THREE: *No. They said that, you know, this is high school, and, you know, you can sit where you want to sit, as long as you are doing your work.*
THE COURT: *Now that is the last witness for the day.*
The Court adjourned.

Back at school there was concern that, with Dr. Reid and so many administrators, teachers, and aides at Court, there might be trouble. But the school held together. There were five suspensions, most of them from excessive tardiness.

Three-fourths of the white student body returned to school. I was surprised until I caught the tail-end of a TV news story in the school audio-visual room after lunch. There had been a parents' meeting at the high school Thursday evening. Dr. Reid was televised telling them, "I think there are some of you who are working for the NAACP to close the school. When the teachers of your youngsters are being accused of racism, where are your children? Instead of in this school supporting the teachers, they're out in the street." His voice moved from an angry crescendo to an almost silent "out in the street."

Some parents still protested. Virginia Sheehy of the South Boston Information Center countered, "Before we support the teachers, they have to stand up and be counted."

Bill Hamann did not testify about the chant—"Two four six eight, assassinate nigger apes"—that Student Number Two alleged she had heard both outside and inside his homeroom on Friday, October 24. Later, when I asked Bill about the incident, he told me, "I didn't hear anything."

Another teacher of the handicapped, who works with Bill, said angrily, "This is a witch hunt. You couldn't find a nicer guy than Bill Hamann."

The *Globe* headlines read: STUDENT PICKS WRONG MAN IN TESTIMONY IN CHARGES OF S. BOSTON HIGH RACISM.

Saturday, November 22

The evidentiary hearings on South Boston High continued at the McCormack Federal Building. Metal detectors, used for the first time at the entrance to the courtroom, turned up three knives and an "inoperable zip gun" among the would-be spectators.

Mr. Fremont-Smith protested the student witness "rooting section" in the court and requested that they be asked to wait outside during testimony.

*MR. FREMONT-SMITH: I say it makes it difficult for a witness to give an impartial answer, and I notice that, for instance, when I asked whether the majority of the white kids at South Boston were trying to be decent and the witness hesitated and looked at the group and then said, "No."
. . . This is a very important proceeding because it does involve the good name and careers of individual teachers and it also involves the future of the school in South Boston and the whole community.*

THE COURT: Well, I really thought about that yesterday and that request is denied.

The first witness of the day, Student Number Four, a senior transfer from the Jeremiah Burke High School, alleged that Donald Bilotas, or "Big Red," a teacher-aide, had participated in an assault on a black student, and had encouraged "Paul's gang" to harass black students in the high school. The sole accuser of "Big Red," she alleged she saw him come over and make like he was trying to help the black student, but all the time he was kicking him in the head. When she tried to "pull some of the whites" off the student, a state trooper grabbed her by her hair, handcuffed her, and led her away.

In cross-examination, Mr. Portnoy, defense counsel, offered the Court incident reports that he felt contradicted Student Number Four's affidavit:

MR. PORTNOY: Your Honor, I believe it demonstrates that the witness was involved in another incident and taken to the detention room and that she could not have been involved in the late incident because she wasn't physically there.

THE COURT (after examining reports): It doesn't prove a thing. Excuse me. In my view, it doesn't prove a thing.

What I want you to do is save your rights here and we are going to have this marked for identification. If you think it proves a thing, you can argue it some day to the Court of Appeals.

Judge Garrity again repeated the purpose of the evidentiary hearings.

THE COURT: The court is going to find out what the situation is there and what, if any, affirmative action is being taken to alter the situation or to better the situation.

Now, one of the problems, as I see it in South Boston High School, is that the faculty has decided not to cooperate with the CCC Mediating Board. That is what has been reported to me. I heard this morning that the faculty now has had a change of heart. I think that is very, very welcome, as I said at the outset of the hearing today, but that is not going to dissuade the Court from investigating the facts.

Now, you have Mr. Brociner's affidavit and he is going to be the next witness and his affidavit has to do with the faculty meeting, to which the last statement in the affidavit is the following: "The faculty was very much against this idea, that is, cooperating with the CCC Mediating Board, and many white teachers expressed the opinion that the CCC was a creature of Judge Garrity and should be kept out of the school."

Well, now, is that true or not? Let's have Mr. Brociner here. He is going to be called upon to testify by direct questioning, which can be objected to and answered, and then cross-examination.

Mr. Kenneth Brociner, a political science major in college, a "close friend" of plaintiff lawyer Roger Rice, and a substitute teacher on October 15 and October 24 at the high school, was sworn in. Mr. Pressman began the direct questioning of the witness.

Again Messrs. Fremont-Smith and Portnoy protested: They had "never seen" a copy of the affidavit.

THE COURT: Well, I think we should take a short recess. We will take the morning recess, and you and Mr. Fremont-Smith and anyone else that hasn't seen that affidavit should do so.

After the morning recess, Mr. Pressman resumed examination of substitute teacher Mr. Brociner about the October 15 faculty meeting when the "question of the CCC acting as a mediator came up."

MR. PRESSMAN: You say there was "a hostile reaction?" To what?

MR. BROCINER: To the idea of the CCC coming in. It was hostility mixed with some ignorance because a lot of the faculty did not know who the CCC was, but there was a feeling like: We don't want them in the school. They are outside people. We are the experts. We are the professionals in South Boston High. They are just Garrity's "preacher," for lack of a better term.

They didn't use this word. There was a lot of resentment against Judge Garrity. . . .

A lot of discussion — some of the discussion — was some people made statements such as: They are Judge Garrity's people. We don't want them in.

It might not have been as explicit as that, but the connection was very obvious.

MR. TIERNEY: *Objection, your Honor.*

THE COURT: *Overruled.*

MR. BROCINER: *I just came to it. . . . People left the meeting with an open mind. Some members of the Faculty Senate at South Boston High were delegated to meet with one or two members of the CCC to discuss what they wanted and whether or not they would be allowed to come in.*

The next witness, John Cunningham, faculty senate president, testified about the rejection by the faculty of the services of the CCC Mediating Task Force. He explained that two attempts last year by outside mediators — the National Center for Dispute Settlement and the Hartford General Assistance Center — were unsuccessful in their efforts.

Before lunch recess, Mr. Tierney, defense counsel, addressed the Court.

MR. TIERNEY: *Your honor, pardon me. Before we recess, could the Court indicate what witness will be called after Mr. Cunningham?*

THE COURT: *I don't know. I just don't know. I will try to figure that out.*

MR. MOLONEY: *But if we don't know what the witnesses are, there is nothing we can accomplish during lunch to prepare for this afternoon.*

THE COURT: *Well, maybe you will enjoy your lunch more.*

Mr. Cunningham continued his testimony when the afternoon session resumed. Asked to compare the situation this year with last year in "respect to racial confrontations," Mr. Cunningham testified that the situation at South Boston High was better this year than last, up until October 7; from then on, it was "more difficult and more disruptive" than the same period last year.

MR. CUNNINGHAM: *I could make a comparison of, say, the week for — two weeks before Michael Faith was stabbed — and the week of October 6th and the week of October 14th. That was comparable. I think they are both parallel. The reason I say that they are parallel is because in the weeks previous to the stabbing of Michael Faith, there was a lot of white community involvement and, at the same time, in the week of October 6th and the week of October 14th, the black community had been involved. This is the comparison that I would make.*

We, as a faculty, feel that if the black and white communities will stay out and let us handle the problems and do not do any agitation in the communities with the students, then we feel that education and the carrying out of the duties of a normal high school would be able to be accomplished.

Ms. Sandra Lynch, counsel for the Massachusetts Board of Education, picked up on classroom seating.

MS. LYNCH: Mr. Cunningham, could you tell me whether you have ever received any instruction, either orally or in writing, about how students should sit in the classrooms and what actions you should take if there are segregated seating patterns in the classroom?

MR. CUNNINGHAM: No, Ms. Lynch, I have not received any.

Dr. Reid was not scheduled to testify. However, late Saturday afternoon, despite the protest of Mr. Tierney, the Court called "the Doctor" to the stand.

Dr. Reid testified at length and spontaneously on what things improved through Phase 2 desegregation and "those which have deteriorated." On the "plus side," he summarized, attendance of white students has improved; students "within the class talk to each other much more"; students "are more comfortable"; the "faculty is much better organized" and "have more confidence in themselves and their ability to handle the situations as they arise." There is "very little graffiti"; "no mass movement of students through the building"; "no serious injuries"; "one unified police force, rather than a division of authority"; and a "better record system."

Dr. Reid noted that, of the youngsters who had testified, "only two" of them were at the high school last year. By contrast, he said, "The youngsters who were with us last year seem to do very well this year. They appear to know our style and what is expected of them and I think we get along much better professionally and personally than we did a year ago."

Dr. Reid then turned to the negative aspects, as he perceived them, of Phase 2 desegregation at the high school.

DR. REID: These things are all on the plus side. On the minus side, and the one that concerns me mostly, is that I think my faculty morale has deteriorated. This is a matter of great concern. I think I have a good faculty. There are many excellent people on it. You can take a hundred faculty of schools in the state and I will match them with them.

I think they are somewhat discouraged that this year hasn't gone better. We were somewhat optimistic that Phase 2 would go better. I think they are concerned that they are under attack from many sources or they feel they are under attack from many sources. I think that they feel that people think they aren't doing a good job, when I know they are, and I think they are discouraged and disappointed, but, hopefully, they are not demoralized.

I think they feel that they are being put upon. They have a program working with the University of Massachusetts in reading. They have a program in mathematics. These were developed over the summer and they are in operation. They have three in-service courses going on in how to teach reading in the content area.

We have an active program with the Gillette Company, with the Federal Reserve Bank, and I think they feel that they are doing everything that is reasonably possible within the time they have available and within their mental and emotional capacity to do these things, and I think they feel that people are trying to force other things upon them which, perhaps, they cannot absorb at this time, with the other things that they have going.

Dr. Reid listed two other "minus" factors: "more individual fights" and a "higher suspension rate," and a third: *"I don't think community support has improved in either community, and this leaves us in many cases, I think, at the mercy of factors which are outside the school and over which we have little or no control."*

Shortly before Court adjourned at four o'clock for the weekend, Dr. Reid tripped himself in his efforts to be completely fair when he responded to the Judge's question, "Have you any reason to doubt the accuracy of any of the things that they [the student witnesses] stated?"

DR. REID: In a few cases, but, basically, I think the reports were honest.

THE COURT: But you did obtain from them, as you watched them, a feeling of credibility, did you, and believability?

DR. REID: I think basically, the youngsters were honest. This is one of my basic premises.

THE COURT: I am the fact finder here. That has certainly been my conclusion as well.

THE COURT: Is there anything else you want to add before we adjourn?

DR. REID: I have nothing further to add, sir.

Before adjourning, Judge Garrity noted, *"It would be a terrible injustice to Mr. Scalese to conclude from that testimony that he did what was alleged. After all, he had been embarrassed, and I think unintentionally wronged. . . . But, to the Court, it is far less important that Mr. Scalese did not do this than that somebody did it.*

"The Court's principal inquiry is not who hit who. The inquiry is: What has happened? What is the situation? Is the situation at South Boston High School such that a person, whether it is Mr. Scalese or Mr. Smith or Mr. Jones or whoever, could, with the hilarity of observers, get up and dance like a monkey and make sounds and scratching noises?"

The Sunday *Globe* capsuled Dr. Reid's testimony in banner front page headlines that left Dr. Reid, until he could clarify his meaning, twisting slowly in the wind: BLACKS' CHARGES AFFIRMED BY REID. The *Herald* ran a picture of Dr. Reid standing beside the three boxes of incident reports and captioned: SOUTHIE HEADMASTER SAYS TESTIMONY OF BLACK STUDENTS BASICALLY HONEST, BUT. . . .

In his "rationale" for the receivership of South Boston High, Judge Garrity summarized Dr. Reid's testimony on the faculty:

Part of the problem at South Boston High School has been the attitude of the faculty as a unit toward the changes that have accompanied desegregation. . . . As a unit, . . . the faculty has, in Dr. Reid's phrase, felt "put upon" by desegregation, and this attitude has impeded integration of the school.

The positive efforts the faculty had made, which Dr. Reid mentioned, besides those he failed to cite—the sensitivity courses, crisis-prevention courses, proposal writing, innumerable voluntary after-school faculty meetings—were all disregarded.

Over the weekend, blue-collar workers from Louisville and Boston demonstrated in Washington at the National Democratic Issues Convention. They carried AFL-CIO banners against forced busing. The police force was ominous: helmeted riot police standing with water guns, night sticks, and tear gas. Prior to the demonstration, each member of Congress had received a letter from Mr. Andrew Biemiller, director of AFL-CIO's Department of Legislation, stating that a vote against forced busing is "an action deemed an anti-labor vote."

Out of the entire Congress, Mo Udall was the only legislator who met with a delegation of the demonstrators, and he lectured them: "Now you see what poor black children have been going through for the past [so many] years."

Monday, November 24

Dr. Reid was the first and only witness in the morning session at the federal court house hearings. Defense counsel probed to clarify some of the points raised during the two earlier sessions.

MR. TIERNEY: *Doctor, you state under "Teacher's Role" in this [Head-master's] Bulletin 3 the teacher should be fair, be consistent, and be impersonal. Could you explain what those instructions mean?*

DR. REID: *Basically that you treat every youngster alike, you are consistent in your rulings, you use judicious judgment in making decisions, and you treat it as an offense against the school, not against yourself. Impersonal, as you note, is underlined. It is a very important factor in the philosophy.*

MR. TIERNEY: *What is the seating policy in general at South Boston High School?*

DR. REID: *The seating policy in general depends upon the individual teacher. In high school, many teachers allow youngsters to choose their own seats. Some insist upon an alphabetical arrangement, and others just rearrange the class with flexible furniture in whatever way is best suited to conduct the class. In the assembly hall, all seats are assigned by the headmaster.*

MR. TIERNEY: *Now, Doctor, directing your attention to October 10, did you have occasion to meet with a group of black students at South Boston High School?*

DR. REID: *I did.*

MR. TIERNEY: *Could you tell me who was also present at that meeting?*

DR. REID: *There were numerous members of the faculty. . . . There were numerous members of the state police in the vicinity.*

MR. TIERNEY: *Did Student Number Three have occasion to make a statement at that time, Doctor?*

DR. REID: *She did.*

MR. TIERNEY: *Would you please repeat that statement for us?*

DR. REID: *We are going to close this school.*

MR. TIERNEY: *Now, Doctor, one of the black students' demands was that there is a core group of twenty or thirty violent white students. What was your response to this demand?*

DR. REID: *There appeared to be certain troublemakers among both black and white students. Cumulative files are kept on all reports, and when evidence is sufficient, students are called to the office for discussion, warning, or suspension, as the case may be. It takes time, effort, and documentation to prove such cases, but under the due process rulings of the court, it must be done.*

MR. TIERNEY: *Have the complaints received by yourself with respect to racial slurs and assaults come with the same frequency from both black and white students?*

DR. REID: *I would say so.*

MR. TIERNEY: *Would you state, Doctor, that your disciplinary standards are strict at G Street?*

DR. REID: *We tend to go by the book. We have standards which we expect youngsters to measure up to.*

MR. TIERNEY: *And in your professional opinion, Doctor, as an educator, is strict discipline a necessary predicate for an appropriate learning environment?*

DR. REID: *Reasonable discipline equitably applied is essential for any educational environment, in my professional opinion.*

MR. TIERNEY: *Doctor, did you have occasion to discuss this summer with Mr. Perdigao the upcoming football season?*

DR. REID: *I did.*

MR. TIERNEY: *And did you render certain instructions to him, Doctor?*

DR. REID: *I said I thought it was essential that we have black boys on the team, but then I modified it, I said on the squad, and, if they are capable, on the team, in order to have a successful season.*

MR. TIERNEY: *In your opinion, then, as an educator, there is teaching and learning going on at South Boston High School?*

DR. REID: *There is. I think people who walk through the building can see this for themselves.*

Mr. Richard W. Coleman, counsel for the Boston Association of School Administrators and Supervisors, AFL-CIO, continued the cross-examination of Dr. Reid.

MR. COLEMAN: *Dr. Reid, on Saturday afternoon, in answer to Judge Garrity's question about whether or not you thought the student witnesses were testifying truthfully, you said basically you thought you did, and some of the media over the weekend took this statement and kind of headlined it. Would you explain whether you intended to mean that you believed everything the students said or what you intended by that answer to the judge?*

DR. REID: *I think it is part of an educator's philosophy that you have to accept students at face value until they prove themselves otherwise.*

When a youngster comes to the office, you ask him why he was sent there. He will say, "Oh, I don't know. Miss So and So sent me down here." You say, "Well, John and Mary, you wouldn't be down here if Miss or Mr. So and So didn't have a reason." They say, "Well, perhaps you are right. Maybe I was talking out of line. Maybe I was walking around the room," so forth. If you talk with the youngsters, sooner or later you come up with a reasonably accurate story. This is our procedure. We find on an allegation, incidentally, that if you get a report from a youngster immediately following the allegation, you get a fairly good, substantial, honest report. After he has talked with his friends, it becomes less so; after he talks with his parents, less so; and after he talks with community leaders —

Here Dr. Reid "paused and shrugged his shoulders," a reporter noted.

MR. COLEMAN: *Did you —*

DR. REID: *Most high school students are basically — if they have confidence in you, will eventually come out with the truth.*

MR. COLEMAN: *Now, to the extent that their testimony implied that there was a discriminatory pattern of operating South Boston High School, do you agree with that?*

DR. REID: *I deny that. As far as the administration is concerned, the youngster is a student there, and he is treated as a student.*

MR. COLEMAN: *Would you briefly state what your present opinion is as an educator as to the implementation of Phase 2 at South Boston High School, and your thought as to whether the school should be closed or moved?*

DR. REID: *It has been difficult, more difficult than we expected. We had hoped this year would go more smoothly. The school should remain open. It can remain open. We should run it as school, upholding the standards which we expect of high school students scholastically and in conduct, and if we do this, as I am sure my faculty will, there is no reason why the school can't — shouldn't remain open and there is no reason why youngsters who want an education shouldn't get it.*

MR. COLEMAN: *Concerning the seating in the cafeteria, I believe you testified that it was somewhat better this year as far as being integrated.*

DR. REID: *Yes. Youngsters tend to sit at their own tables, but the tables — within groups, but the tables are scattered over the cafeteria this year. The youngsters sit at tables in various places at the cafeteria this year, and occasionally you see youngsters sitting in mixed groups.*

MR. COLEMAN: *Do you think it advisable to attempt to do anything about forcing them to mix more in the cafeteria?*

DR. REID: I do not.

MR. COLEMAN: There was testimony concerning an incident, I believe it involved Student Number Two, in the cafeteria, where you were described as saying that her act in sitting at a table where there were some white girls was a provocative act. . . . Would you explain to the Court what happened?

DR. REID: There are two groups of girls, one white and one black, who are on the north wing of the building at the same time, in business classes. There is considerable antagonism between these two groups. We know it. We are very conscious of it. We keep close surveillance. When they go to lunch, they tend to sit at adjacent tables, and we are very conscious of the fact. The fact that I was three feet from the thing when it — I saw the incident is indicative of our concern about the situation. It was, and I repeat, a provocative act at the time.

MR. COLEMAN: In what way?

DR. REID: Because the young lady I suppose in the old fashion waltzed through a group of white girls coming back. There was room at the end of the table. She sat down there, and she deliberately moved over to the other table, where there was — quite definitely she wasn't wanted, and I think the act was deliberately provocative. Perhaps the fact she got into a fight the next day proved the point.

MR. COLEMAN: Were you ever aware of the allegation that the nurse claimed to charge ten cents for a bandaid to a black student?

DR. REID: No, I am not aware of that.

MR. COLEMAN: Or that she was using dirty swabs to swab—

DR. REID: I think that is an insult to the lady's professional and personal integrity.

MR. COLEMAN: If crowds gather outside the school in apparent violation of the Court's order, whose responsibility is it to disperse the crowd?

DR. REID: No crowds have gathered outside the school.

MR. COLEMAN: Was there such a crowd on October 10th that you are aware of?

DR. REID: No, there was not.

MR. COLEMAN: In responding to the White Student Caucus Demands, did you print up the statement that they had in their demands that music soothes the savage beast?

DR. REID: I did not.

Mr. McMahon questioned Dr. Reid on the feasibility of clustering at the high school.

MR. MCMAHON: *Was there ever a proposal from a member of the faculty or the faculty senate to adopt a modified cluster approach?*

DR. REID: *We have discussed it.*

MR. MCMAHON: *What would be a cluster approach, in your understanding?*

DR. REID: *My understanding is that the — some five or six rooms would be set aside in one area of the building, and the youngsters from five or six home rooms, a hundred twenty, a hundred fifty youngsters, would stay within that area exclusively.*

MR. MCMAHON: *And the effect of such a proposal is to reduce down the extent of student need to travel within the building?*

DR. REID: *That is correct.*

MR. MCMAHON: *Is it feasible to adopt a modified cluster approach in South Boston High School?*

DR. REID: *The people who went to the University of Massachusetts this summer said they investigated at some depth. They do not think it is particularly feasible at the high school because of the variety of subject matter which is taught and the rooms which are widespread for special education of one type or another, plus the fact that the toilets are all located on one side of the building or the other. We did try to put the homerooms in a group. I am not sure this has been successful as we had hoped.*

Mr. Portnoy, feeling perhaps that the defendant teachers Scalese and Perdigao and the aide Bilotas had been undermined by Dr. Reid's Saturday testimony, now cross-examined Dr. Reid.

MR. PORTNOY: *Dr. Reid, on Saturday I believe you testified that you had read the affidavits of the student witnesses. Is that correct?*

DR. REID: *I have.*

MR. PORTNOY: *And you also testified that you had been present throughout these hearings. Is that correct?*

DR. REID: *I have.*

MR. PORTNOY: *I believe it was Judge Garrity who asked you if, in substance, or — the substance of the allegations made by the plaintiffs were or appeared to you to be correct or true.*

THE COURT: *I said, "Have you reason to doubt the general accuracy," or something to that effect. . . . No. I said, I know, "Have you reason to doubt it."*

MR. PORTNOY: *Do you recall that question as the Judge has now rephrased it?*

DR. REID: *More or less, yes.*

MR. PORTNOY: *Do you recall your answer?*

DR. REID: *I said basically I think youngsters are honest.*

MR. PORTNOY: *Basically you believe the youngsters who had testified were telling the truth, is that —*

DR. REID: *But I believe I made exception that there were some things in here which were not. I think I — the record might show what the exact words were.*

MR. PORTNOY: *All right. . . . I am just going to focus in on a couple of specifics. Dr. Reid, you heard testimony about alleged incidents involving Mr. Scalese of your faculty, is that correct?*

DR. REID: *I have.*

MR. PORTNOY: *Did you believe that testimony?*

DR. REID: *No. I think the charge is ridiculous.*

MR. PORTNOY: *Have you read the affidavits that deal with specific allegations against Coach Perdigao?*

DR. REID: *I have.*

MR. PORTNOY: *Did you believe those allegations?*

DR. REID: *One of the statements in which my name was used I believe is correct.*

MR. PORTNOY: *Can you tell us what that statement was?*

DR. REID: *The statement that I sent the young man to the coach with a note. That is correct.*

MR. PORTNOY: *Dr. Reid, you have also heard testimony about an alleged incident involving an aide named Donald Bilotas. Do you recall that?*

DR. REID: *I heard the testimony.*

MR. PORTNOY: *Do you know the aide Donald Bilotas?*

DR. REID: *I do.*

MR. PORTNOY: *Did you believe that testimony, the testimony that you heard?*

MR. ERIC VAN LOON (plaintiff lawyer): *Objection, your Honor.*

THE COURT: *Overruled. Overruled. Let's get the answer.*

DR. REID: *I believe that Donald Bilotas was trying to save this youngster from further injury and that the kicking thing is not the true version.*

MR. PORTNOY: *Thank you. I have no further questions.*

The afternoon court session was again dominated by the Scalese allegations. Student Number Nine, a senior who was at the Burke High School last year, repeated charges similar to those made by Student Number One.

Student Number Ten, a senior from the Burke High School, testified that, on Thursday morning, October 9, he had pointed out Mr. Scalese to Miss Peters of the B.U. Crisis Intervention Center as the man he saw standing in the doorway making gestures like a monkey.

STUDENT NUMBER NINE: *Then he just put his arms up there, you know, put his lips like — you know how apes does.*

MR. VAN LOON: *How long did that happen, did that continue?*

STUDENT NUMBER NINE: *Maybe four or five seconds.*

Judge Garrity briefly interrupted the afternoon testimony.

THE COURT: *Before we start with the questioning of this witness, perhaps I can inject a favorable note into the proceedings. Here is a note from Father Groden. It says, "As of 2:50 p.m., Monday, November 24, 1975, the faculty of South Boston High School voted overwhelmingly to cooperate with the Mediating Board of the Citywide Coordinators Council." Signed Michael F. Groden (Executive Director).*

Mr. Scalese took the stand, and was sworn in.

MR. PORTNOY: *Do you ever recall an incident occurring in your classroom where a student asked you the question, "Where do niggers come from?"*

MR. SCALESE: *I definitely do not remember — I never heard of it, period.*

MR. PORTNOY: *Mr. Scalese, you have heard the allegation of certain gestures that you are alleged to have made at that time.*

MR. SCALESE: *I have.*

MR. PORTNOY: *Can you think of any motions or actions that you may have taken at that time that might be misinterpreted to be such a gesture?*

MR. SCALESE: *I cannot.*

MR. PORTNOY: *Did you make such a gesture?*

MR. SCALESE: *I didn't make any such gestures.*

MR. PORTNOY: *You are sure of that?*

MR. SCALESE: *I am positive.*

MR. PORTNOY: *Did you make any funny noises with your mouth?*

MR. SCALESE: *I did not.*

MR. PORTNOY: *Mr. Scalese, have you ever stood on top of a desk at South Boston High School and made monkey-like gestures?*

MR. SCALESE: *I have never — I don't believe I have ever been on a desk, period.*

MR. PORTNOY: *Mr. Scalese, how do you feel about the desegregation process at South Boston High School?*

MR. SCALESE: *How do I feel? As a teacher?*

MR. PORTNOY: *As a teacher.*

MR. SCALESE: *As a human being? It is the law, for one thing, directed by the Court. It is directed by our — my boss, if I may say that, Dr. Reid, to carry out to the fullest — it was directed the first day of school, and as a teacher, to me it doesn't — doesn't make any difference to me. I am paid to be a teacher, and I have always done my best one hundred percent and I figured I would continue on to do the same thing with this new — implementation of the desegregation plan.*

MR. PORTNOY: *Mr. Scalese, do you have any idea why these charges have been made against you?*

MR. SCALESE: *I do not.*

MR. PORTNOY: *Any incidents at all that you can recall with blacks in South Boston High School that may have led to this?*

MR. SCALESE: *No. Could I sort of brag about myself at this time? I never have any trouble with any students, black, white, anything, and I believe the office can verify that. . . . I have a very good, excellent, . . . excellent rapport with all students, all my students.*

The hearing adjourned until Tuesday.

It was a quiet day in school. Later Ms. Murphy and I filed affidavits with Mr. McMahon in his law office. Her affidavit described our misadventure at the NSCAR meeting at Northeastern University, on Friday evening, October 10, and answered the charges of Student Number Five. We did not know that her accuser had already been excluded as a witness on motion of the plaintiff lawyers even before the hearings began.

The second paragraph of Student Number Five's affidavit alleged that, on Friday, October 10, *"at Northeastern University, Mrs. Murphy had an encounter with Student 20. Mrs. Murphy told Student 20 that: 'You're in a no-win situation.'"*

Ms. Murphy responded, *"At no time during this conference did I say 'You're in a no-win situation,' to Student 20 or to any other student."*

In his affidavit, paragraph 3, Student Number Five alleged, *"The second school day after that, October 15, Student 20 and I were in Mrs. Murphy's English class in second period. Mrs. Murphy wrote an exercise in my workbook about the different uses of the word there (their, there, they're). Some of the sentences said: 'Who says it's ----- school?' and '----- always fighting.' She also wrote '----- to blame for all the trouble ----- causing' and 'Everyone should realize ----- in a 'no-win' situation if they lose ----- cool.'*

These are the kinds of things Mrs. Murphy said to me. Student 20 and I took my workbook down to the office and had a copy made and filed an incident report about it."

Ms. Murphy responded: *"Student Number Five was in my second period class. He had declined since September to perform any class work or assignments including tests and quizzes. When I asked him to explain his refusal on several occasions, he replied that he would do no work because he was being transferred back to the Jeremiah Burke. He would only copy occasional sentences from the chalkboard. I added the sentence completion exercise to the copy book page annexed to his affidavit to encourage him to complete an assignment requiring him to create sentences about what was relevant to him. I had just corrected such student writings containing similar sentences. I frequently write out exercise completions and add encouragements to the students as I did in his case."*

Student Number Five further alleged, *"Mrs. Murphy doesn't seem to like some black students. Every time I say something in class, she makes a smart remark back. She also hands out lots of conduct cards for minor things like asking a question in class."*

Ms. Murphy responded, *"I do not understand paragraph 5 of [his] affidavit. I can say that I hand out few conduct slips to either black or white students."*

Ms. Murphy made no response to the last allegation: *"I have talked to Dr. Reid about Mrs. Murphy. When I told him about the situation, he said, 'I had better put you in another class.' I answered him by saying: 'But, Dr. Reid, she is stepping on people with the tricky use of words that some of the kids don't even understand.'"*

Tuesday, November 25

More testimony on the Scalese allegations opened the fourth day of evidentiary hearings at the Court House. Miss Lyda Peters of the Boston University Crisis Intervention team, a graduate of Regis College, testified on her affidavit: On the morning of Thursday, October 10, Major Gilligan of the state police met in the teachers' room off the cafeteria with about fifteen black students—among them the Ad Hoc Black Caucus—and parent surrogates from the black community, including herself, Percy Wilson, Mrs. Ruth Batson, and Ellen Jackson of Freedom House. Dr. Reid was also present. At the meeting students complained about a teacher who had made "monkey-like gestures" at them. When Mrs. Batson then asked if any student could identify this instructor, *"One of the students raised his hand and* said, 'I could.'" Ms. Peters then accompanied Student Number Nine and another member of the Crisis Intervention Team to the teacher's room. They "*knocked on the door, and the students opened up the door and went into the room, pointed to the teacher there, and said, 'That's him.' . . . As he [the teacher] came to the door, I said to him, 'What is your name?' He said to me, 'Scalese.'*"

Rosalie Packard, a business teacher, whose homeroom is across from Mr. Scalese, testified next on her affidavit as an eyewitness to the alleged "monkey" incident.

MR. PORTNOY: Do you know where Mr. Scalese's homeroom is?

MRS. PACKARD: Yes. It is directly across the corridor from mine. Room 219.

MR. PORTNOY: Focusing your attention, if you can, on the morning of October 9, 1975 — to help you in that regard, that was the morning after the black students refused to get off the bus and went to Lena Park, the morning afterwards, which I believe has been identified as October 9, 1975 — do you remember that morning?

MRS. PACKARD: Yes, I do.

MR. PORTNOY: Do you recall an incident that occurred on that morning during homeroom period outside of your room?

MRS. PACKARD: Yes, I do.

MR. PORTNOY: Could you describe your involvement, if any, in that incident as best you can?

MRS. PACKARD: I heard a loud commotion and I went to investigate, and when I opened the door, there were a group of black students in the corridor near the stairwell. . . . I held my door ajar because I wanted to keep my students in the room, and I saw Mr. Bilotas and Mr. Dowdell performing their duty. They were trying to contain the youngsters, find out where they were going, and then I saw Mr. —

MR. PORTNOY: What is Mr. Dowdell's duties, if you know?

MRS. PACKARD: Mr. Dowdell is an English teacher at the building, and one of his administrative assignments is to keep the corridors clear, to encourage students to go to their homerooms as quickly as —

MR. PORTNOY: And Bilotas, you know who he is?

MRS. PACKARD: Yes. He is an aide stationed in the locker area near Room 217.

MR. PORTNOY: I see. Go on.

MRS. PACKARD: . . . and I saw Mr. Scalese come to his door, and he was — he had his hands on the flaps of his pockets, and there was a lot of noise going on, and . . . we saw later that Mr. Dowdell and Mr. Bilotas had the situation well in hand. They were trying, you know — trying to calm the kids down, find out where they were going, and then — after I saw Mr. Scalese look at the crowd, saw that everything was in good hands, went back into his room, then I watched Mr. Scalese sit down, and then I walked back into my room.

MR. PORTNOY: *So you were standing in your doorway directly opposite Mr. Scalese's doorway during the entire time he was in his doorway, is that right?*

MRS. PACKARD: *Yes.*

MR. PORTNOY: *Did you hear Mr. Scalese say anything or make any noise during that time?*

MRS. PACKARD: *Well, no, I couldn't, because there was a lot of noise and confusion, a lot of talking going on at one time, so I couldn't pick out any one conversation at one time.*

MR. PORTNOY: *Did you see Mr. Scalese do anything at that time? Did he grab any of the students or make any motions with his hands?*

MRS. PACKARD: *No. He was just fixing the flaps on his jacket and — but he didn't touch any of the students.*

MR. PORTNOY: *Did you see anything that might be interpreted as a monkey-like gesture made by Mr. Scalese?*

MRS. PACKARD: *No, I didn't.*

MR. PORTNOY: *Is it fair to say that Mr. Scalese was under observation by you or within your sight during this entire period?*

MRS. PACKARD: *Yes.*

Mrs. Packard's testimony concluded the "Scalese allegations."

Dr. Reid resumed the stand for the defense counsel.

MR. MOLONEY: *With respect to an incident at the school, inside the school, under what circumstances do the state police take some kind of action?*

DR. REID: *If there is physical violence, they intervene immediately. If there appears to be the imminence of physical violence, they are supposed to move toward the area and put themselves in between the prospective combatants and avoid the incident.*

MR. MOLONEY: *But not otherwise?*

DR. REID: *Not otherwise.*

MR. MOLONEY: *Do the state police treat all students, insofar as you know, in an equal fashion?*

DR. REID: *From my observation, they treat all students alike.*

MR. MOLONEY: *Black, white, male, female?*

DR. REID: *Well, I think they like to treat the girls a little differently, but sometimes it is extremely difficult.*

MR. MOLONEY: *All right. So far as you know, have they acted reasonably under the circumstances?*

DR. REID: *I am perfectly satisfied with the action of the state police.*

Mr. Van Loon, plaintiff lawyer, followed Mr. Moloney in cross-examination of Dr. Reid.

MR. VAN LOON: *You stated that the white community and the black were not giving the school the needed support. Have you spoken with members of the white community about giving support for the school and why they were not, in your judgment?*

DR. REID: *I think this goes back to July of 1974. We have had dialogue from time to time on that basis.*

MR. VAN LOON: *Would you say that a majority of the [South Boston] community as you know it, to the extent you have had contact with it, do feel opposition to this Court's order?*

DR. REID: *My analysis of it?*

MR. VAN LOON: *Yes, sir.*

DR. REID: *My analysis is that the majority of the community would like to go along in a peaceful method in getting an education for the children of the community.*

MR. VAN LOON: *Would you say that the opposition to the Court's order, then, is just from a few scattered individuals?*

DR. REID: *I would say the vociferous opposition is from a few individuals.*

MR. VAN LOON: *Well, there are organizations in South Boston, are there not, Dr. Reid, that are actively involved in opposition to the Court order?*

DR. REID: *That is correct.*

MR. VAN LOON: *Would the South Boston Information Center be one of those organizations?*

DR. REID: *I believe it is well known.*

MR. VAN LOON: *Doctor, who is the president of the Home and School Association in South Boston this year?*

MR. TIERNEY: *Objection.*

THE COURT: *What is the objection?*

MR. TIERNEY: *Your Honor, you stated at the outset of the hearing that the intent of the hearing was to investigate whether your plan was being* implemented in South Boston High School. Now I know and I believe everyone in this courtroom realizes that there is opposition within the community to the plan itself, but my understanding of the scope of the hearings was that we were going to be directing our attention to whether the plan itself was implemented by the staff and faculty at South Boston High School.

THE COURT: Well, that is one inquiry, but to the extent that it is not being implemented in the high school, the Court naturally and inevitably, it seems to me, must be interested in the next question, which is why. . . . Everyone knows it [the community] is opposed. It is a question of how active and how virulent is the opposition.

I do not know the answer to that question, and that is what these matters tend to indicate, but the next question is, what action is being taken by the administration of the school and of the district — and I am talking about Dr. Reid and Mr. McDonough — to insulate the school from the opposition that surrounds it. I cannot conceive of anything more relevant than the questions that Mr. Van Loon is asking, and your objection is overruled. So put the question again.

MR. VAN LOON: Dr. Reid, who is the president of the Home and School Association this year?

DR. REID: Mr. James Kelly is president of the South Boston High School Home and School Association.

MR. VAN LOON: And is Mr. James Kelly also active in the work of the South Boston Information Center?

DR. REID: I understand he is.

MR. VAN LOON: Dr. Reid, the white students' demands that were presented to you on Friday, the tenth, reprinted in the column [of the South Boston "Tribune"] on October 16th. . . . do you have any opinion as to whether those white students' demands were formulated in any way with participants from the Information Center?

DR. REID: I have no knowledge specifically as to who helped the students prepare these, but most demands are prepared with the assistance of adults.

MR. VAN LOON: When you say most demands, do you mean most demands of white students at South Boston High School?

DR. REID: I mean demands of both groups at South Boston High School.

MR. VAN LOON: Was the reason that a racial-ethnic council was not formed at least at South Boston that the white parents refused to elect representatives to it?

DR. REID: I would have to check the record. I think we had insufficient *black representation and no representation — no official representation from the white community.*

MR. VAN LOON: *Is there a racial-ethnic council in operation at the school this year?*

DR. REID: *There is. There is a full membership on it.*

MR. VAN LOON: *And when was it elected?*

DR. REID: *At the time that the Court designated. Some night in October.*

MR. VAN LOON: *How many white students attended South Boston High School on Monday, October 27th of this year, National Boycott Day?*

DR. REID: *Forty-two.*

MR. VAN LOON: *And what is the normal white attendance?*

DR. REID: *Three hundred fifty to four hundred.*

MR. VAN LOON: *Dr. Reid, are mass student absences, for whatever reason, disruptive of the educational process?*

DR. REID: *They are for the students who are absent.*

MR. VAN LOON: *Are they also disruptive, Dr. Reid, for the students who are present, because when the absent students return, the teachers have to go over the material that the absent students missed?*

DR. REID: *Perhaps, but they also maybe help the youngsters who come, because they get individual attention.*

THE COURT: *We will take a five-minute morning recess now, and then we will have Major Gilligan on and off. Then we will resume with Dr. Reid.*

After recess, Major Charles Gilligan, commanding officer of Eastern Field Operations and Task Force Commander for Unit 1 of the Massachusetts state police, South Boston High School, took the witness stand as the Court's witness. Mr. Timothy Wise, assistant attorney general for the defendant State Board of Education, examined him.

MR. WISE: *And could you tell the Court, please, what preparations you made in the state police for your work this year in covering South Boston High School?*

MAJOR GILLIGAN: *We devised a training program.*

While in this training program, we talked about situations that we were involved in last year. . . . Many of us are parents ourselves. We have children of high school age. We love our children, each and every parent that sends their children to South Boston High or any other high school. We are worried about the safety of our children, and we were going to do something about the safety of their children. Because of the love of our own and feeling that the love of their children was just as important, we talked about this in the in-service training program and what we would do as far as using minimum force against any student who was disruptive. This we have done.

And I think we have done a great job there. My men have been terrific. They are the best there are, the best trained, the best disciplined, and that is what we rely on. . . . Even outside of the school, we have never drawn a stick nor clenched a fist, and the same goes for inside of school.

THE COURT: *How much has the size of your force inside South Boston fluctuated since school opened in September?*

MAJOR GILLIGAN: *The inside, we never ran any less than 85 to 90 men, sir.*

THE COURT: *And do you say this year the situation is more or less orderly from the standpoint of fist fights than it was a year ago? If you can make a comparison. Maybe it is impossible to do it that way.*

MAJOR GILLIGAN: *Well, the reason I think it is an unfair comparison is because the students changed.*

Before Major Gilligan stepped down, Mr. Pressman requested information on the number of black troopers assigned to the high school on the day selected by the Court, November 18.

THE COURT: *Well, do you know offhand of the 90 how many are either black or other minorities?*

MAJOR GILLIGAN: *This is the grand total. Boston residents: black male, one; white male, one; white female, zero. Nonresidents: black male, one; white male, 85; white female, two.*

THE COURT: *Yes. I have got it. Total of ninety. Of which there were two blacks and two females.*

MAJOR GILLIGAN: *Yes, sir.*

THE COURT: *All right. Well, that is it, and thank you very much.*

MR. TIERNEY: *Might the Court ask the major to briefly describe how the decision was made to have a police presence in South Boston?*

THE COURT: *Well, yes.*

MAJOR GILLIGAN: *To my information, it came through the Court to the Mayor to the Governor, and the Governor went back through the secretary and down to the commissioner, and they felt police —*

THE COURT: *Well, believe me, I can tell you it did not come from the Court. In fact, it was contrary to every standard we were endeavoring to set to have police inside the school, but that does not mean that there was not a proper basis for the decision. I just did not participate in it.*

So, thank you, Major, very much.

Charles Barry, secretary of public safety for the Commonwealth, next testified that the decision to place police inside South Boston High was "a joint decision," made by himself, the Boston Police Department, and the school authorities.

After Secretary Barry, Dr. Reid again resumed testimony.

Although the prosecution had excluded Student Number Five from testifying, Mr. Van Loon questioned Dr. Reid about the propriety of the spelling exercise Ms. Murphy had written in his notebook.

MR. VAN LOON: Did you believe that the — or was the writing of those sentences, those particular ones, in your judgment improper activity for —

DR. REID: In general, I questioned whether it was a misguided effort in which the teacher, who I think is sympathetic to students, was perhaps disturbed over a situation which occurred at a meeting she attended at Northeastern University, and she was upset over the situation and thought that this might be a teaching lesson for herself and the students in the class.

THE COURT: All right.

MR. MCMAHON: Your Honor, may I move to strike that portion of the testimony which characterizes what the teacher's opinon was?

THE COURT: No, no. That is all we will have on that particular subject.

MR. VAN LOON: Could I ask simply one last question concerning that?

THE COURT: Such as?

MR. VAN LOON: Was Dr. Reid surprised at such conduct by one of the members of his professional staff?

MR. MCMAHON: I object.

THE COURT: That is excluded.

MR. VAN LOON: Dr. Reid, is the athletic program an important part of the school's activities?

DR. REID: I consider it such.

MR. VAN LOON: Do you believe, Dr. Reid, that joint black and white participation on the school's sports teams could help to ease the tensions that come frequently with desegregation?

DR. REID: It may very well.

MR. VAN LOON: Dr. Reid, did you testify in a deposition in this case last Tuesday your understanding that the black students had all quit the team?

DR. REID: That was my information.

MR. VAN LOON: And from what source did you receive that information?

DR. REID: The coach.

MR. VAN LOON: So that to the best of your information right now, the reason for them not being on the team is that they all quit. Is that a fair summary?

DR. REID: One — The first time I checked after the preliminary practice, one had withdrawn or dropped out or hadn't come to practice. The next time I checked, two had been dropped for smoking. The next time I checked, the others had thrown their equipment at the bus, I think, and whether that accounts for five or six I really don't know.

The student allegations against Coach Perdigao dominated the afternoon hearing. Students Number Ten and Eleven alleged that black students at the high school were required to ride to football practice on a separate bus on more than one occasion; black students did not receive football equipment during the first four days of practice after they had joined the team, and were not allowed to play in the October 23 game against Dorchester High at White Stadium; Coach Perdigao did not remove a racial slur written on the blackboard during a team meeting.

After the October 23 game, which ended in a near riot, Student Number Ten alleged, *"I was standing near the buses, and heard Perdigao saying to the players, 'Get back on the bus. Just get them in school tomorrow. Get back on the bus. Get them in school tomorrow.'"*

MR. PORTNOY: There was a lot of commotion around the buses at that time, is that right?

STUDENT NUMBER TEN: Right.

MR. PORTNOY: Were a lot of people yelling?

STUDENT NUMBER TEN: You could say that, yes.

MR. PORTNOY: And you are positive you heard Coach Perdigao say these words, is that right?

STUDENT NUMBER TEN: Right.

Students Number Eleven and Thirteen charged Perdigao with giving them the "run around" when they tried to go out for the team in the early weeks of school.

Under cross-examination, both Students Ten and Eleven admitted that white recruits as well as black recruits rode to practice on a "second" bus, which was reserved for the squad — black and white — who joined the team after several games had been played, and that black students had asked to ride on a separate bus, which would take them to the Bayside Mall, Columbia Point, instead of back to the high school after practice. They admitted Coach Perdigao had cited a school rule that equipment was not to be issued to students until after they had attended five practice sessions, and that they had received the equipment at the same time as the white recruits who joined the team late.

Student Number Ten admitted he did not "see" the racial slur on the board during an indoor team session, but that "one of my friends had told me that"; further, Student Eleven testified that another racial slur had been left on the blackboard because assistant coach Samuel Pearson, a black, told Perdigao, "That must have been left over from the day before, because I am certain none of your players would write that."

Coach Perdigao, the last witness of the day, testified after the students. He had been informed in August of his appointment as head football coach.

MR. PORTNOY: How were you informed?

MR. PERDIGAO: I was informed by Dr. Reid, by telephone. He called me, he asked me if I wanted the job, and I said I did.

MR. PORTNOY: Did you have any discussion with Dr. Reid at that time about football at South Boston High School?

MR. PERDIGAO: Yes. The main concern as far as football was that— last year we did not have a football team, and the main concern was to field a team, and naturally an integrated team.

MR. PORTNOY: This was sometime in early August?

MR. PERDIGAO: Yes. It was sometime in early August.

Coach Perdigao had, he said, tried to recruit blacks for the team, but they would not come out. He had advertised the football tryouts for two weeks in the Bay State *Banner,* the black community newspaper, with no results. Furthermore, blacks did not report for practice.

THE COURT: It is, of course, obvious that we are not going to conclude with Mr. Perdigao today. So the hearing in this case tomorrow will resume at twelve o'clock noon.

Now we will just recess.

South Boston High remained quiet. When I asked my senior class for a modern example of a scapegoat, other than Snowball in Orwell's *Animal Farm,* one boy offered, "Dr. Reid." I agreed. I said, "The white community has to support him. He is a fine man. Not to support him—as the Black Student Caucus voted—would play into the hands of the people who want to close the school." I said, "*You* know Dr. Reid. Why would *you* take Dr. Reid's statement reported by the press out of context, when you know newspapers don't always print the truth."

Bill said, "You should go around to the classrooms and say that."

I answered, "You have to do that yourselves."

Bill pointed to a black football player standing at his locker in the hall outside, with his bodyguard, a hefty boy, almost seven feet tall and weighing over two hundred pounds. Bill said, "See that boy? He made our coach look bad. We'll get him."

I said, "Don't talk like that."

Wednesday, November 26 (the day before Thanksgiving holiday)

I arrived at the high school about 7:35 A.M. The troopers, preoccupied, were heavily at their duty. Groups of troopers and aides had gathered in a circle on the first floor. Billy, the aide, explained the excitement, "Judge Garrity is here."

The judge went through the metal detectors, removing his watch, belt with metal buckle, glasses, keys, change. Even then the nails in his shoes activated the metal detector.

Judge Garrity especially wanted to satisfy himself that Mrs. Packard could see Mr. Scalese's room from her own. Ms. Murphy had been stationed by Mr. Goorvich to supervise Mrs. Packard's class, since Rosalie was in court. When he passed by, the judge met Ms. Murphy and told her she would not be asked to testify. "Your affidavit is more than sufficient," he said.

Ms. Murphy then introduced Paul, who had been named in several affidavits, to the judge. He told Paul, "I've heard a lot about you."

I did not see Judge Garrity, but heard from the students that he walked the corridors surrounded by plainclothesmen, U.S. marshals, the court-appointed "experts" Dentler and Scott from Boston University, and a law clerk. One of my sophomore girls observed, "He don't care about us." I corrected her English.

Since there were only two white sophomores in the class — the day before the Thanksgiving recess — I asked them to write a composition about busing. Jack, a voracious reader, perfect in attendance, who had received a full sports scholarship next year at a prestigious private academy, refused. "My language would be too bad," he said.

Margie wrote:

> My opinion of busing is not a *right law* or court order which ever you call it. I don't like it. I'm against it, and I'm sure everybody else is except Judge Garrity. I believe South Boston High School is going to pieces. I think Doc Reid is doing every thing he can, accept what

he can not do is to stop force busing. Blacks & whites can't get along in this school because the whites don't want them in our school and they don't want to come. I think they should stop this busing and go back to the regular way but the politics don't care their own kids are in white private or black private schools. Also another reason is to balance the school. But when somebody ends up killing someone then what will they say don't close the school still, did you ever go see *Jaws* when they wouldn't close the beaches they left them open because of the Mayor. Well that's what its like, and further more I don't want to keep walking into South Boston High feeling like a prisoner.

Only four seniors—all of them white students who had been bused from South Boston to Roxbury last year—were in class today. Bob spoke of the positive aspects of his experience at Roxbury High—the nice bus ride in the morning, the blacks who waved to them as they rode by. "And the blacks are from a different culture; they're different, and it was interesting to know them. You have to love your neighbor, and at the end of your life, that's all that's going to matter—whether you obeyed the Ten Commandments."

I asked Bob about the educational level at Roxbury. He said, "They're just as bad as they are here. And they're not as prejudiced. You can walk around in Roxbury without being killed, but in Southie, you couldn't go in some of the little streets our bus went on without going to the hospital seriously injured. It used to be better in Southie."

Shortly before the school day ended, George Croft, *Globe* reporter, stopped by on his way back to the federal court house. "Judge Garrity is getting fed up with the testimony and wants to wrap the thing up," he said.

A trooper exclaimed, "*He*'s getting fed up!"

"Senile," another muttered. They are very angry with the judge.

In court, before testimony resumed, Judge Garrity explained that his "unexpected" visit would be very "helpful in understanding the evidence and the contentions." Taking note that it was the day before the Thanksgiving holiday—"students planning to go away for Thanksgiving, that sort of thing"—he remarked on the low attendance, with about half the classes having eight or fewer students, and many with only two or four students.

Dr. Reid again led off the testimony.

THE COURT: There was mention also in your direct testimony about seats in assemblies being assigned by the headmaster, if I understood correctly.

DR. REID: That is correct.

THE COURT: Could you elaborate on that, please.

DR. REID: We have had six assemblies this year. I insist that all the assemblies be integrated, and the way in which we do it is to assign each homeroom certain rows and seats in the auditorium, and each class goes as a class, seniors, juniors, right down the line, to a distinct assembly. The two exceptions were the day we had the "Up With People" show. The seniors and juniors went together, but again went in assigned seats, and the sophomores and freshmen went together but in assigned seats.

THE COURT: With respect to the "Up With People" singers, there was a concert at the Hynes Auditorium the night they were here, and I sat at a table of six or eight members and talked with the officials of the "Up With People" organization. I met them, and there was a meeting before the — or it was like a reception before the concert.

These people, that is, both the young people and the officials of the operation, told me that the only school in the city where they were unable to elicit a response from the audience was at South Boston High School. Would you say that is an unfair or inaccurate report?

DR. REID: I would say that is reasonably accurate in regard to the older assembly. With the younger assembly, I think it was a much more relaxed audience.

THE COURT: I don't mean — I am not really talking about their relaxation.

DR. REID: Well, I mean participation. Participatory.

THE COURT: At the Hynes Auditorium, I saw all sorts of business people and others really, you might say, taken over. They were clapping their hands and stamping their feet and responding to all the — you know, show of the singers and dancers and whatnot, and, as I say, both the young people in the group and the older people said their experience in the city was inspiring to them except at South Boston. They were unable to come across, they felt, and naturally I wondered if you observed the same thing.

DR. REID: I would say so, but the fact that we had the assembly is perhaps a major achievement.

THE COURT: There was reference in your testimony about immediate suspension for the possession of weapons, I think. What is covered by the term weapon? Someone said that he was suspended for having a fingernail file, and I wondered —

DR. REID: That would be classified as a weapon, sir.

THE COURT: Well, can you give an additional definition of the word weapon?

DR. REID: *This is printed in the student handbook. It is also posted in the main lobby. I quote: "All persons entering the main building or L-Street must pass through the metal detectors as a condition to entering the building. Students and others must surrender items listed in the laws of Massachusetts, Chapter 269 (Annotated) Paragraph 10 and 12, plus but not exclusive of the following: firearms of any kind; any knives, razors, or other objects sharpened into blades; clubs; athletic equipment, such as baseball bats, hockey sticks; umbrellas, karate sticks; moon chucks, or rods of any kind; pipes, brass knuckles, and other metal objects; screwdrivers, wrenches, hammers, or other metal tools; chains; whips; ropes, or any combination of objects fashioned into such; combs and picks with metal teeth; rattails; scissors; metal nail files; hat pins; mace and other chemicals such as spray paint and spray deodorant; bottles and cans; alcohol, illegal drugs; fireworks. Possession of any of the above may result in suspension."*

THE COURT: *Well, thank you. And is that definition disseminated to students and teachers?*

DR. REID: *It is, sir. A copy is given to each student, and a copy is mailed to each family. It is posted in the lobby.*

THE COURT: *Well, fine. What extra-curricular activities are there at the school other than athletic, if there are any?*

DR. REID: *A number of years ago, we took most of the so-called extra-curricular activities and put them right into the curriculum as such. Drama, for example, is a part of the curriculum. Journalism is part of the curriculum. Music activities are part of the curriculum. They are built into the school day program because of the difficulty at that time with the extended day, we didn't have —*

THE COURT: *Is there a glee club or band or orchestra, or something like that?*

DR. REID: *We have had glee clubs from time to time. We are less successful with the instrumental music.*

THE COURT: *So that if by extra-curricular is meant outside the class-room, the extra-curricular activities are athletic.*

DR. REID: *After school time, I would agree, your Honor.*

Judge Garrity also questioned Dr. Reid about the "creaky" third floor, but Dr. Reid assured him there was "no question about the structural soundness of the building."

THE COURT: *Anything else?* (No response) *Thank you again, Doctor. This looks like the real end of your testimony. It has been closed about four times already.*

DR. REID: Thank you for the opportunity.

THE COURT: Now, please. Let us have Mr. McDonough. I want the district superintendent to be on and off.

I was there this morning—the attendance was about 75 percent of a week ago Tuesday, which we selected as an arbitrary day, and it turned out to be, I think, about average. This was at G Street, 540 students. Today when I was out there, I think it was 402, about three-quarters.

MR. MCDONOUGH: Right.

THE COURT: I would estimate that half of the classes that I saw at G Street had, I would say, eight or fewer students in them. I would say maybe a third of them had fewer than six students. It was not unusual to see a class with two students in it or four, or very low numbers, and I think I am understating it.

MR. MCDONOUGH: Well, I think, you know, you can really see it from the figures. The most I have ever seen up there recorded I think was 603 some day last week. But the thing that to me that is overriding it is that there is learning, there is teaching going on there, and I think that frankly under the circumstances dictated by Phase 2 that you cannot go by previously accepted standards of teacher-student ratio.

MR. TIERNEY: And how many times have you visited South Boston High School?

MR. MCDONOUGH: Between eight or ten times since October 1st.

MR. TIERNEY: And it is your opinion, then, that teaching and learning is going on at the high school.

MR. MCDONOUGH: It is my strong opinion that teaching and learning are going on at the high school. Right.

THE COURT: By what do you judge that, Mr. McDonough?

MR. MCDONOUGH: Well, I judge it by the—probably twenty-three years' experience of my, you know, being in schools, being in classrooms.

THE COURT: What do you look for when you walk the halls or visit the classrooms to determine whether teaching is in progress?

MR. MCDONOUGH: One of the things obviously is are the students, you know, paying attention to whomever is addressing them; do they seem interested; is the teacher active; is there any dialogue going on; is there order.

THE COURT: Well, thank you.

Now we are going to resume with Mr. Perdigao.

Coach Arthur Perdigao was the last witness. A teacher-coach now in his twelfth year at South Boston High, he was head swimming coach, assistant junior varsity baseball coach, assistant football coach, and as of August, 1975, head football coach. The football team for the past ten years had had an all-white membership, but he had fielded an integrated baseball team last year, and anticipated no trouble from his new assignment.

On October 21, prior to the White Stadium game, Mr. Perdigao testified he had been warned by one of the black recruits that Student Number Thirteen "had been talking on the bus that he was going to set me up."

MR. PORTNOY: *Those were his exact words?*

MR. PERDIGAO: *Those were his exact words.*

MR. PORTNOY: *Did any of the recruit players play in the game with Dorchester High on Thursday, October 23, at White Stadium?*

MR. PERDIGAO: *No recruits played at all, because they had only been out for five days.*

MR. PORTNOY: *Can you tell us what happened after the game?*

MR. PERDIGAO: *Well, I think the — as far as the game, after the game itself, the game was a good game, it was a tie score, eight to eight, and at the end of the game, we had to walk off to the side of the track. We had to walk to the track, where there was a minibus for the cheerleaders and two yellow buses behind, parked behind on a sort of inside runway, and that is where the team members reported to.*

MR. PORTNOY: *Well, did all go smoothly? Did the team report there after the game?*

MR. PERDIGAO: *No. What happened was that the — once the game was over, the team automatically — we walked from there as a group to the buses, and we got to the end where the buses were, there was a gate, and as we turned the gate, there was a group of blacks in the stands standing on the side of the — right on the stairway going down, and they were starting to yell, "Southie eats shit," and then it started building and building.*

MR. PORTNOY: *Was anything thrown at that time?*

MR. PERDIGAO: *Not at that moment. At that moment I looked — turned and looked. I had seen this, and I told the members of the team to get on the bus. I said, "Get on the bus," because I was afraid of any confrontation. I wanted to get them on the bus at the time. While they were going, they turned and looked up and saw it, so I just tried — I just tried — I pushed a few of my own players just to try to get them on the bus so nothing would happen, and then there were things that were thrown at us.*

As the confrontation escalated, Coach Perdigao's only concern was to get the team back on the bus. The recruits, black and white, who had not played in the game, were in the stands near the buses. The cheerleaders were lying on the floor of the minibus to avoid the flying rocks. The white recruits returned to the bus. The black recruits—two of them—threw their duffle bags at the coach and swore at him.

MR. PORTNOY: At any time during this incident, did you make the statement "Get on the bus. You can get them in school tomorrow"?

MR. PERDIGAO: I would never make a statement like that.

THE COURT: No, no. That is not quite the question. The question is not whether you would; it is, Did you?

MR. PERDIGAO: No, I did not. The only thing I did say was to get on the bus, and my main concern then was safety.

Coach Perdigao was absent, sick from the tension, on the following school day, Friday, October 24. When the black recruits appeared Saturday on the practice field, Perdigao told Coach Pearson "that due to disciplinary reasons and also safety reasons, the blacks were off the team."

MR. PERDIGAO: After I said that, Coach Pearson just took the ball players back. He said okay, and he just took the players back in his car, and he drove off.

Mr. Pressman cross-examined Mr. Perdigao.

MR. PRESSMAN: You testified that you tried to get the ad [for the black recruits for the football team] *in the Bay State "Banner" on August 28th. Is that right?*

MR. PERDIGAO: I believe I said that.

MR. PRESSMAN: And the first day for physicals had been the twenty-fifth. Is that right?

MR. PERDIGAO: That is correct.

MR. PRESSMAN: And you said that the ad didn't get in until September 5th. Is that right?

MR. PERDIGAO: First of all, what I would like to say is that the South Boston "Tribune" is a South Boston paper, and Columbia Point is also a—part of South Boston. As far as the black community in Columbia Point, if they read the South Boston "Tribune," they would have been informed at the same time.

MR. PRESSMAN: You think the people in Columbia Point would be reading the South Boston "Tribune"?

MR. PERDIGAO: I don't see why not. They do live in South Boston.

MR. PRESSMAN: Was there any other way that that meeting for physicals was advertised besides—

MR. PERDIGAO: *That was the only way we knew of. That was the only means which we have in which to advertise it.*

MR. PRESSMAN: *Well, as to any of the black students who turned in completed cards at the beginning of the year and then, your testimony is, did not come for practice at the end of the day, did you try to contact any of them to encourage them to come for practice at the end of the day?*

MR. PERDIGAO: *As far as I was concerned, whether the student was black or white, if they desired to try to come out for football, everyone would be given an opportunity. I felt if anyone did not show up the following day, they were not seriously interested.*

MR. PRESSMAN: *So the answer is no, you didn't.*

MR. PERDIGAO: *I did not seek out blacks or whites as far as the — to find out why they did not show up, right, if that is what you mean.*

MR. PRESSMAN: *I believe you testified that when you looked up in the stands at the time of the trouble at White Stadium, you didn't notice any particular black recruit. Is that right?*

MR. PERDIGAO: *That is correct.*

MR. PRESSMAN: *You said that the following Saturday after the White Stadium incident, you suggested that the blacks should not appear at practice for safety reasons? Is that right?*

MR. PERDIGAO: *I said that when Coach Pearson came to the field with three black players, I told Coach Pearson that there was a disciplinary reason, and as far as a safety reason.*

MR. PRESSMAN: *What safety reasons did you mean?*

MR. PERDIGAO: *Well, as far as I was concerned, after the incident at White Stadium that Thursday, the following Friday I was informed by the news media and some fellow teachers that informed me that the high school blew up as far as — there was a lot of — there were a lot of incidents there.*

MR. PRESSMAN: *Well, what did you think would happen at the football practice?*

MR. PERDIGAO: *At that time, I felt that — I did not feel that at that time that anything could be accomplished as far as the tension involved with the student body and as far as the team was concerned.*

MR. PRESSMAN: *What do you mean, the team? The white players and the black players? What do you mean?*

MR. PERDIGAO: *The team that was on the field at that time was all white.*

MR. PRESSMAN: *Had there previously been any expressions by the team about having black players?*

MR. PERDIGAO: *No, there was no problem.*

MR. PRESSMAN: *What were the disciplinary reasons?*

MR. PERDIGAO: *Consisted of smoking and throwing the equipment at us.*

MR. PRESSMAN: *All the black — Two people had thrown bags?*

MR. PERDIGAO: *Two people had been throwing bags. Then the following Monday when I talked in school, the teacher informed me that another black had thrown — had thrown his equipment, but he did not have it in his bag, it was loose equipment, at us.*

MR. PRESSMAN: *What about Student Number Eleven? Why was he off the team?*

MR. PERDIGAO: *I told you, as far as safety, I felt — that I could not at that time integrate the team as far as safety reasons.*

MR. PRESSMAN: *You put him off the team because of that reason?*

MR. PERDIGAO: *He was with the crowd —*

MR. PRESSMAN: *You just said before that you didn't see any black recruits in the crowd.*

MR. PERDIGAO: *Well, tell me one thing: Why — if he was not there, why didn't he come back with the rest of the team from the —*

MR. PRESSMAN: *If you thought it wasn't safe for blacks to come out on the football field on Saturday, why would it have been safe for them to get on the bus on Thursday?*

MR. PERDIGAO: *Because there were two separate buses.*

MR. PRESSMAN: *Well, wouldn't the new white recruits be riding on the second bus?*

MR. PERDIGAO: *The second bus would be taking black recruits back to the Mall. The first bus would be taking the white recruits back to the high school.*

MR. PRESSMAN: *Who was put off the team for smoking?*

MR. PERDIGAO: *Kevin [and] Bruce. When we first got on the bus at the high school, both the whites that were dressing for the varsity game were on one bus. The new recruits, both black and white, were on the bus also. So finally, when we got ready to leave, I walked on the bus, and as I looked up, I saw there was — Kevin was there smoking a cigarette right in front of me and just laughing.*

MR. PRESSMAN: *Well, did you see Bruce smoking?*

MR. PERDIGAO: *After I told Kevin to put out the cigarette, I said there is no smoking allowed. Then I was informed by my assistant coaches Crowley and Apprille that once the bus had stopped at White Stadium, Bruce had come off the bus with a — and he lit up and smoked right in front of the two coaches.*

MR. PRESSMAN: *Was there some previous day when you told players they would be put off if they smoked?*

MR. PERDIGAO: *It has been a policy in the past. As far as new recruits, I did not say it to them, but I did say it to them at the time on the bus, and that is what disturbed me about Bruce. . . . It wasn't the case of being seen smoking. In all my years of coaching, I have never had an athlete smoke right in front of my face in complete disrespect. This was the matter. This was a case of defiance right in front of you.*

MR. PRESSMAN: *Wasn't the real reason you put the blacks off for the safety reason?*

MR. PERDIGAO: *I said it was a combination of disciplinary action and safety.*

MR. PRESSMAN: *No further questions.*

Donald Bilotas, a South Boston High dropout, was the last witness. An aide assigned to the corridor outside the locker room, at Room 218, he testified that, on the morning of October 24, when he was alleged by Student Number One to have kicked a black student being jumped by Paul's gang, he was in the nurse's room. He had accompanied a black student there after a fight and had remained there at the nurse's request. The alleged black victim of "Big Red" did not submit an affidavit and, finally, could not be located to testify.

MR. VAN LOON: *One last question. When these motions were filed, or whatever — Well, did you go by the nickname "Big Red"?*

MR. BILOTAS: *No, I didn't. I do now.*

MR. VAN LOON: *Well, how did it come about that you got involved in this?*

MR. BILOTAS: *The nickname? In this courtroom?*

MR. VAN LOON: *Yes.*

MR. BILOTAS: *God only knows. I don't.*

MR. VAN LOON: *Who first told you that there was something in court accusing you of something?*

MR. BILOTAS: *I had a talk with some people from my union, and they said that these allegations were made against a "Big Red," and there are two other aides in the building that have red hair and they are both short, so they, you know — they figured "Big Red," they took me, but they still had no idea if it was me or not, and they took a couple of names. I remember the "Big Red" appeared in the paper for one or two days, and all of a sudden my name came out in black and white.*

MR. VAN LOON: *Thank you. No further questions.*

The court adjourned until two o'clock on Friday afternoon for final arguments.

In his "rationale" for the receivership of South Boston High School, Judge Garrity described his visit to the school as follows:

> *In the classrooms, with perhaps a half-dozen exceptions, an inconsiderable amount of instruction appeared to be in progress. Granted, some aspects of teaching are impossible to observe or gauge in a brief visit and the court did witness observable instruction in progress in some classes, such as chemistry and the sheet metal shops. However, in most classrooms there was no dialogue between teachers and students nor observable test-taking in progress and most students appeared to be paying little if any attention to the teachers.*

Friday, November 28

Lawyers presented final arguments in the evidentiary hearings on South Boston High School.

Eric Van Loon, scorning "the notion that perhaps some blacks are trying to stir things up there in order to have the school closed," summarized. The "teaching-learning-violence" situation inside the school is "far worse" this year than last. The time for halfway measures is past. The plaintiffs ask:

1. *A court order to close the school.*
2. *A report from the Boston School Committee in one week on the availability of an alternative building, or a report on the feasibility of dispersing students and faculty throughout the city.*
3. *A plan for the School Committee to investigate those promoting the student boycotts.*
4. *A declaratory statement that Scalese and Perdigao are in violation of the Court's order barring discriminatory conduct.*

Although plaintiff lawyers had excluded Student Number Five from testifying, and Ms. Murphy, therefore, had never been permitted an opportunity to rebut her accuser in open court, Mr. Van Loon, in his closing argument, cited sentences from Student Five's notebook page ("They are the cause of all the trouble," "They are in a no-win situation") as proof of the faculty's unwillingness *"to really get together and try to make desegregation work at that school."*

Mr. Philip Tierney, attorney for the School Committee, summarized:

Just as there was heavy involvement in the school by the white community prior to the Michael Faith stabbing last year, there has since October 6 been heavy involvement by the black community. There has, in fact, been "a well-planned but ill-conceived and founded effort," made by a core group of black students in concert with certain leaders of the black community and plaintiff lawyers, to close the high school "in a community that has come to symbolize resistance to the Court's order."

Once students are away from and out in the community, their concerns are magnified. The evidence is clear as to the preparation of the affidavits.

Mr. Timothy Wise, assistant attorney general, listed the recommendations of the State Board of Education:

1. *The school should remain open.*
2. *A formal student grievance procedure should be established.*
3. *Ombudspersons, one white and one black, should be appointed to handle grievances.*
4. *A greater participatory role should be assumed by CDAC (Community District Advisory Council). Civil rights prosecutions could be instituted where appropriate.*
5. *More black faculty and staff should be assigned.*
6. *Faculty should receive desegregation training.*
7. *The police presence should be continued — possibly federal marshals inside school.*

There is cause for great concern, but closing the school might only "increase racial tension there and elsewhere."

THE COURT: Now we will simply recess.

Monday, December 1

Dr. Reid met with the faculty after school to review the evidentiary hearings at the federal court. It had been his unilateral decision to reject the services of the B.U. Crisis Team, he told us.

Tuesday, December 2

Judge Garrity visited the school again to "finish up," he said, where he left off—to observe students in the corridors, the locker rooms, and the cafeteria during lunch periods. The first time, on Wednesday, November 23, his visit lasted from about 7:30 A.M. to 9:03 A.M. Today's visit lasted from about 10:15 to 11:30 A.M. Mr. Corscadden, assistant headmaster, and

Dr. Reid accompanied the judge, but Garrity later released Dr. Reid because he didn't want to keep him from his regular duties.

Interviewed on the high school steps later, Dr. Reid, pleased, told the reporters, "The students were quite excited the judge came down to see the school again."

Wednesday, December 3

Another quiet day. The students are waiting for Judge Garrity's decision whether to close the high school.

Tuesday, December 9

The Lord Mayor of Dublin visited South Boston High today. When Dean Yarborough, one of the two new black administrators assigned to the high school, interrupted my class to discuss with me final arrangements for the visit, Sandra walked out after me. "There aren't any other blacks in there," she complained. Dean Yarborough and I were both pained—I because, if I'd been there, she would not have left; and Dean Yarborough because, he said, "I've been living in a world of whites all my life."

The visit was scheduled for the library. I prepared the students by suggesting that they would rise for an older or distinguished person, and asked if they would do so for the Lord Mayor.

Lord Mayor Patrick Dunne arrived; everyone stood.

The Lord Mayor described for the students the difference between the office of the mayor of Dublin and the mayor of Boston: In Dublin, the mayor is more manager than executive head, and serves as chairman of committees within the council. The Dublin mayor is not in charge of making appointments, "thanks be to God," said Mayor Dunne, because in the past this sometimes led to "political jobbery."

It was a charmed meeting of statesman and students that turned to wonder as the Lord Mayor produced from a pouch a "piece of living history"—a six-and-one-half-pound, solid gold ceremonial chain of office, attached with a medallion of King William of Orange.

A student and teacher went around the library exhibiting the chain to the students, who were impressed with all that solid gold, or because the Mayor "took time to visit South Boston High School, when he could have gone to some other high school." Cynthia, a black girl, said, "The most important thing I liked about him was that he is Irish, and I love to hear Irishmen speak."

In return Dr. Reid presented the Lord Mayor with a tie clip and Mrs.

Dunne with a charm replica of the Dorchester Heights Monument, pointing out its historical commemoration.

Afterward students stayed to have their pictures taken with Dr. Reid, some putting the chain around his neck: William Reid and William of Orange. It was a golden glow in the morning.

Dr. Reid stopped by later in my cafeteria study, obviously pleased about the Lord Mayor's visit. He talked to the trooper, one of his former students at Hyde Park High, who had earlier described Dr. Reid to me as "a student's teacher — very approachable and student-oriented."

Dr. Reid was relaxed. The school was working the best ever, two days before the anniversary of the Michael Faith stabbing. There were only fifty state police now assigned in the school, and a promise of none in January. There had been no racial fight for almost two weeks. Today was Dr. Reid's "last hurrah."

In recognition of the return to normalcy, it was decided for the week of December 8 to 12 to allow dismissal of white students before the blacks. Inadvertently Mr. Goorvich dismissed the "bused students" at the same time as the "walkers."

"Get ready," Major Gilligan ordered the troopers in the lobby. But, blacks and whites — bused students and walkers — among them Paul exulting on his tiptoes about "our turn to go first" — peacefully left the building into the drizzling snowy rain.

It was not yet 3:30 when the waitress at Amrheins Restaurant on Broadway told us that Dr. Reid was "out" and the school in receivership.

Effective tomorrow, South Boston High and the L-Street Annex would be run by the Court, not by the School Committee. Dr. Reid and the entire full-time academic administrative staff at both schools, together with Coach Perdigao, would be transferred.

The Court found, on plaintiff motion, *"that the black students at South Boston High School are not receiving the peaceful desegregated education to which they are entitled under the Fourteenth Amendment to the Constitution of the United States; and secondly, the Court's desegregation plan is not being carried out at South Boston High School.*

"Mr. Perdigao was under an affirmative obligation to conduct the football program on a desegregated basis, and in the Court's opinion and finding, Mr. Perdigao failed to fulfill that obligation. . . . The record of Mr. Perdigao's direction of the football team's program at South Boston High School failed to meet the requirements of the Court's order."

Judge Garrity explained that he had returned a second time to South

Boston High, December 2, *"because I could not really believe what I saw there on my first visit."* The court would not order the school closed because *"the situation can be turned around there, and quickly."* The *"racial tensions"* and *"educational deficiencies"* could be more readily cured by other measures. *"The combination of Southie pride and Roxbury courage,"* the Court said, *"when it is made to work and when it is put to constructive use, can make this school the best high school in the City of Boston."*

The Court addressed specifically the white students' allegation, picked up by counsel, of *"conscious effort of the black community and the black students to create incidents to provoke the closing of South Boston High School."* The Judge found *"not a scintilla of evidence"* presented before him to back up such an allegation. *"Did the black parents and leaders of the black community want the school to be closed?"* he asked. *"Absolutely yes. Of course they wanted and have moved and have come into Court to seek that the school be closed, but that thought is not a novel thought with the black community. Didn't the mayor himself and the Commissioner of Police himself urge that the school be closed? Mr. Cunningham, President of the Senate, on the witness stand said that in his opinion, the situation was deteriorating there and it was not unlike the situation that built up previous to the tragic Michael Faith stabbing a year ago last October.*

"So I cannot imagine that, given the background of things that happened last year and this year at that high school, there would not be a sensible and perfectly logical and understandable petition on the part of some members of the black community, especially the parents of those youngsters, to have that place closed so that the children would not have to attend school there, but in a more friendly atmosphere, but that is quite different from saying that there were false stories and false reports manufactured in order to do injury to the people of South Boston. . . . They were told in good faith. That does not mean that every word that was stated was true, but there was [no] community conspiracy on the part of the black community to deprive South Boston of its closest and properly called neighborhood high school."

Public reaction to the receivership was intense.

Boston Police Commissioner diGrazia defended Dr. Reid as a "fine gentleman" and called his dismissal "unjust." He said, "The man has overextended himself . . . in trying to work with the community that didn't appreciate what he was doing, with a lot of students who didn't appreciate what he was doing, who was truthful with his community . . . pupils . . . teachers, and truthful with the judge when asked to testify.

"I think it was a complete and just unbelievable action that Bill Reid was released of his duty as headmaster. I think it was an injustice to him and an injustice to the students of the school."

Senator Bulger of South Boston accused Garrity of "punishing his victims."

Mr. Kelly of the South Boston Information Center charged the teachers with remaining silent, when they should speak out. They know what's going on.

Jim Doherty, assistant headmaster, called the order "an asinine decision based on fictionalized evidence."

Black Representative Royal Bolling from Dorchester called the move "innovative and imaginative," while Representative Mel King from the South End said the receivership would put the other schools in the city on notice that integration would take place.

My father said, "It will save Dr. Reid's life, if he can throw it over his shoulder. In effect, Garrity closed the school."

Wednesday, December 10

It was a foggy day, the school shrouded in mist. TV cameras lined up behind the huge white printed letters on the sidewalk: P R E S S. It was 7:35. I was five minutes late. The teachers had not signed in, but were meeting in the library, an aide in the lobby told me.

Upstairs the teachers sat heavily at the library tables, depressed and angry, talking about "making a stand." The minutes ticked by; it was time for students to arrive. Dr. Reid looked in the door.

"If you want to help me, then go to your classrooms. You're professionals. Do your job," he growled, and shuddered his jowls. The teachers stood up immediately then, went downstairs, and signed in.

The buses emptied. The black students came in, avoiding my eyes when they passed. Black and white students roamed the corridors in packs. I trailed after them. Troopers were already tailing them with walkie-talkies, sputtering their movements to other floors. Students I knew, I took by the arm and coaxed to their homerooms. At the second floor landing, a band of white students, blocked on the staircase by troopers, stood dueling verbally with a teacher. Paul came pivoting into the area, attracted by the action, and was hustled off.

On the third floor I saw Dr. Reid. I asked, "What do you want me to do?"

"Get them to their classes," he ordered.

When I was in the 300 area, I noticed a boy — the one the seniors had told me "made our coach look bad" — watching the corridor from the window of his homeroom. Two white boys went to the room. Within minutes, chairs were flying. I found a trooper around the corner. Others came running, and the Boston cop, Marie. We held students back from the next room, some fighting with the troopers. Once in the melee I found my hand pulling at the arm of a trooper, his wrinkled face ashen from the violent struggle. I let the arm go. The troopers brought the black boy, a cut on his hand, out of the room and down the corridor, past students who had bolted from their homerooms and were lining the walls, their faces gray with fear. Then the bell rang for the first class of the day.

As I passed room 304, thudding bodies burst the glass door window outwards.

I went downstairs to the second floor. Students had ganged up outside the auditorium and near the staircase landing. Whether by accident or intention, a white and a black boy collided. The white boy flared and flashed out. "Stop it," I ordered. I was amazed; they looked at me, then the black boy walked off.

A few steps away outside the main office door, aides struggled with a black girl in throes of epileptic seizure. Afraid of being caught in a crush, I moved down the corridor. At the next stairwell, beside the main office, two troopers struggled to move a black girl downstairs; she bit one of them in the thigh. Another small black girl, in a panic, was trying to move down the stairs to help her friend. Dr. Reid was blocking her, holding on to the bannister in front of her, his arm trembling violently in waves. I tried to calm the girl, then said to Dr. Reid, my voice high and frantic, "You have to close the school."

Dr. Reid said, "Go to your class."

I picked up my books from the library and went upstairs. As I reached the third floor, I sobbed. Out of the corner of my eye I saw a student and trooper look at me, startled.

The violence lasted ten minutes, according to the newspapers, and was confined to the second and third floors. I must have seen it all. In class there were three students waiting patiently for me with another boy who didn't know where he belonged. Gary, the only white student there, looked around and said, "Small class, eh? You can't have a class unless 60 percent of the class is here."

We talked a little about the trouble in the school. Gary said, "We were getting along. But Garrity blew it yesterday. Now there will just be fights."

Ralph told me the blacks, angry about the fire-bombing of the NAACP headquarters in Roxbury, had come in to fight.

Cynthia said, ruefully, "I shouldn't have come in. I knew I shouldn't when I heard about the fire bombing on the radio this morning." But they settled down to work on *Oedipus Rex*.

The class lasted one hour. Dr. Reid put his head in the door once and said a few encouraging words.

My seniors asked me, "Why don't the teachers take a stand? The teachers are the school. They take the administration and Perdigao now, and then they'll pick the rest of you off one by one, until you're all gone. You have to speak up now, before it's too late." They said, "The senior class is dwindling to nothing. A student gets an assault-and-battery charge, and he doesn't come back."

By 10:30, when Dr. Reid held a press conference outside the school, it was calm. Dr. Reid commented on the receivership, "If Judge Garrity chooses to remove me, that's his prerogative. Someone has to be the scapegoat in these things. I'm the boss, and I can understand why I should be moved. But it's unjust to include my assistants in the order, if it's aimed primarily at me. Why it should go to them, I do not know. They operated under my instructions. It was all my responsibility.

"I don't know what the future holds for me, but I don't think anyone could have worked harder to implement the desegregation order and maintain the integrity of the school than I did."

He told Eleanor Roberts of the *Herald*, "Actually, the situation was far better than it was a year ago. Then it was mass confrontation. Now, it's a one-to-one confrontation, quickly and easily broken up in twenty minutes. I only wish Judge Garrity had visited the school a year before he did."

Dr. Reid called the decision "unfair and not impartial." He said, "I don't think Judge Garrity acted as impartially as the blindfold of justice would require."

After saying he did not believe receivership was the solution to the problems at the school, Dr. Reid commented wryly, when asked about his replacement, Mr. McDonough, area superintendent, "I hoped the judge would have made Dentler and Scott receivers instead of McDonough because they were the experts who concocted this plan and I think they should have been appointed."

At the end of the school day, the walkers left first, then bused students. There was no trouble. On my car radio I heard Tom Atkins comment, "Integration is worth a fire bomb."

Afterward, the faculty met again in the library to discuss and vote on a response to Judge Garrity's decision. A few teachers felt Dr. Reid had not supported the faculty sufficiently in court, and that he didn't deserve our special support. Most did. A union representative assured the faculty and staff that they had the full support of the Boston Teachers Union.

The faculty response to Judge Garrity's decision on South Boston High read:

> The faculty at South Boston High School has been silent during court proceedings because we felt that our colleagues would be exonerated of the unjust allegations brought against them.
>
> The faculty strongly disagrees with the court's findings of fact which were not substantiated by the testimony of the student affiants. The statements of the court are vague and phrased in generalities. The following statements, specifically, are objected to by the faculty:
>
> 1. *"I really couldn't believe what I saw on the first visit."*
>   QUESTION: What specific things did he see that were so unbelievable?
> 2. *"Mr. Perdigao has a more specific obligation to take affirmative action."*
>   QUESTION: Is a man who is not an attorney expected to understand all legal ramifications and complexities of the court order?
>   QUESTION: Under the new federal court rules, is it expected that a man is considered *guilty until proven innocent?*
>
> The faculty further strongly disagrees with the findings of fact by the court as follows:
>
> 1. *"There is a lack of support by the predominantly white faculty and staff of South Boston High School."*
>   QUESTION: What are the specific allegations constituting "lack of support"? What precisely is meant by the "implementation of the court order"?
> 2. *"The high school faculty has undercut the smooth implementation of court-ordered desegregation."*
>   QUESTION: What, specifically, are the acts that have undercut the implementation?
> 3. *"The faculty had failed to cooperate with the Citywide Coordinating Council and with a separate task force established by Superintendent Fahey."*
>   ANSWER: Under direct testimony in court, it was pointed out under oath, by the faculty senate president, that since both groups presented us with no formal plans to alleviate tensions and that since last year mediation

teams were unsuccessful, we requested that they come back with a plan. Also, in reference to the Superintendent's task force, at no time did the faculty reject their offer. Once again, we ask them to return with positive suggestions.

4. *"Racial slurs and epithets were heard by the school staff but the staff failed to take any corrective disciplinary action."*

   ANSWER: There are records of incident reports regarding racial slurs and epithets that are now presently part of the court's record. These reports deny this finding of fact.

5. *"Racial mistreatment has not been restricted to black students but . . . also to black teachers."*

   ANSWER: All black and white staff members have been subjected to racial slurs, epithets, and verbal abuse.

   White students as well as black have been the objects of continuous racial abuse.

The school is now under federal receivership.

We, the faculty, believe that we have worked diligently and in good faith to implement desegregation under the court order.

The court in its findings of fact and other statements has castigated the faculty unjustly as the villains in this tragic situation.

If these previous points are not clarified by the court, it is an indication to the faculty that the Court has no faith in the faculty's ability to implement the federal court order. Moreover, if this is true, we feel that the court should also transfer the entire faculty. We make this statement in support of those staff members, Dr. William J. Reid, Mr. Arthur Perdigao, and those assistant headmasters who are to be transferred.

(Signed) FACULTY MEMBERS:
South Boston High School

Judge Garrity responded to the letter five days later in his 25-page memorandum giving his "rationale" for the receivership of South Boston High School.

Thursday, December 11

Police presence was increased outside and inside the high school in anticipation of trouble, but there was none. Outside on a lamppost a sign flapped in the wind: REMEMBER BLACK TUESDAY.

Major Gilligan, as planned several weeks ago, talked to my senior class about safety in the school.

Honest and thoughtful with the students, he answered their questions about the life of a trooper, mentioning its snares — alcohol and women — and discussed TV police stories with them.

Asked how the police were able to clear themselves of the student allegations of police brutality, Major Gilligan explained that the black aide had been hit with a lock, not a stick, as she at first claimed. The police lieutenant had checked out the rumors immediately with the troopers involved and filed reports, so they had all the documentation they needed.

Interviewed outside, Dr. Reid told the news media that the mood of the teachers reflected "perhaps a little discouragement, a little resignation, some indignation, eventual acceptance of the inevitable."

The Boston police arrested Siegfried today and are holding him without bail for an alleged murderous assault with a baseball bat on a white man last August at Columbia Point.

Friday, December 12

Mrs. Rita Graul, ROAR chairperson, announced that, because the people of South Boston are no longer free, they "plan to commemorate their loss by keeping their children away from every classroom in the city on mourning day."

Outside the high school — beside rows of cameramen — mounted police, fleets of white Boston police cars, helmeted TPF, and buzzing helicopters readied for the "mourning parade."

Inside, troopers sat talking together at the students' desks in empty classrooms. One trooper caught asleep standing up explained, "If you only knew how boring it is!"

Six white students were in attendance at the high school because they must if they want to participate in sports.

In my sophomore class, there were two blacks. Richard, one of my best and most intelligent readers, had been out of school so long I didn't recognize him. By lunchtime he was in the holding room with Ralph, who told me they had beat up Paul, the "big slob."

Throughout the day, Dr. Reid called staff to the office to arrange with them for an orderly transition of administration. He seemed relaxed. Once I overheard him answer the phone in his office. He quoted figures and repeated, "Disillusioned, disillusioned, disillusioned."

There was no parade. The emergency police finally abandoned lines. The buses roared up the hill and departed with the bused students. As teachers walked to the parking lot, the white students placed a funeral wreath on the school steps.

At Amrheins Restaurant after school, our waitress told us with delight, "We pretended to be having a big mourning parade, but that was just a decoy. We're not going to set our kids up to have their heads beat on by the police anymore. We just stalled our cars, or walked off and left them on the expressways. Let the police tow them, if they want. All you need is a few cars in front of the TUNNEL and across the Expressway, and the traffic doesn't move. If they want to play games with us, we'll play games with them." Then she asked, "Were you delayed going to work today?"

Associate Superintendent of Police Joseph Jordan, wide-eyed with amazement, explained that he had no knowledge of this preconceived and obstructionist plot to create a massive traffic tie-up. Virginia Sheehy of the South Boston Information Center also expressed surprise. It was a great idea, she said; she only wished she had thought of it herself.

Senator Edward Kennedy has announced in favor of the receivership. He said that, although it was "regrettable that events in South Boston led to the need for Judge Garrity to take the action, it was far less drastic than other measures he could have taken."

Senator Brooke from Massachusetts, the only black senator in Congress, also supported the decision, saying, "If quality education is a byproduct of our desegregation orders, so much the better," but it is not the reason for those orders. "The Constitution does not demand quality education. It demands equal educational opportunity." Quality education is a matter for local, state, and federal policy, he said. Equal educational opportunity is a matter of constitutional law.

Monday, December 15

Before school, troopers were feeling along the walls in the classrooms.

"Another bomb scare?"

"No, looking for contraband."

Midmorning there was a white student walkout. No troopers were in the lobby, but the new court-appointed receiver, Mr. Joseph McDonough, was — red-faced, pleading with the students: "You'll close the school, you'll close the school." They hesitated at the door. Dr. Reid repeated the warning. I continued upstairs. In the past I would have pleaded with them, too, but now I didn't bother.

This was a "trial" walkout. Leaflets passed out and signed by the White Student Caucus read: "By doing this the white student body hopes that in the future the white students may be able to leave the school by a system of signals when they feel the black students are provoking incidents that lead to the closing of Southie High."

There were five white seniors waiting for me in class. One said, "Garrity won't take the school. They'll give it to him."

After school, teachers had been scheduled to take the reading course under the plan worked out with the University of Massachusetts, in order to meet the wider range of reading skills found in the classroom since desegregation. One teacher commented, "You may as well leave. You get just as much credit." We didn't stay, abandoning the building to the buzz of the saw and hammer of nails carving out the new cooking room and administrative office cluster at the back of the foreshortened auditorium — the first evidence of Judge Garrity's determination to make South Boston High the "best school in the city."

We stopped in Amrheins Restaurant on the way home. The waitress who served us wore a black arm band with the legend: R E S I S T.

Tuesday, December 16

Before school, Mr. Kelly of the South Boston Information Center was at the high school to represent a group of fifteen of the eighty white students who had walked out yesterday and been suspended. Each student would have to return with a parent, he was told, because the policy for lifting suspensions had been changed. Mr. Kelly agreed, as long as the policy was kept for black students as well: no double standard.

The trooper sergeant in the lobby told me, "You seem very depressed. I spoke to you twice yesterday, but you didn't answer."

Paul passed by the black lobby holding room, provoking an instantaneous outcry. A tall and slender trooper stalked behind him at a distance.

Teachers met after school. They determined to protest the receivership by asking for transfers. One teacher posed the question, "By asking for transfers, are we being used to close the school?"

Dr. Reid commented to Ken Botwright of the *Globe:* "I feel no bitterness or recriminations toward Judge Garrity, because he had his job to do. I did my job the best way I knew how. It's obvious I was not successful. We should have had 4,400 pupils in the entire complex last year and we wound up with 2,000. This year, we should have had 1,300 in the main building and we have 600. I'm like a hockey or baseball coach who's judged by results. If your results are not satisfactory, you get a new boss. The judge apparently was not satisfied with me, so. . . ."

Dr. Reid felt, however, that presuming the two Citywide Coordinating Council monitors had accurately reported the tensions and conditions in the building, Judge Garrity's receivership action appeared to be "more stringent than the CCC reports warranted."

He conceded the "fight" had taken a lot out of him, but the Lord had given him good health, and he didn't feel he'd been beaten or defeated.

"Many of the kids were appreciative of my position," he told Eleanor Roberts of the *Herald*. "They felt I was in a tough spot and they would say, very casually, 'Tough day.' That was all. But you knew they understood."

Today ROAR occupied the Government Center offices of Senators Brooke and Kennedy, House Majority Leader Tip O'Neill, and Congressman Moakley. ROAR vacated Senator Kennedy's office when he agreed to meet them on January 4.

Wednesday, December 17

Early before school Dr. Reid bent over the morning *Globe* spread out on the office intercom cabinet reading Judge Garrity's "rationale" for the receivership of South Boston High School. His face was florid, his manner absorbed.

Angrily and publicly he characterized the judge as "naive" to draw conclusions about the school on the basis of two visits. He called Garrity's finding on the school's student and faculty attendance figures an "out-and-out lie," and challenged the judge to prove his statements.

Dr. Reid said, "We have teachers sign in every morning. We know who's here and who's late and who leaves early. We can account for every teacher in the building."

He denied that aides were functioning as teachers. He said, "No aides are teaching here. The only time an aide is allowed in the classroom is when he is invited by the teacher or perhaps when a teacher has to leave the room."

Dr. Reid suggested that the judge call in the attorney general to investigate.

The judge's statement about the attendance figures is an indication of his prejudice that the teachers were not in good faith and were acting, including Dr. Reid, "against implementation" of his plan. The judge, overlooking court testimony that the October 22 meeting was after school and voluntary, used the attendance figures for this voluntary meeting as proof of administrative misrepresentation of regular faculty attendance. Incredibly, he assumed that the whole school—including the ten stairwells, gyms, shops, library, bookroom, and faculty lounges—"froze" while he and his assistants took an attendance count. The actual tally of teachers arrived at by the court is not recorded.

In his "rationale" for the receivership of South Boston High, Judge Garrity had written:

> As for teachers, the roster of names and addresses filed by the defendant school committee at the outset of the hearing on plaintiffs' motion lists 100 teachers and 6 administrators. However, nowhere near 100 teachers could be found on the premises during the court's visits. On the second visit, when 99 teachers, including 6 substitutes were carried on the roll, we made an unsuccessful effort to locate clusters of teachers not then teaching or present in corridors, store-rooms, shops or laboratories: only a total of 10 teachers were in the two teacher lounges at the time. Additionally, some classes were being conducted not by teachers but by aides, thus further reducing the number of teachers to be seen. During the testimony, a faculty meeting on Oct. 22 was described and it was stated that about 40 faculty members were in attendance. This testimony corroborates the court's impression that on both visits the number of teachers listed in the teachers roll as being in attendance on those days was substantially overstated.

I was angry, so angry I was getting a headache. Teachers were sputtering with rage.

A trooper sergeant commented to me, "You have to fight back."

In my sophomore class, students were discussing among themselves before class a book about a student plot to take over a school, discovered just in time by the principal. "Do you see any comparison between the book and this school?" I almost asked. But I was silent. Every day now I question: Are the students relating to me, or to an outside voice from the community? It is the delicate web of caring and trust between teacher and student that the hearings have damaged.

One of the students who had writen an affidavit against Coach Perdigao told his English teacher, "Hey, he's a nice guy!"

She commented to me, "It's too bad he didn't wait a little longer to find that out."

Judge Garrity had been apparently heavily influenced in his decision by Dean Robert A. Dentler, Boston University adviser to the judge on Boston school desegregation. Mr. Dentler told the judge, "There is very abundant research literature that a school administrator can affect the educational environment powerfully, and in a very short time—more or less overnight."

In an interview in today's *Globe*, Dentler revealed that he and Dean Marvin Scott, also from Boston University, had briefed the judge on how to assess the school. "We were advising before, during, and after on the nature of urban high schools in general—and of Boston in particular—for months," he said.

Teachers at the high school are so depressed that to lift a paper, even, seems an exercise in futility. "The school is dying," said Noreen Curley, a teacher-nun. "I'm only one person. I'll just do what I can do."

Robert Donovan, faculty senate member, told a *Herald* reporter, "We've been busting our backs for a year and a half and all he [Judge Garrity] does is kick us."

Thursday, December 18

Receivership was necessary to protect black students from the onslaught against their constitutional rights, said Mr. Pressman, the NAACP lawyer.

The receivership is unconstitutional, Raoul Berger, professor of American legal history at Harvard, believes. "Law made by judges, based on oracles, social scientists, crystal ball gazing, and personal feelings requires, as in the case in Boston, more and more oppression and enforcement. It is like prohibition laws, unenforceable," he said. He suggested that, for the Bicentennial observance, Americans should concentrate on "grounding judges flying by the seat of their pants in the courtrooms. . . ."

In my opinion, Garrity's "rationale" is full of potholes.

I did not go to school today.

Friday, December 19

Classes were small again. In class, one senior boy put his head down on his *Hamlet* text. Remembering Judge Garrity's "rationale," I reprimanded him with, "What if Judge Garrity were to come by and see you. I'd be in trouble."

The other seniors asked excitedly, "Is Garrity here? Is he here?"

I said, "No, what *if!* Like Snowball, he's everywhere."

One boy, who had not finished reading *Animal Farm*, asked, "Is Snowball the fat pig?"

"Yes."

"Oink, oink," he responded.

In his "rationale" for the receivership, as proof of apathetic and inadequate teaching, Judge Garrity had written:

> *We observed a student in the front row of a classroom with his
> head on his forearm, apparently sleeping, and saw him in the same
> position a minute or two later, although his teacher was in the front
> of the room within a few feet.*

After lunch, students were dismissed so that the faculty could meet with
Mr. Joseph McDonough, district superintendent, and now receiver, a taller,
thinner, and younger man than Dr. Reid.

"When you hit bottom, where can you go but up?" he began. He
continued, "If I had known Dr. Reid would not be at South Boston High,
I would have refused this job." Reminding us he had defended the faculty
in open testimony in Court, Mr. McDonough rejected the transfer requests
of the teachers. He said, "There is no way I am going to destroy the
education of five or six hundred kids by permitting transfers until June."

Receiver McDonough then listed his two priorities: one, to find a building
administrator to replace Dr. Reid; and two, in Garrity's words, to "review
and evaluate qualifications and performance of all faculty, guidance, and
other educational personnel and in light of the special demands and strains
on such persons in the days ahead at South Boston High School." Teachers
not determined to be a "proper" person for the school would be transferred.
His judgment of teachers, Mr. McDonough said, would be based on four
criteria: their effectiveness, rapport, indicated willingness to work, and
desire to be at South Boston High School.

Receiver McDonough added that he might ask the president of the faculty
senate to be part of a review panel to judge the "fitness" of the faculty.
John Cunningham replied, "No way will I judge the faculty."

Monday, December 22

There was a snowstorm today. No school. Teachers had planned
to picket outside Judge Garrity's court at the federal building, then hand
in applications for transfer to other schools. There are sixty requests. The
demonstration was postponed.

Tuesday, December 23

A "Snow Day" again. No school. The snow silenced the rage of
the faculty demonstration. The out-of-town teachers scattered for the long
holiday. Alone, Dr. Reid left the school for the last time. Silent, secret snow.

Asked whether, if people had been more cooperative, the desegregation
process would have worked, Dr. Reid told Eleanor Roberts of the *Herald,*

"Oh, sure, the way the Ten Commandments would work if the people were cooperative."

Senator Brooke met with a group of ROAR delegates. He promised them he would "fight day and night" for the defeat of a constitutional amendment against busing.

Thursday, January 1, 1976

The court has a choice, Judge Garrity explained, either to close the school or make it more attractive to students so they won't be "hanging around street corners wasting their lives away."

Therefore, in addition to the estimated $20,000 expended for work completed by the end of the Christmas holiday, Judge Garrity has ordered $111,900 for repairs at South Boston High: new formica tops and a paint job for the 60 cafeteria tables; a paint coating for classrooms, gymnasiums, auditorium, and shops; new tile floors for all classrooms; replacement of 190 ceiling tiles at the L-Street Annex; and for the teachers' and aides' lounges, $500 worth of chairs and tables.

My father compared the situation at South Boston High to D. H. Lawrence's short story, "The Rocking Horse Winner": Garrity makes movement, but no progress. The more hopeless, the more furious the rocking back and forth, back and forth.

Sunday, January 4

Senator Kennedy kept his promise to ROAR and met with a group of students from the Boston public schools, then a group of teachers and aides, and finally with the parents. ROAR members stood with lists at the door of the John Fitzgerald Kennedy Federal Building, carefully screening those they would allow upstairs through the tight security. The senator was on the firing line for five hours.

When Senator Kennedy, in blue suit and ankle-high, soft black leather shoes, came to our group composed of teachers from around the city and aides from South Boston, his face was already flushed from his meeting with the students. He was interested in the conditions in the schools, he told us, and wanted to know how he could be helpful.

John Cunningham, faculty senate president, began: The faculty felt the receivership was unjust; the facts brought out in court did not substantiate the action taken by Judge Garrity; the faculty felt undermined and destroyed. He then summarized events at the high school from October 8 on. Mr. Doherty continued, pointing out the injustices in the conduct of the hearing and in the judge's decision. He accused Judge Garrity of depriving Arthur Perdigao of due process of law, but added that, for family reasons, Coach Perdigao did not want to press charges. On January 9 the receivership decision would go to the Court of Appeals, he said, but Garrity had crafted his decision cleverly, because a "finding of fact" could not be appealed. Mr. Doherty concluded, "A lie is given and is halfway around the world before the truth comes out."

Senator Kennedy asked about the suspension rate, why 50 percent of the total suspensions in the city came from South Boston High. He noted that the race issue in Boston had been exploited for political reasons. He paraphrased H. L. Mencken: "For every difficult problem there is an easy solution — and a wrong one."

Once an aide with ROAR membership, who was at the high school last year, interrupted Senator Kennedy. He angrily overpowered her. "Can I talk? Can I finish? We're not on City Hall Plaza now," he said, referring to the day in early September 1974, when he had tried to address the antibusers, but was pursued inside the JFK building by flying egg and tomato.

Joan, another aide, pleaded passionately. "Our backs are to the wall, Senator. Our husbands work in factories or on the docks, when there is work. The kids come home from school crying. We have nowhere to go. But you, Senator, can go back to Washington. You don't even listen to us. Nobody cares."

A gym teacher accused Senator Kennedy of being insincere, charging that his record of support for low-income housing in the suburbs was unsatisfactory. He retorted, "I've been listening to your complaints about defamation of character for an hour now, and *you* accuse me of being insincere. I have a right to know what you are talking about. Be specific." When she hesitated, he replied, "If you can't think now, write me a letter then."

Senator Kennedy concluded that he would like to keep open the line of communication with us. The teachers responded affirmatively.

I had almost decided not to attend the meeting with Senator Kennedy, but I was glad I went because I found he did listen, he did feel, and he was concerned.

Downstairs we saw the waitress from Amrheins Restaurant. "We'll dynamite the high school," she told us.

"Please wait until we get our things out of the building."

The new year at South Boston High will begin with an interim acting headmaster. After twenty-five refusals from around the city, Mr. Corscadden, assistant headmaster in charge of mathematics, accepted the position.

Monday, January 5

Trouble was anticipated today. An indictment of South Boston allegedly by Charles Gilligan of the state police was reported in the suburban Beverly *Times* by a young Emily Lodge. Gilligan—recently promoted to lieutenant colonel—printed a retraction that only made him appear as if his feet were caught in molasses. "I'm the goat, I'm the goat," he cried.

I called the managing editor of the Beverly *Times* after school to ask whether he didn't think there might be as much alcohol consumption and as many marital problems in suburban Beverly as in South Boston. He was angry but said, "Yes."

The classrooms were so cold, the drafty windows rattled by the nor'easter blowing in from the Atlantic, that four teachers brought their students— among them Paul—down to the warm cafeteria study. Since the publicity of the court hearings, his appearance alone can provoke an incident. When some black students jumped up on the cafeteria tables and challenged him to fight, he was taken out. The study quieted then, except for Donna, a 766 special needs student, who taunted, "Paul, Paul, Paul, Paul." I went over and told her, "You're deliberately provoking." Then, remembering Dr. Reid, the words choked in my throat. But she looked afraid at my anger, and quieted immediately.

Almost the same word I had used with Donna, taken out of context, had been used as damaging evidence against Dr. Reid.

In his "rationale" for the receivership of South Boston High, Judge Garrity had written:

> There is no administrative policy as to seating arrangements in classrooms, the matter being left up to the individual teacher, so black students all sit on one or the other side of the room or all toward the front or rear. A plan to have desegregated assemblies, but having homerooms sit in assigned rows, is, according to the only testimony as to its implementation, not being enforced. Students of separate races sit at separate tables in the cafeteria at lunch time; no effort is made to "break the ice" between the two groups such as by having teams of white and black aides eat together; on the contrary, a black girl taking a seat at a cafeteria table at which some white girls were already seated was reprimanded by the building administrator for having made a "provocative move." The black girl had previously

*testified that she did this because there was no room for her at an
adjacent table at which her black friends were seated.*

After school, at a faculty meeting, Mr. Corscadden asked for the support
of the teachers. There was "no way" he would let us experienced teachers
transfer to another school. He was introducing a three-minute warning
system between classes and asked us to cooperate. The introduction of the
warning system and the removal of the forbidding list of contraband weapons from the lobby wall above the metal detectors were the only innovations
of the first phase of the new "creative" receivership.

Tuesday, January 6

There was a power failure in the school today and no heat. The
temperature was 12° outside, 40° inside. The bused students were sent
home, and about 100 walkers. The teachers waited in school from 7:30
until 9:30 for permission from school headquarters to leave also, complaining
of cold feet and catching cold. "What are we?" asked Mr. Fred Murphy.
"Sheep! We're sheep. That's why we're here. Let's demand to leave." There
was loud assent.

Wednesday, January 7

I asked the seniors in class whether I should submit a transfer
request. I had thought they would be unanimous in urging me to protest,
but instead they were angry. Only one of them, a girl, argued that the
faculty *had* to make some protest against the accusations implied in the
judge's decision. The other students were concerned only that their teachers
might leave.

A coalition of 30 "concerned students" from the high school and from
activist groups such as the Boston Anti-Repression Organization, the October
League, and the Communist Youth Organization, called again from Freedom House for the closing of South Boston High. ROAR protested that the
groups were only trying to stifle resistance.

Thursday, January 8

School began two hours late. Sixty-two black students got off the
buses at the high school, then stood on the steps, refusing to go to their
assigned classes. They were suspended. They boarded the buses and returned to the pickup site, where they had been leafleted on their way to
school.

The white students were upset. Fifteen members of the White Student Caucus walked out of the high school and marched to School Committee Headquarters with James Kelly of the South Boston Information Center to confront School Superintendent Marion Fahey. A smiling School Committeewoman Pixie Palladino from East Boston met and welcomed them.

They complained, "We don't want to have anything to do with the biracial council. Mr. Corscadden said we will not have any protection if we don't have the council."

Superintendent Fahey waxed angrier and angrier and louder and louder. I think she may have frightened them. She said, in fully articulated words, "If the troublemakers are surfacing, and if they are there to interrupt the educational process in the school, I have stated over and over they shall be removed. My number one concern is safety and security, and my second is educational programs. I want every student in a program of learning. . . . I do not want any student in the system out of the school. That is why I am superintendent. That is my obligation."

The students' faces showed no reaction. They spend more time protesting than in school.

Miss Fahey promised she would send a team to investigate.

Teachers stayed after school a half-hour to write letters home to the parents of the suspended black students, boycotting because, they claimed, they had tried unsuccessfully to meet with Mr. Corscadden and discuss discrimination in favor of whites at the school.

Friday, January 9

Classes began at 9:20, not 8:10 as scheduled. Black students suspended yesterday were refused permission to return to class unless accompanied by a parent. One black woman came to represent her niece as well as her daughter, but was informed she could represent only her own child. "In the vernacular," remarked one administrator, "we said, 'Fuck you.'"

One trooper told me he has to go home and drink after putting up with the "shit" in the school. He didn't see how the teachers could stand the insults and disrespect.

Ms. Murphy was in the hallway today when Dan came up to her, complaining about a fresh black girl. Ms. Murphy asked, "The pretty one, Lila?"

"No, that funny looking one," he answered.

Ms. Murphy said, "It's not so long ago since I was a teenager. There's nothing harder than to be a teenager and ugly. Think about that." She cleverly switched his thought direction from race prejudice to the problems of all teenagers.

My senior class was my largest—six students.

At Amrheins after school, we gave the ROAR waitress copies of Major Gilligan's retraction. She said, "We heard the Major was all right from people who know. The Establishment just wants to drive a wedge in wherever they can. We know their games. We won't let them."

Monday, January 12

A mild snowstorm today. No school. Dorchester Heights, the impregnable fortress that defeated the British in the winter of 1776, is still a threat to the buses that must climb the slippery Heights to the high school.

A week has passed now to reflect on the changes in the past year. *THEN:* We had a headmaster who knew our strengths and weaknesses, whose fairness and judgment we relied on. His stature added dignity to the struggle. *NOW:* It's catch-22, a comedy, and we watch the exits and entrances of the players of the complicated plot: Enter Receiver Joseph McDonough on December 10, 1975, exit Dr. Reid on December 23, 1975; exit Receiver McDonough on January 5 and enter Superintendent Marion Fahey as Receiver on January 12 with acting interim Headmaster James Corscadden. Judge Garrity supported the appointment of Mr. Corscadden, one of the administrative staff under court order to vacate, although the black plaintiffs reminded the judge of his inconsistency. Now administration, reprieved until June, and staff careen along together; all of us without distinction have a hand on the steering wheel. The judge, although he issues all orders relative to the well-being of the school—teachers and students—has turned down the faculty request to meet and communicate directly with them. *THEN:* The black plaintiffs said, "Get rid of Dr. Reid or close the school." *NOW:* After three days of school, black students, 62 of them, refused to get off the buses and were suspended. The allegations are the same as before: *then,* Dr. Reid wouldn't talk to them; *now,* Mr. Corscadden won't talk to them. *THEN:* Massachusetts was the most liberal of the United States, the only state to vote for George McGovern in the 1972 presidential election. *NOW:* George Wallace has opened an office in South Boston. *THEN:* Boston was solvent. *NOW:* Boston is $33 million in debt, and is anticipating the largest tax rise in its history.

But there have been a few pleasant changes. Marie, the Boston cop, who took a few punches from the 766 kids and came gallantly to the fights, who guarded the toilets for a year and a half, joined the Boston mounted police and a better life. *LAST YEAR:* We had neither football nor hockey team. *NOW:* Both teams are the city champions.

Tuesday, January 13

Spanish-speaking students at South Boston High School, who claim they have protested to Judge Garrity for months, gave public notice that they will boycott until their grievances at the high school are adequately addressed. According to media reports, they feel discriminated against because they are Hispanics. They claim they are subjected to harassment and police searches; their culture and language are not respected by administrators and teachers. "They are forced to speak English, even among themselves, and are being denied the right to speak, be taught, and learn in their national language," the *Herald* read.

Ironically, in his "rationale" for the receivership, Judge Garrity had observed from his two brief visits to South Boston High, "Generally speaking, except for the special needs and bilingual classes, the whole place was devoid of the youthful spontaneity that one associates with a high school."

Mr. Corscadden explained to the media that this was the first he knew of the problem. Some grievances are "legitimate," he said; he'd do what he could.

Contrary to the newspaper report, I had only seen them moving in a giggle of girls, chattering in Spanish among themselves, and sometimes delightedly in Spanish to a trooper. I had felt they added an international charm to the school and had wished I could communicate with them in their language, although Ms. Murphy *had* remarked to me earlier in the year about them that she "hated to see another group of lepers"—the isolated groups of students in the school—the Hispanics, the 766 special needs students, the holding rooms of black and white students.

Wednesday, January 14

Paul was involved in two fights today and sent home, but not suspended because he hadn't started the fights. He was still outside the school at dismissal time in his pointed stocking cap. The black students emptied out of the buses and the boys—not the girls—went after him.

Today the U.S. Court of Appeals upheld the Phase 2 desegregation plan on every point.

Friday, January 16

At 7:40 A.M., the troopers, looking at the dreary, empty corridors, asked, "Where are all the students?"

The attendance is dropping. My total attendance for the day was sixteen sophomores and six seniors.

There is terrible depression everywhere in the school.

At Amrheins, the ROAR waitress told us she had kept her two children out of school by continually moving, rather than send them where she didn't want them to go. She seemed very weary.

Monday, January 19

At Hyde Park High, a black student burned the American flag in the auditorium.

Wednesday, January 21

At Charlestown High there was a sit-in and a walkout of forty students. In East Boston, 300 students demonstrated for the second day in a row, turning over cars and briefly blocking the Callahan Tunnel at the airport exit to protest Phase 2B desegregation next year, when their community high school will be converted into a citywide magnet school.

Hyde Park High was closed after a "very large confrontation." A school department official, a witness, said a group of 300 blacks held a sit-in in the basement cafeteria, sent a delegation to meet with Headmaster Best, and then decided to return to classes. When the bell sounded, "turmoil" broke out. "There were several hundred kids fighting all over the place. They were like soldiers—fighting and falling down." Steel chairs flew. Wastebaskets hurtled outside through the broken windows. One girl related to a *Globe* reporter, "I have black and white friends. I didn't believe they would do anything to me. Then suddenly they were punching me. I was on the ground. I covered my head so my face wouldn't get hurt and screamed."

The Hyde Park High faculty voted to close the high school until Monday.

Friday, January 23

There was more atmosphere of violence in the school than for many days. Once again the troopers stood, backs to the front lobby doors, facing in toward the metal detectors.

Wearing black gloves, the troopers moved to the back and sides of the cafeteria until I finished taking attendance in my study there—perhaps because Paul had come down with his class. Their hands were cold, the troopers said, but I heard that the gloves were a precaution; one trooper had been bitten on the hand.

Paul is accompanied to classes now by an aide.

At Hyde Park High, the faculty has adopted a stronger disciplinary code and has demanded the assignment of 100 police to the building for the reopening of school Monday.

Monday, January 26

Ms. Murphy, accompanying Paul to his homeroom before school, walked into a fight between black and white girls outside Miss Wynne's homeroom, near the World War I memorial plaques. Miss Wynne, fearing that one white girl might be strangled, tried to break the black girl's headlock, but was knocked to the floor. Paul ran to the defense of his favorite teacher, fragile Miss Wynne, but was wrestled to the floor by two troopers, then escorted downstairs. When I arrived, Miss Wynne was picking up her things, crying.

One of my classes was bad. A 766 special needs student ran in and out of the adjoining room until I called an aide. And Lillian, a black girl, refused to be quiet and swore aloud—"fuck," "shit." When I finally called an aide, she left, whispering in my ear, "Hussy." She reads at a sixth-grade level in a tenth-grade college-preparatory course, but there is no opening in the remedial reading classes. Coming up the stairs later in the day, she poked me in the back.

There were 35 suspensions today at South Boston High.

Wednesday, January 28

Teachers are out regularly now in large numbers: 14, 18, 16. "You have the name, so play the game," one said.

Thursday, January 29

Mr. Byram Cossie, the black principal of a school in South Africa, was the second visitor in our Distinguished Visitors Series—a joint project of Dean Yarborough's and mine.

Mr. Cossie was so honest about the flagrant abuse of human rights along color lines in South Africa that I was nervous about student reaction. Armed robbery, he told them, is punishable by hanging, especially if involving blacks and whites. A black man must carry a passbook with him at all times; not to do so is a punishable crime. A black man receives a salary five-eighths that of a white man. The students reacted positively, however, some remaining afterward to pose for photos with Mr. Cossie.

Sunday, February 1

Of the three final candidates for headmaster of South Boston High, Jerome Winegar, a forty-year-old assistant principal at the Wilson Junior High in St. Paul, Minnesota, and administrator for that city's extensive network of alternative programs, seems to be the choice. Superintendent Fahey will make the final selection.

Interviewed in the Sunday *Herald,* Marion Fahey called the Hyde Park High confrontation the worst in the city, and suggested that Louise Day Hicks should leave the running of the schools to the School Committee before they erupt into the streets. Besides Mrs. Hicks, Superintendent Fahey attacked the School Committee, ROAR, Mayor White, faculty senates, as well as South Boston High teachers for having failed to accept her Task Force; in summary, she sided with Judge Garrity and for the "improved education" she sees.

Monday, February 2

I sat at lunch with a colleague, who had witnessed her first fight outside her classroom last Friday. In a year and a half—the first fight she saw. Nothing in her teenage years—except remotely, perhaps, celluloid images on a movie screen of *Blackboard Jungle* and *Rebel Without a Cause*—had prepared her for the "unsavory event"; she cried all weekend.

I said, "You get used to the fights, become apathetic." She was shocked. I hardly care now who is involved in a fight. Kids are involved in fights when they "go looking for them" for the most part. Some never get in fights.

During lunch break, one of my five sophomore students was suspended for fighting. I said, "Take your book home and finish the work, so you can pass." A push, a punch, and they're out. How can they learn?

Today the Boston School Committee summoned Superintendent Fahey to an emergency meeting, then left her waiting twenty minutes on the committee platform. Chairman John McDonough reprimanded her: She should not have made political statements; her remarks bordered on hysteria; she was an agent of the School Committee, elected by the people. Miss Fahey hung her head, and her mouth drooped. But she "stonewalled it," Mr. McDonough said later. She defended her interest in the safety and education of the children of Boston with stock answers: "I'm for quality education; busing is the law. . . ." She pronounced every word exactly and slowly, enunciating each *d* or *t* or end-letter to its fullest measure, a technique which gives substance and strength to words that otherwise would seem inconsequential.

Tuesday, February 3

There were only five students in my senior class. Bill's father died. The hockey team lost to Roslindale High yesterday—their first loss—no Bill.

There is very low teacher morale at South Boston High.

In an article on Jerome Winegar by Muriel Cohen of the *Globe,* Mr. Winegar allegedly described the classes at the school, after a brief visit, as "dull"; criticized as insensitive the pinpointing of hair picks as weapons, and said only those who use them should be penalized; commented that there were no art, music, and acting programs at the school, like so many "working class schools." Mr. Winegar had been promised by Superintendent Fahey that, as headmaster, he could hand-pick his staff and, further, make those teachers who do not transfer, take in-service training, over and over again, until they are "blue in the face," in order to learn how to deal with minority students and with confrontations.

Mr. Corscadden commented on the *Globe* article, "Look at the teachers now. You don't even hear a whimper of protest."

After school at the Crisis-Prevention seminar, the psychiatrist confessed that the receivership of the high school had made him angry because, from his contact with them in the seminar last year and this, he found them to be "caring teachers."

Wednesday, February 4

ROAR met with Superintendent Fahey at School Committee headquarters today to demand an apology or her resignation. Belatedly attempting to align herself with the teachers, Miss Fahey alleged ROAR had attacked the teachers—a charge ROAR denied. Twenty Boston Tactical Patrol were present to ensure order. ROAR hissed at them.

Thursday, February 5

The sophomores read with interest a *Scope* magazine drama, "Sarah-T—Teenage Alcoholic," as part of my mini-course, "Solving Teenage Problems Through Literature." Black students identified drugs as the major problem in Roxbury; South Boston students named alcohol as the major drug abuse problem of their community.

Again, like last year, when asked to write a page from Alice's diary, sophomores wrote, not about drugs, the theme of the book *Go Ask Alice,* but about what they see around them:

Excerpts from Alice's *Diary:* At South Boston High

Dear Diary,

I know I am not going to like this new school because there are cops everywhere. I tried to take just one aspirin to get over my headache and bingo an aide grabs me and brings me to the office. The atmosphere isn't the friendliest here either. Well, got to study for a test. Bye.

A white sophomore boy

Dear Diary,

Today I started in a new school, South Boston High. It is really different here it's kind of scary. When I first came in I had to go through a metal detector I had to take everything out of my pockets. My classes were all right but once you get out in the hallway you didn't know what's going to happen. Today I saw two fights. I don't know if I am going to like this new school. There seems to be to much trouble. Talk to you later. Luv ya.

A white sophomore girl

Dear Diary,

When I walked into school today, I went through the usual thing: going through the medal detectors then going up stairs to get my books and put my jacket away, then waiting in class for about 15 minutes after the bell rang. I went till the basement so I could take my pill for the first couple of periods because I need something to get me through these days at school.

After my two periods which were so boring I had to take something to get me going again I went to one of my friends to get something to hold me over for the rest of the day.

Well I finally got through it (school) so I have nothing to look forward to till another day at school.

A white sophomore boy

The six new offices for administration and counseling, constructed at the rear of the assembly hall, opened today. The office space, long Dr. Reid's first priority, will alleviate the congestion and tension in the front office.

Paul, despite a ROAR protest, has been involuntarily transferred to English High.

South Boston Heights Academy, a new alternative school on Broadway, has been accredited for 434 students in grades 1 to 12, a third of them in grades 9 to 12.

Friday, February 6

Four Boston police were suspended for participation in the Rabbit Inn incident on October 5, 1974, in South Boston, two of them for six months without pay, charged with "assaulting and beating citizens, use of excessive force and filing false reports" concerning the incident; two others for one month without pay for submitting "false reports." Still nine other officers received letters of admonition, promising close scrutiny of their future conduct, although no formal reprimand was placed in their personnel file. °

Wednesday, February 11

Mr. Kelly of the South Boston Information Center complained of reverse discrimination and announced that, just as the blacks had made their advances by street violence, so would they.

Thursday, February 12

Two hundred ROAR members emptied out of buses, then broke up a meeting of the Citywide Coordinating Council at English High School. Mr. Gartland, president of the CCC, disbanded the meeting at 8:10 P.M. after all parent attempts to talk were drowned out by ROAR, leaving Mrs. Pixie Palladino, School Committeewoman from East Boston, triumphant on the stage, an enormous smile on her face. Beside her stood Paul, wearing sun glasses, basking in the triumph of the moment. He is not yet mature enough to act in his own best interest.

Friday, February 13

Mr. Best, headmaster of Hyde Park High School, was removed by Superintendent Fahey, and the vacancy filled by a football coach from Roslindale High, despite faculty support of Mr. Best and their criticism of the "shabby and unprofessional" manner of his removal, with rumors of his departure rife for weeks in the city.

° The Massachusetts Civil Service Commission later overruled Police Commissioner Robert diGrazia, exonerating and reinstating the officers with full back pay.

Sunday, February 15

There was a "near riot" outside South Boston High after police tried to detour one section of a "Fathers Only" antibusing march from the parade route. Helmeted police, their visors down, met the marchers with drawn clubs, horses, and dogs. One man threw a tear gas cannister; it was returned by the police. In the confrontation that followed, the crowd swelled from 400 to 1,000. Seventy police and forty civilians were injured; thirteen adults were arrested.

ROAR charged police brutality. They demanded the disbanding of the TPF and the resignation of Police Commissioner diGrazia. In turn, diGrazia, sitting beside a display of sticks, rocks, and bottles allegedly used against the police, promised he would get tough now with the "hoodlums"; he would file charges and prosecute. He would no longer continue the low police visibility policy of September 1974; he hoped no one would challenge him.

Mr. Kelly of the South Boston Information Center, flanked by a South Boston marshal, Mr. Warren Zaniboni — an aide last year — countered that there would have been no violence if the police had not been present. There would be a parade next week, he promised, with or without a permit.

Vacation week, February 15 to 22

There was rioting in Charlestown three nights in a row. Youths attacked the police with bottles, stones, sticks, clubs, tire irons, and tear gas.

Channel 5 TV broadcast an appeal, in the name of sanity, against busing East Boston students next year. The Boston School Committee also asked Judge Garrity to keep a minimum (not maximum) of 25 percent of the East Boston high school and middle school students in the community. Garrity will take the appeal under advisement. He asked the public to consider the human suffering caused by opponents of school desegregation: students vomiting, parents near nervous collapse.

Senator Bulger called his comment "the most contemptible and hypocritical outburst the judge has yet made on this case."

Judge Garrity finally allowed twenty-two Hispanic students, boycotting classes at South Boston High since January 12, to transfer to Roxbury High.

On the national scene, President Ford criticized "wrong remedies" used by some courts to desegregate. He said, "I think in some areas judges have used the remedy of busing without tearing up the fabric of the community and it depends upon the wisdom and judiciousness of the judge who has to deal with reality."

Monday, February 23

Back to school. There was graffiti everywhere on the South Boston High building—doors, steps, sidewalk, streets: GARRITY FEDERAL HIGH SCHOOL, RESIST, STOP FORCED BUSING, FREEDOM ENDS HERE, REMEMBER BLACK TUESDAY.

The senior boys are angry because Jerome Winegar comes from a *junior* high school. The ROAR waitress at Amrheins is angry because Winegar is a member of the NAACP and the American Civil Liberties Union.

Wednesday, February 25

The faculty are upset about a directive to seat students alphabetically, in accordance with Headmaster's Bulletin Number 20, December 5, 1975, which reminded teachers of the court order, 1974: "There shall be no segregation of students within schools, classrooms or programs in the school system."

In the classrooms students sit for security in groups, near their friends. What point is there in making a student sit next to someone whom he may dislike or is afraid of, or of disturbing students who are getting along all right and would only perceive the alphabetical seating as the meddling of Judge Garrity? There *is* no point, at least not now. Is South Boston High the only school in the city that has to seat students in alphabetical order? Not fair!

In the Crisis Prevention seminar after school, teachers discussed with the psychiatrist the forced alphabetical seating of students for desegregation. No one knows who is responsible for the order.

I had suggested to a rebellious sophomore class that I would just read the student names alphabetically so they could see where such an arrangement might seat them. After class, Lillian came up to ask me about Ray, whom she would be sitting next to under the tentative arrangement. "Is he . . . Is he . . ." but she didn't know what to say or how to finish. Finally she asked, "Does he have skin your color?"

Some teachers have solved the problem by simply submitting alphabetical seating plans of classes to the front office without moving the students.

Friday, February 27

Classes were light: in my four classes, fourteen sophomores and four white seniors.

Two black girls came to my senior class with a petition for the retention of one of the administrators ordered removed by Garrity. The class was silent. I restated their petition and asked, "Doesn't anyone want to sign?"

Bill said, "They caught me downstairs."

Matthew said, "He suspended me. I'm not signing."

Two pretty girls said, "I don't know him."

When the petitioners had left, Matthew said, "I wasn't suspended. I just said that."

Bill said, "Why didn't they take around a petition for Mr. Perdigao and Dr. Reid? I can't wait to get out of this school. Wait until the new headmaster Winegar comes. He's a member of the NAACP."

I said, "That stands for the National Association for the Advancement of Colored People. It doesn't have to mean anything except he wants the advancement of blacks in jobs, housing, opportunities. There's nothing wrong with that." But I admired their sophistication in handling the petition. I had no idea what they were thinking, until they told me. Such aplomb. A statesman couldn't do better.

Seventy white students boycotted today, protesting the alphabetical seating. Mr. Corscadden explained that the purpose of the new arrangement was to further promote desegregation in the classrooms, to "break up cliques of whites and blacks who sat in separate groups."

Sunday, February 29

The "Fathers Only" antibusing march in South Boston was peaceful. Senator Bulger addressed the crowd of more than 3,000 men, urging them to go to the polls and send the government a message to "get off our backs. . . . leave our children alone."

Wednesday, March 3

The conservatives—George Wallace and Henry Jackson—won in the Massachusetts presidential primary.

Some girls in the library were reading and talking about the *Globe* article on Jerome Winegar—whom they referred to as "our principal." They reacted to two items: that he allegedly was responsible for the classroom alphabetical arrangement suggestion, and the choice of the primary colors for the formica on the lunchroom tables. One scoffed, "It makes the tables look like a nursery school."

Wednesday, March 10

At the Crisis Prevention seminar after school, I asked the psychiatrist about the color symbolism in *Lisa Bright and Dark,* the story of a teenage schizophrenic. The association of black with death, blindness, or fear was universal, Dr. Kantar believed, not limited to Western culture. He mentioned that patients tended to use brighter colors in painting therapy as they became more able to cope with their problems.

In turn, the psychiatrist asked if anyone was trying to sabotage the new headmaster, Mr. Winegar. I said, "You sound like Judge Garrity," then remembered that some students, under the direction of a black teacher devoted to Dr. Reid, were tacking up on classroom walls a quote from Mr. Winegar that only "renegade" teachers had applied to him for jobs at South Boston High. A definition of "renegade" was attached.

Thursday, March 11

Ms. Sharifah Zuriah Aljeffri, cultural affairs asistant of the USIA in Kuala Lampur, Malaysia, our third international visitor, talked to my senior class about similar cultural problems shared by Malaysia and America.

Ms. Aljeffri told the class that there were two forbidden subjects in Malaysia: race and language; Malaysia had had race wars. Malay, she said, is the first language, English the second language of a country which shares three cultural identities: Malay, Indian, and Chinese. The English conquerors had divided them: The Malays were farmers, the Chinese were bankers, and the Indians were merchants. Now there was an effort to mix up the occupations of the different races, and, therefore, the races.

It was good for the seniors to see the problem of race from a different perspective, and the need to solve it — perhaps artificially.

Ms. Aljeffri was curious about how the students spent their leisure time.

"We play sports — football, hockey, baseball," Tony told her.

"And what do the young ladies do?" she inquired.

"They watch us," said Tony, getting in his shot before the girls could speak.

At the end, Sean, with typical Southie enthusiasm, rushed up to Ms.

Aljeffri and pinned a Southie 1975-1976 button on her. Dean Yarborough asked me if I had planned Sean's enthusiastic dash. I said, "No, I am very honest with them."

Sunday, March 14

St. Patrick's Day Parade—the Bicentennial anniversary of the expulsion of the British from Boston—shorter than usual. Many bands were afraid to participate. Fort Devens commander Colonel Rittgers barred his troops from marching, despite protests to Washington by Louise Day Hicks.

Monday, March 15

To celebrate St. Patrick's Day, Moira Jenks, book reviewer for the *Herald American,* gave a slide talk on Ireland for all students in my Irish literature classes assembled in the auditorium. Her husband, Homer Jenks, managing editor of the Sunday *Herald-Advertiser,* accompanied her. Later I saw him standing outside the front office, looking at the sports trophy case.

"Dr. Reid was very proud of them," I said.

"Yes, I know. We photographed him here on his last day," he replied.

Tuesday, March 16

In my sophomore Teen Lit class we began *The Contender,* the story of a black youth who uses boxing to hoist himself from the ghetto. Kim protested, pointing to the publisher's blurb on the back cover: *Don't get friendly with whitey.*

"I'm not reading this," she said.

I was angry. "Almost every book and film we've seen this year has been about whites," I replied. "We read *Of Mice and Men* and no black student protested the use of 'nigger' in the story, or took the insult personally. I expect you to be mature and fair." Kim was mollified then. The black students were silent.

Thursday, March 18

Today Jim McLoughlin, teacher, circulated a petition to retain Jim Corscadden as headmaster. I looked at the petition, then asked, "Why didn't we do this for Dr. Reid? If not for him, then I don't want to sign for anyone else." I was embarrassed, but didn't sign; 95 percent, however, did sign.

Ms. Murphy, still angry that Mr. Corscadden had not blocked the transfer of Paul out of South Boston High, and concerned that black parents would perceive Paul as a touchstone for the treatment of equivalent black types, also refused to sign. She argued that the parents—by which she meant the ten parents on the biracial council who had selected Mr. Winegar as their choice for headmaster—felt that the faculty was going against them by signing the petition.

Monday, March 22

Just a few troopers on duty—fewer than a busful. I walked through the North Cafeteria. Empty now. In the past the troopers sat there and read or talked when they weren't on duty upstairs.

Tuesday, March 23

Commissioner Anrig of the Massachusetts Board of Education declared Massachusetts now free of illegal racial imbalance in its schools.

A social worker from South Boston told me it is impossible to tell the effect busing has had on the psyche of South Boston kids because they would rather tangle with the police than a psychiatrist: Police are status; a psychiatrist is a stigma.

Dentler and Scott, desegregation "experts," requested a year's delay in the conversion of East Boston High to a citywide magnet technical school.

Wednesday, March 24

I gave my students the "Chitlings" test, saved from a predesegregation 1974 sensitivity course I took. I wanted to prove, to myself mostly, that there is a black vocabulary that is not tested in I.Q. tests.

The black students, in fact, did very well; the whites listened. One white boy wrinkled up his paper, but several white students knew some of the black dialect words, and they acted like advance scouts for the students who were complete holdouts.

One of the "Chitlings" questions was about "hambones." I asked what they were. Celia said, "Oh, never mind."

Sandra said, "Well, tell me, then." Celia did.

Students discussed the meaning of "Uncle Tom" and "oreo" and then which character in *The Contender* was accused of being an "Uncle Tom" and why.

I asked whether prejudice hurts the victims. They agreed.

Friday, March 26

Sandra was the only black in class today. She was unconscious of that fact.

I gave the class the "Bitch" test—shortened by me diplomatically to "B" test—which I had also garnered at the predesegregation sensitivity course. Only one girl, Angela, put her head down on her desk and watched sideways.

Tim, a sophomore, had refused to do the "B" test and wrinkled up his paper. I asked him to run the filmstrip, *Roots of Prejudice,* through the projector. I asked Tim, "Are you prejudiced?" He nodded his head. I said, "I'm prejudiced, too. Everyone is to some extent, some more than others. We just have to try to be as fair and honest in our dealing with others as we can." I wanted him to see that he was not alone, and no less worthy than the rest of us.

My seniors posed another problem. They mimicked the black dialect when they guessed at the vocabulary in the "Chitlings" test. I tried to discourage them, unsuccessfully, by exaggerated facial grimaces, which the two black girls, sitting on either side of me in the horseshoe seating arrangement, couldn't see. The black girls, who had joined my senior English class after Christmas vacation, used to sit beside one another, but had separated themselves without a word when I began discussing an alphabetical arrangement in the class. Bill had threatened, "I'd like to see anyone try to tell me where to sit."

Before class today, Bill gave out tuxedo rental card advertisements for the senior prom. He gave them to all the white students, then hesitated and asked Rose, "Are you a senior?" Then he gave her one, too.

Tuesday, March 30

I was in class with my seniors when Ms. Murphy came in. Quite accidentally, she had found Senator Bulger and Mr. Corscadden sitting together in the front office with James Coleman, the "Father of Busing," and had managed to get passes for us to the State House that afternoon where Mr. Coleman was scheduled to deliver a speech on busing. After she had gone, I told the class, "Ms. Murphy is the eyes and ears of the school."

Senator Bulger and Representative Ray Flynn sat on the speaker's platform behind Mr. Coleman. Pixie Palladino sat to the side of the platform.

Warren Zaniboni of the South Boston Marshals was in the visitor's gallery. "They're here, they're here!" Ms. Murphy exclaimed.

School desegregation had not proved to be the "panacea for black achievement" originally anticipated, Mr. Coleman said, in terms of the three goals of school desegregation policies: eliminating de jure segregation, benefiting achievement of disadvantaged children, and achieving social integration.

His remarks about Boston were specific:

> Boston presents an example though far from the most extreme, of what happens when extensive desegregation is imposed in a central-city school district. In the five years before desegregation, there had been a loss of approximately 4.5 percent of whites per year. In 1974, when desegregation took place, there was a loss of 16.1 percent, over three times as great. And in 1975, the additional loss, using figures for December 31, 1975, is 15.5 percent if students are kept on the rolls who never came to school throughout the fall. If they are not included, the figure is even worse, a loss of 18.9 percent of the 1974 white enrollment — or altogether, in two years, a loss of 32 percent of the 1973 white enrollment, almost one-third.
>
> Altogether, then, when we look at the effects of school desegregation for the third goal, the goal of achieving social integration in America, the results are mixed. In small school districts, in rural areas, and in countrywide metropolitan districts, then extensive school desegregation, even compulsory racial balance, has not led to social segregation through a loss of whites from the schools — so long as the proportion black in the schools is low. Because it has not led to demographic instability, it has probably been beneficial, in both the short run and the long run, to the goal of social integration. But at the other extreme, that is in large cities, with available suburbs, and with a moderate to high proportion black, school desegregation, in particular compulsory racial balance, has proved disastrous to social integration, by greatly accelerating the loss of whites from the cities, and leading to racially divided metropolitan areas, with a black central city and white suburbs. The extent of this impact is not yet evident, because it is a snowballing effect, which has had only a short time to operate. But it is a policy that, carried out in the name of accomplishing the first goal of desegregation, that is elimination of de jure segregation, acts to defeat the third goal, the goal of achieving social integration. . . . Rather, straightforward elimination of de jure segregation in large cities would constitute primarily a redrawing of school attendance zones to eliminate gerrymandering, and would have little impact, one way or another, on the third goal of achieving social integration. That goal must be achieved by much more long range policies, involving residence at least as much as schools, policies that recognize both the needs and desires for ethnic community and those of ethnic integration.

Finally, James Coleman put his finger on the heart of the controversy:

> Any policy should not by design or consequence be punitive on families or children, whether in the name of redressing past wrongs or for other purposes. Much of the error in school desegregation policy has been the result of an unarticulated punitiveness which has no place in achieving positive social goals.

No question-and-answer period followed Mr. Coleman's speech.

Wednesday, March 31

In reading *One Flew over the Cuckoo's Nest* with the sophomores, I told them, "Don't read the swears."

They said, "We know those words."

I countered, "Your parents would be angry with me."

They said, "Our parents don't know what we're doing."

Lillian would not read the part of stuttering Billy, although she had accepted the part. She told me, "That's what you think of me. You send me to a reading tutor."

"It's just a part in a play," I urged. "You're only pretending to be someone else." Lillian had started remedial reading with tutors from the University of Massachusetts but refused to return when they asked her to write her autobiography.

The Crisis Prevention seminar met after school. I asked Dr. Kantar about the class reading of the play, *One Flew over the Cuckoo's Nest*. How should I react when the white students overdo the black dialect in the play, or when, for example, they read black dialect in the "Chitlings" test with exaggeration and relish? Do I say anything? Sometimes I know there has been malice because, in one case, I knew the boy. And what about the parts of blacks in the play—do I assign them to blacks?

"Ask the students how they feel about reading the dialect. It will give them a chance to express how they feel; and you won't be singling out the black students and putting them on the spot. It will show the black youngsters that there is someone there who cares about their feelings. Let them know that it bothers you, at least." About the assignment of parts, the psychiatrist commented, "You wouldn't assign females to males."

Thursday, April 1

Jerome Winegar was selected by Superintendent Fahey. He will arrive on April 19. The teachers with their petition, the parents of the South Boston Home and School Association, and the Boston School Committee have all publicly opposed him, but on he comes. Why?

Saturday, April 3

I went to a testimonial banquet for Arthur Perdigao. Arthur received a tremendous ovation, and Dr. Reid round after round of applause. Two priests, Father James Lane and Father Arthur DiPietro, flanked the ends of the head table.

A *Globe* sports reporter gave the address: There had been only three coaches at South Boston High School in fifty years, and it was a measure of the greatness of Coach Perdigao that he overcame obstacles like playing on four different fields and still led the team to city championship. He compared the Southie team to Notre Dame—so good that everyone wants to play against them, to get a piece of the action. Nowhere, not even at the Olympics, had he found a spirit like Southie's—it was unique. He praised their loyalty and courage, and asked them not to become divided, a message echoed by the priest who followed.

Arthur Perdigao spoke little, but said the team gave him "courage."

Football team members—only the white team members were there—were awarded gold medals and blue jackets. When Bill came into the team line-up, one of the younger boys, I noticed, patted him on the head. Later, my seniors, Bill and Tony, elegant in suit and vest, came over to me.

I said, "You look gorgeous."

They replied, "So do you."

Ms. Murphy was wearing a long black dress and black shawl with shiny beads. Alluding to her activism at school, she said, "The devil is very attractive."

A man beside me at the banquet, a postman, predicted Southie would not hold together. Those who can run, will run. Why should they stay where there is no field to play on? In Southie, there are training groups in baseball from the time kids are babies. Black kids from Roxbury can't play baseball, but they have to be on the team. "We can't win with them," he said. Again, the fear of the downward pull.

I met Dr. Reid afterward, the first time since his departure. I told him, "The snow muffled your going. We couldn't say goodbye the way we wanted."

Monday, April 5

In class I worked individually with the black students. Boycotting white students from South Boston and Charlestown marched to City Hall to protest Jerome Winegar, to demand a uniform code of discipline and a moratorium on busing, like East Boston, for two years.

The students met with City Council President Louise Day Hicks, in whose City Hall window the ROAR sign has hung for weeks. "They came in to get out of the cold," she explained, and were treated to refreshments. The students forwarded their grievances, then stood and pledged allegiance to the flag in the empty City Council chamber.

At the nearby federal building they made an abortive attempt to present their demands to Judge Garrity. Then, across City Hall Plaza in the path of the 250 departing boycotters came Theodore Landsmark, a black lawyer. Several youths attacked Landsmark in the face with the staff of the American flag they carried, breaking his nose and glasses. They knocked him down, and kicked him. One of my sophomores, identified by police from blow-ups of the news photo, took part in the attack.

An angry black Representative Mel King warned everyone that Boston was not safe; they should stay away from the Bicentennial celebrations. Mayor White countered that he could not guarantee the absolute safety of everyone in the city; his own aide had been shot through the head in the Back Bay on the night he passed the bar exam.

After school, the South Boston High faculty met in the library to hear the results of a telephone conversation with Jerome Winegar, still in St. Paul, Minnesota. The faculty senate president presided, reviewing the topics discussed:

Question: How many teachers are going to stay, how many to go?
Winegar: Anyone who wants to go, can. Only an idiot would clean house. He would observe at first. The process of change is very slow — but speeded up by the teachers.
Question: State troopers?
Winegar: He knew only what he read in the papers. He would have to analyze the situation when he came.
Question: Could you clarify your statements as reported in the article by Muriel Cohen that appeared in the Boston *Globe?*
Winegar: His statement on Afro picks was made not to the press, but to the administration. *Re* sensitivity training: This might occur in any school with black students. *Re* classes being dull and unimaginative: He had not been in a single classroom for any reporter to be able to quote him.

Tuesday, April 6

White students reported back today. I told them how disappointed I was about the attack on Landsmark, that they only hurt themselves by such incidents. Subdued, they looked toward their classmate's empty seat. A member of the integrated basketball team, the boy had never shown the slightest racial anger.

Wednesday, April 7

There were no problems in school, though buses were stoned at Technical High, and there were more stonings in the Mission Hill area of Roxbury.

My sophomore involved in the flag attack on Landsmark was back in class. I gave him a small part in the drama we were reading.

At the Crisis Prevention seminar after school, we discussed the incident. All the teachers agreed that the student body was depressed and ashamed about the incident. The boy was not "crazy," as one of the teachers, disgusted, speculated. But, Dr. Kantar said, the boy should be aware, as he probably is, that he did wrong, even though some community people might think or tell him he was cool.

The Massachusetts legislature fulminated about the Landsmark incident, resorting to epithets like "sons of bitches" and "bastards." Republican Whip William G. Robinson of Melrose introduced a resolution condemning the beating. It should be formulated, Representative Mel King, Black Caucus leader, had advised, not in terms of black and white, "but in terms of what's right and what's wrong. . . . You're either in support of what those bastards did, or you're not."

Landsmark, his face swathed in white bandages like a mummy, said, "It is the community leaders who manipulate and use the community for their own selfish gains and whose ambitions work to undermine the security of the community at large. Racism diverts people from the real issues, which are more economic than racial."

Judge Garrity today ordered the Boston School Committee to appoint Jerome Winegar as headmaster of South Boston High School. The School Committee complied with his order but "under protest and legal duress." Pixie Palladino voted against the hiring.

Friday, April 9

At the Bicentennial Ethnic Heritage meeting at the State House, I met Monsignor Geno Baroni, president of the National Center for Urban Ethnic Affairs in Washington.

Monsignor Baroni had urged blacks to go to the suburbs; it was a mistake to bus in the urban centers. He had said as much to Judge Garrity, but the judge didn't listen, he told me. Fr. Baroni, when asked about the Center's stand on busing for racial integration, had answered, "You should put the [children of] Ph.D.s on the first bus, [the children of] masters' degrees on the second bus, and the [children of] working people on the third bus. . . . It's a real matter of economic segregation here, and the burden is being put unfairly on the poor blacks and the working-class whites."

Monday, April 12

Graffiti is wild on the streets: GO HOME JEROME, RESIST on the school doors, with splashed red paint on the floors, and broken windows in the high school.

Tuesday, April 13

Mr. Jerome Winegar visited Superintendent Marion Fahey. A few ROAR parents waited outside her office to heckle him. Unruffled, he explained that he liked this part of the country, had long wanted to live here, and that this was a professional "opportunity" for him.

Thursday, April 15

After school in the high school library there was a voluntary, informal meeting of staff with Headmaster Winegar and Superintendent Fahey. A taller, bigger man than most, solidly set down in his shoes, with a face heavily pocked and wearing glasses, Mr. Winegar seemed basically honest and decent.

Mr. Winegar said he would like to make things work for the staff, students, parents, and community. "I know it is not going to be easy. There was a lot of resistance to my coming. We will keep goals in mind, and work toward those goals." He appeared calm and took notes on the comments and questions.

When Mr. Winegar said he had been calumniated and misquoted by columnist Muriel Cohen in the *Globe,* he struck a common chord with the staff. They attacked Marion Fahey instead, and through her the judge: her invisibility, ignoring them.

Saturday, April 17

South Boston men stoned two black bus drivers. White men came to their aid.

Monday, April 19 (Spring vacation, a week of violence)

It was unusually hot today — a record-breaking 94°. Richard Poleet, driving through Roxbury at 10:15 at night, stopped for a traffic light. As the light changed and his car moved forward, black youths pelted his car with rocks, one of them smashing through his windshield. He fell over sideways, his car veering out of control and sideswiping the car of a Puerto Rican who had stopped for the light on the other side of the street. Then Poleet's car came to a stop. The youths beat his face, hanging out the car door, to a pulp with rocks and fists. One stole his wallet. The Puerto Rican pulled the fire alarm. Then the youths fled. Police later counted fifty rocks around the car, and a chunk of concrete a foot long.

A witness identified the attackers.

A white retarded girl is on the critical list at City Hospital. Her father, trying to find his way out of a dead-end street in the unfamiliar Columbia Point housing project, had found his car blocked by angry black youths with bricks.

In the nights that followed, there was rock-throwing in Hyde Park, West Roxbury, Roxbury, and Roslindale. Firemen answering alarms were stoned.

In South Boston, the marshals warned outside agitators to stay away.

Boston is now a city "in trouble." Because racial polarization had reached the "flash point," Maceo Dixon said, he was canceling a probusing march for Friday. Instead, at noon Mayor White and Senators Kennedy and Brooke, the standardbearers of the American flag, led an army of men of good will in a "Procession for Peace" from the Boston Common to Boston City Hall.

Later, Senator Kennedy answered questions for a Boston *Phoenix* reporter:

Question: If you were a resident of Boston and had school-aged children, would you send them to the public schools in Boston today?

Kennedy: Probably not.

Question: Why not?

Kennedy: Because I can afford to send them to private schools. Because I think I can get a better education for them.

Question: Especially in view of the current tension in Boston, could you blame any Boston parents, black or white, who'd be afraid to send their children to school when it reopens after spring vacation?

Kennedy: That's obviously a subjective kind of decision. Could you blame someone? No. But would you hope they'd send the children? Yes.

Question: Would you favor extending the Boston school desegregation plan beyond the city limits?

Kennedy: I don't think that makes sense.

Monday, April 26 (Vacation ends)

The outside doors of the school have been coated over with paint to hide the angry graffiti. Inside the school, the rooms have all been painted; lunchroom table graffiti has been obliterated by new rainbow-colored formica tops; floors have been tiled; new equipment provided for the gym. There are window shades at every window; four small and two large new administration offices have been constructed at the back of the auditorium under the balcony; a copier has been installed in the business office for the teachers to use at will.

Today was Jerome Winegar's first day as headmaster.

At the school doors, the white students demonstrated and refused to enter the building. Two boys were arrested for refusing to obey police orders to move. Jerome Winegar told the media cameras, lined up behind the large P R E S S lettering on the sidewalk, "I would have been a fool if I didn't expect this."

During my senior English class, with three white students in attendance, four bells sounded.

"A bomb scare," I explained. They were upset and nervous; I wasn't.

After the black students had been evacuated to the Bayside Mall, the whites waited in the cold and wet outside without coats until the building had been searched.

"How come they let the niggers go first?" Sean asked.

By the time the all-clear sounded, it was lunchtime.

Tuesday, April 27

The school was quiet. Class day rehearsals are in full swing.

During a break, I talked to a trooper who had grown up in South Boston about the "tough-guy" reputation of Southie kids. He said, "I literally had to fight my way from corner to corner. My last name was Lithuanian, though I had an Irish mother. The kids would mispronounce my name and I would fight. I wanted to get on the athletic team. I had to fight five guys. I fought three one day, and got so tired, I quit. They let me fight the other two the next day. But that was thirty years ago."

Thursday, April 29

Hyde Park High evacuated for a bomb scare. Outside the students divided up racially and threw rocks at each other. Police were sent there from South Boston. The school closed for the day.

Headmaster Winegar placed letters in the faculty mailboxes, asking to meet individually with all teachers, whether or not we had asked to transfer out.

Friday, May 7

It was Senior Class Day.

No administrators attended the activities, or addressed the 40 parents. Mr. Winegar had a previous engagement in Chicago, which he was unable to break, he said. A few troopers leaned against the auditorium wall, sipping coffee, then walked out.

The art background and costumes of the class show were magnificent, but some seniors had been smoking marijuana and others forgot their lines. The old nauseous fear, which made hair stand on end, swept briefly back when two black girls mimed a song from *West Side Story*. "Somewhere, somewhere . . . There's a place for us, A time and place for us. Hold my hand and we're halfway there . . . ," they sang. Their voices were flat, I thought, not realizing they were only miming the record. At the end, the Southie audience, always liberal with either criticism or praise, booed.

An administrator commented later that they could feel the sadness wafting up to them in the front lobby from down below at the reception and dance, where a few seniors, including one black girl from Puerto Rico, clustered together at the back of the gym and danced, watched by 40 state troopers.

Friday, May 14

It was the seniors' last day.

I left my class of four sophomore boys and went down to the first floor, where the senior homerooms had been clustered together for safety purposes. I collected books from students and gave ivory elephant pins to any of my seniors I could locate.

I said good-by to Tony. Good Tony: hockey star, football star, Pinocchio in the class day show, beautifully balancing himself with supertrained muscles. He called me "kid" — "So long, kid. Take care of yourself." He had tears in his eyes.

I said good-by to Rory, with his Irish red hair, who told me yesterday, "The judge didn't take the school; he took the community. The people don't care anymore. How do I know? Look at their houses. They paint all over them: RESIST and NEVER. The kids sleep until afternoon, and hang around the streets all night, drinking beer. Look at Landsmark. Those kids knew the police were there, but they didn't care. No, they'll never accept Winegar."

I said good-by to Matthew, who shares with me a fondness for Kurt Vonnegut novels.

Gentle, very literate and married Ruth from Roxbury was not there; nor Rose, a Muslim in turban, long dress, and smile, who came closest to death when she tried to save her dog caught in the railroad tracks; nor peace-loving Bob, who had enjoyed riding the yellow bus to Roxbury last year, and who had already left for the armed services. Bill, football and hockey star, was not there either—good Bill, whose mother was dead and whose father had died just before they won the city hockey championship. Nor the Southie girls, so sweet and gentle you would almost not know they were in class. All special people; they were survivors.

Sean grabbed his elephant pin and left in a hurry, going off with a roar with the other seniors through a line of troopers and administrators blocking out a one-way exit route from homerooms to the front door.

A mother, an aide who worked in the business office, became hysterical as she saw her son marched out through the line of police. "That's my son," she cried. "He's not a prisoner from Walpole."

True. So much school time has been wasted, what loss would there have been if the other students had been sent home early to allow a dignified and warm good-by for seniors who have put up for two years with all kinds of indignities?

Monday, May 17

The state troopers heralded spring with short-sleeved shirts but not, like last year, their Smokey-the-Bear, wide-brimmed hats. They have been demoralized also and can see the discipline slide without Dr. Reid.

Wednesday, May 19

Today was the bimonthly faculty meeting, Mr. Winegar's first. Although he knew he was being nicknamed "Howard Hughes" because of his invisibility, he still hoped to see all the staff personally; he had only 20 teachers left to see. Then his door would be open the way it should be.

In his administration, Mr. Winegar said, he might retain one administrator, but the rest would leave. There would be no heads of departments. Instead, an administrator would be assigned to attend the department meetings. Neither of the administrators he would bring in—Tim Murphy nor Ron Rosenbaum—was from his junior high school in St. Paul, but had come originally from the New England area. Tim Murphy's specialty was an alternate "school-within-a-school," and Mr. Rosenbaum's specialty was "disturbed" schools.

Mr. Winegar did not believe in working from the top down. Teachers should initiate change, he said, and he would support them.

In a grand gesture, Mr. Winegar said he would recommend that the L-Street Annex, formerly housing the ninth-grade overflow from the high school, be returned to the residents of South Boston, as promised, because he could not come up with an alternative plan for its use by the June deadline.

The meeting was then open for questions from teachers. Some of them I found plaintive:

Will you jump into a fight when one starts, like the rest of us?

Will you tell the press about our being good teachers, as you've told us?

Will you institute the "sweep" of corridors again to get students back into classes? He would, he promised, or get them somewhere else.

Andy Vaccari from guidance tendered an opinion that "merit" was important, not "quotas." "Yes, Andy, I agree with you," Mr. Winegar said, "but the court stipulates a certain minority."

The meeting at last expended itself with an indictment and defense of last Friday's dismissal of the seniors. Mr. Gizzi, administrator, said, "When we explained to the parents that it was better not to have a kid's head split open, they agreed that we did the right thing."

Friday, May 21

During the past week, the "landmark" case involving Siegfried was decided, receiving national attention because it required adjudication on the question: When did death occur? When the brain died, and attending the victim was like attending a corpse?—or when the doctors—two Boston City Hospital doctors—"pulled the plug"—disconnected a respirator, and the victim's heart stopped?

"A human heart can be kept beating in a dish," the prosecutor Mundy argued.

The "grisly" story of Siegfried began late last summer in the wake of the furor generated by the demonstration of blacks to desegregate Carson Beach in South Boston. On August 24, Siegfried, an employee in Mother's Market in Columbia Point, waited across the street until his victim, a white suburbanite who had stopped for cigarettes, left the store. Siegfried then crept up behind the man as he walked to his car and hit him over the head with a baseball bat. The sound of the bash could be heard 200 feet away. Identified by several witnesses from the project, Siegfried pleaded, "Not guilty."

Mundy told the jury: "He did what he did simply because the man was a different color . . . that is the only inference that can be drawn."

Siegfried was found guilty of first degree murder and sentenced to life imprisonment in Walpole State Prison.

Few students were in today, there were so many field trips: to the Salem Museum, to horseback riding, to the Thompson Island harbor program. "We'll soon have a school-without-a-school, not a school-within-a-school," one teacher quipped.

President Ford had instructed Attorney General Edward Levi to find a test case for a Justice Department challenge to court-ordered school busing by means of a "friend-of-the-court" brief filed with the U.S. Supreme Court. Boston was discussed as a possibility. Probusing groups have threatened violence if the court intervenes, and antibusing groups if it does not. Senator Kennedy did not ask the attorney general to stay out of the case, as did the Civil Liberties Union, but for a speedy intercession "if there is to be" one.

An angry Roy Wilkins, executive director of the NAACP, asked, "Why now?"

Monday, May 24

I kept my interview with Headmaster Winegar. Curriculum was his forte, he told me. He had become an administrator to wield curriculum power. Mrs. Geraldine Kozberg, whom he would bring to South Boston High as director of program development, had been his superior in St. Paul and "taught me everything I know," he said.

To me the school psychiatrist commented later, "Oh, he brought his 'mother' with him!"

Wednesday, May 26

It was senior prom tonight. None of the suburban administrators came, nor Mr. Winegar, who had been asked not to, and no blacks. Dr. Reid, the guest of the seniors, moved around among the students and teachers.

Thursday, May 27

There is talk of disbanding half of the $250,000 Citywide Coordinating Council, the CCC. Seventeen members of the CCC, only one of them with children in the Boston schools, used Boston tax money for a mailgram to Attorney General Levi, asking him not to intervene in the Boston busing case.

President Ford is becoming boldly antibusing. Presidential hopeful Governor Jimmy Carter said he is against forced busing, but would uphold the law of the land. He begins his speeches on busing with the comment, "I never saw a rich kid bused."

Friday, May 28

After a fight I witnessed between two girls, I followed the trooper who led the slender black combatant, her blouse pulled open at the neck, down to the holding room. I felt sorry for her. The young trooper, still panting from the exertion, examined his arms for marks. "You look scared," his sergeant observed to him.

I was amazed that the other girl's boyfriend did not intervene. "Why should I?" he asked. "She was winning. Besides, they would just suspend me then."

That was true. There is suspension for the "third-man-in," the hockey rule. "You are automatically suspended because it wasn't your business," Dr. Reid had said.

Saturday, May 29

Attorney General Levi announced he would not intervene in the Boston busing case at this time. In response, Louise Day Hicks sent out signals; she prayed there "will be no violence—people are so frustrated."

Saturday night, torches were thrown through the windows of Filene's, Jordan Marsh, and other downtown stores. The gift shop of the *U.S.S. Constitution* suffered $75,000 damage from fire. A splinter group promised to frustrate all Bicentennial activities this summer in Boston.

Tuesday, June 1

On the sidewalk outside the high school someone had meticulously printed overnight: STOP FORCED BUSING.

Late in the evening a dynamite stick was set off at America's favorite pet rock—Plymouth Rock, blasting its way into the national news.

Thursday, June 3

Judge Garrity ordered the School Committee to approve the appointment of twenty-seven-year-old Timothy B. Murphy and twenty-eight-year-old Ronald S. Rosenbaum to $22,000-a-year positions at South Boston High. They had been working, Judge Garrity said, "day and night in a determined effort to help promote both peaceful and quality education at South Boston High." Tim Murphy would assume the post of head of the English Department.

"He's only two years older than I am," Paul Moran, teacher, complained. "What do you expect in W. Arthur Garrity High School?"

Boston School Committee Chairman John J. McDonough summarized the anger, "If there needs to be any clearer indication that Judge Garrity is running the School Department, this is it. The whole situation has become absolutely absurd. . . . For what purpose are we elected by the people if our decisions on policy and personnel are in fact worthless?"

Sunday, June 6

In a *Herald* newspaper interview with Eleanor Roberts, Mr. Winegar referred to the "super-guy Reid," and said, "He loved those kids. I'm sure he did." It would take a long time for them to build that trust in him — "if it ever comes," he said.

Monday, June 7

At the evening meeting of the biracial council, Ms. Murphy supported, prophetically, it turned out, one of the white parents opposed to the selection of School Committeewoman Pixie Palladino as commencement speaker instead of a more moderate school committeewoman like Kathleen Sullivan. Ms. Murphy cited the disruption of the public assembly at English High, when Pixie had led Paul in breaking the law. Mr. Corscadden, who was also present, explained that the decision had already been made a week earlier, and the programs were in the press.

Mr. Winegar is not aware enough to refuse Pixie a forum.

Today Tom Atkins announced that the NAACP plans no demonstration for this summer, no repeat of the Carson Beach episode in South Boston last summer, and no participation by the NAACP in the march on Bunker Hill proposed by the National Student Coalition Against Racism.

Wednesday, June 9

"Southie is graduating," I overheard a policeman on my way into the John Hancock Hall in the Back Bay. A few helmeted TPF motorcycle cops stood by on the alert, but, with graduation in a building next to police headquarters, and walkie-talkie police communication, there couldn't be much trouble.

Making last-minute preparations on the stage, Mr. Winegar said hopefully, "If all goes well, we're in business."

John Kennedy, Mr. South Boston, led the class of 1976 in procession to their seats. Noreen Curley — Sister Seraphia — reached out and hugged each black girl as she came down the aisle. Ms. Murphy cried. Joan Dazzi, coordinator and choreographer of the integrated class day show, stood at the front of the auditorium with Boston police detective Charlie Famolare, looking out over the graduates as they seated themselves before the stage.

School Committeewoman Pixie Palladino delivered the commencement address. She exalted liberty and freedom. Here Mr. Winegar applauded. Then, diverging from her printed text, she excoriated abridgment of rights, telling the seniors they had gotten a taste of life in the treatment afforded them by Levi, Ford, and the liberal planners from suburbia, who had less intelligence than any one senior had in his little finger.

"She was really getting into it," a few seniors commented later, dismayed at the intrusion of busing into the festive mood of graduation. People unconsciously began to cough and to move around in their seats. About 20 blacks left the hall to congregate in the entrance lobby, yelling, "Get her off, get her out of there." The police restored order there.

Pixie talked about *her* neighborhoods that she would defend: Charlestown, South Boston, East Boston, Hyde Park, failing to mention Roxbury and Dorchester, the black or mixed neighborhoods. A white woman behind me, her face flushed, protested, "I'm from Dorchester."

When Pixie had finished, a black man with seven children sitting in front of me, booed. His children looked at him, startled. I thought, "Kids learning to hate, like in Northern Ireland."

Then the seniors mounted the steps to the stage, received their diplomas from Pixie — including eleven black girls, without protest — and filed past Mr. Winegar, who stood uncomfortably watching, like a cat, ready to reach out his hand if there was a positive sign from a student — barely touching the hand of some, quickly withdrawing his hand when there was no response. Mrs. Barrett, an aide and mother of a graduating senior, had earlier gone downstairs to the dressing rooms and pleaded with the seniors to shake hands with Mr. Winegar. Some did, but I overheard one senior boy in the lobby, "He held out his hand. I raised mine and said, 'Up yours!' I got that much out of him."

One of the black senior girls, presented with a bouquet of roses, was booed loudly by her white classmates. In the November receivership hearings, she had given discredited testimony against Big Red. The girl's mother left with bowed head.

At the close of ceremonies, the seniors tossed their hats in the air, some of them skimming the stage, and one of them sailing directly at Mr. Winegar. "It was deliberate," Joan Dazzi said, standing beside the seniors. Mr. Winegar turned his back as if he didn't notice. "Sure, the kids skimmed their hats on the platform, but I was behind the podium and the other people on the platform had to do all the ducking," he told Eleanor Roberts of the *Herald*.

In all, 45 girls and 75 boys, 12 of them black, were awarded diplomas, though not all seniors were there to receive them.

I saw Bill and Tony in the lobby afterward. They kissed my cheek, but didn't stay to chat: "I've got to hurry."

I felt sorry for Mr. Winegar. "Don't," a trooper told me. "He knew what he was getting into."

Thursday, June 10

The Boston School Committee, on order of Judge Garrity, approved the appointment of Tim Murphy and Ron Rosenbaum to South Boston High.

Friday, June 11

Almost no students were in. The attendance in my three English classes totaled six students.

After school, the faculty met for a social at the Tennis Club in South Boston. Mr. Winegar arrived later with Detective Famolare and other plainclothes police.

Earlier in the day, Ms. Murphy, going out to the Hill Stop Delicatessen to buy a sandwich, had run into two white girl students on their way in to Mr. Winegar's office to present their list of "demands" for next year, including a smoking room and chocolate milk in the cafeteria. She said, "They showed me a small white paper coffin, perfectly made. It said on the top, 'THE LAST BIRD TO FLY IN FROM ST. PAUL.' It never occurred to me to lift the top. I just urged them to hurry to keep their 11:00 appointment."

Ms. Murphy, continually grateful that Mr. Winegar is a doctoral candidate and not a "jock" like the headmaster of Hyde Park High, praised Mr. Winegar, when she had an opportunity, for doing "just beautifully at graduation," and asked him about the girls.

"They came in drunk," Mr. Winegar responded.

"Oh, yes," Ms. Murphy said, "they told me they were going to breathe their beery breath all over you."

Mr. Winegar continued, "They gave me the coffin. I opened it, and there was a dead bird in it. I picked it up, listened to its heart and talked and talked about it until the situation was defused. Then we discussed their demands. I'm just glad it wasn't a rat."

Monday, June 14

Sixty fewer teachers than last year attended the annual faculty party. Their morale has been "shattered" by the receivership, Captain Hurley observed. There were no troopers. Jerome Winegar and his two aides, Tim Murphy and Ron Rosenbaum, sat with the kitchen staff by the front door.

After dinner, Dr. Reid was presented with his portrait in oil painted by a South Boston High graduate to be hung on the school walls with other past headmasters: Dr. William Reid, 1965-1975. The portrait perspective is from below, looking up to Dr. Reid standing at a podium that could be the wheel of a ship. "Orders come and you obey them. You go along with the boss and you make your adjustment," he had told *Herald* reporter Eleanor Roberts on his dismissal from South Boston High School.

The teachers rose and gave him a standing ovation.

Today the U.S. Supreme Court upheld Judge Garrity's Phase 2 desegregation plan, refusing to review the appeals of the Boston School Committee, Mayor White, the Boston Home and School Association, and the Boston Teachers Union.

Final exams were given during regular class time. There was no attempt to hold an exam schedule or film festival like last year. Some students chose to write on "Busing" as an optional essay question. Some random samples were:

I think busing is alright if the parents and kids want to go to better schools. I don't think any kid should be forced to go to a school that he doesn't want to. Desegrating school, to make them half black half white ect. ect. is only going to ruin the kids lives. Trying to make them to be friends with other races is to hard for some kids to ajust. They should have just let us stayed where we wanted too stay, in our neighborhood.

A white girl from Roxbury

Busing in my mind is the most serious problem this country is facing because it doesn't help the school system, when the whites leave the schools, and the white people are forced to a lower level of education to "equal education." It violates both the rights of Blacks and whites to be forced in a bus. It not only fails to "equal education," it also puts the racial situation in trouble putting black against whites.

A white boy

I think that forced busing is wrong. It is a waste of time and money. All the politicians and judges say it is for a better education, if they put all the money that it has cost for the past two years to better schools and better learning devices, I think it would make everyone happier. They almost had to close the schools earlier because they were running out of money. It is just a ridicoulous scituation where the only ones that are getting the short end of the deal are the students.

A white girl

I think busing is for the birds because before busing started most high schools were open. If you had a study period you could go outside if you wanted to and you didn't have to eat the lunch in this school. You could go out and get a sandwich or something. Now most schools in the city of Boston are like prisons especially South Boston High School.

A white boy

I'm all against busing myself because if the community doesn't want you then you shouldn't go. But no one can really stop you from going somewhere that you feel that you have an opportunity to learn even if the tension is high.

A black girl

I think that they should not bus kids from one place to another. Most kids enjoy going to school in there own neighborhood without having to worry about any one stoning the buses or calling you names.

A black girl

It is not worth sending kids to school for the agony and lack of education that they would get if they were bused. It is against the constitution that says we have the right to choose what we want and to be free, and with busing we don't get those rights, and plus I'm prejudiced and I hate niggers.

A white boy

After final exams, I tabulated the cumulative attendance for the sewing teacher, Sara Elbery, who had left a month earlier. I didn't know the students; many of them had not attended school in June. Many had entered late and dropped out early. Of the 31 students assigned to the classroom, nine students—four boys and five girls—had never appeared. From a possible total of 178 school days, the year's attendance read:

| Students | Number of Days | | |
	Present	Absent	Tardy
Boy	118	57	13
Boy	116	60	23
Boy	149	27	9
Boy	56	115	2
Boy	128	43	17
Boy	2	58	0
Boy	14	56	1
Boy	151	24	10
Boy	95	71	0
Boy	39	17	3
Boy	138	37	3
Boy	31	103	0
Boy	48	89	17
Girl	99	76	0
Girl	24	150	0
Girl	119	52	0
Girl	7	117	3
Girl	25	113	0
Girl	71	112	1
Girl	97	76	1
Girl	7	127	0
Girl	61	115	0

September 8, 1975. Boston police commissioner Robert diGrazia, left, and Mayor Kevin White discuss the opening of Boston schools. AP/Wide World.

September 8, 1975. Metropolitan District Police stand guard against the silhouette of the Bunker Hill Monument as Phase 2 desegregation expands to include Charlestown. AP/Wide World.

September 8, 1975. Members of the SWAT team of the Boston Police Department watch from the roof of Charlestown High School. *The Pilot*, photograph by Philip A. Stack.

September 9, 1975. A sanguine Dr. William J. Reid responds to reporters outside South Boston High School on the second day of Phase 2 desegregation. *Boston Herald.*

December 9, 1975. Federal Judge W. Arthur Garrity places South Boston High School in receivership and orders the transfer of the football coach and the entire administrative staff of the school. *Boston Herald.*

January 25, 1976. Members of ROAR demonstrate outside Hyde Park High School. *Boston Herald.*

January 29, 1976. Byram Cossie, principal of Newell High School in Port Elizabeth, Republic of South Africa, poses with students and the author in the library of South Boston High School. Photograph by Dean Yarborough.

March 14, 1976. South Boston politicians celebrate St. Patrick's Day: Senator William Bulger, president of the Massachusetts State Senate, at the microphone; Representative Raymond Flynn; and City Council president Louise Day Hicks. *Boston Herald.*

April 15, 1976. Newly appointed headmaster Jerome Winegar and superintendent Marion Fahey visit South Boston High School. Behind them is interim headmaster Jim Corscadden. *Boston Herald.*

April 5, 1976. Boycotting students attack Theodore Landsmark at City Hall Plaza. Photograph by Stanley Forman (Pulitzer Prize).

September 8, 1976. Phase 2B desegregation begins. It is 6:45 A.M. outside South Boston High School. *Boston Globe.*

May 12, 1977. Police stand guard after a stick of dynamite was discovered in the high school parking lot. "GO HOME JEROME YOU FAILED" graffiti refers to headmaster Jerome Winegar. AP/Wide World.

Phase 2B Desegregation, 1976–77

At the faculty meeting before school opened, Mr. Winegar spoke optimistically about putting files and desks in the front lobby holding rooms, referred to by Judge Garrity as *"dungeons"* or *"oubliettes,"* described caustically in his "rationale" for receivership of South Boston High:

> *These rooms, in effect, isolation cells, are approximately fifteen feet long and eight feet wide with ceilings ten to twelve feet high. There is a row of four to six chairs permanently affixed to the floor in each room, with folding seats. There are no windows. The large, single door to each room is solid wood and is cut into independent top and bottom sections. During classes, only the bottom half is closed. Between classes, both sections are closed and the students within have no visual contact with the corridor. The air inside the holding rooms is stale, and, especially in the white holding room, is permeated with odors from the gymnasium underneath.*

Mr. Winegar expressed disapproval of "all the screwballs hanging out of the holding room doors," hyper students and minor offenders, with "the whole batch going bananas." He would like to find a place more remote from the front lobby, he said, to soften the initial shock on visitors arriving in the school and to deflect insults hurled at them. In fact, no change was made during the year, except for a brief period, when the black students expended their rage by tearing off the wall boards and were placed in the white student holding room instead. But, by year's end, his plan was realized and several new auxiliary holding rooms had been built in the basement— true *"oubliettes."*

Cardboard signs labeled "Senior Advisor Room" were placed above the holding room doors, where they remained for months. The large sign listing contraband weapons forbidden in the school was again lifted to the walls between the black and white *"oubliettes"*: NO TONIC IN CANS, BOTTLES, KNIVES, CHUCKS, METAL PICKS, NAIL FILES, JACK KNIVES, NAIL CLIPPERS, SCISSORS OR GUNS; ALL OBJECTS WITH SHARP POINTS.

After Mr. Winegar had addressed the faculty, Captain George Kimball of the state police spoke. Then Mr. Ron Rosenbaum, new administrator and expert in "troubled schools," put his foot on the cafeteria bench and outlined disciplinary steps he had set up for tardiness. The intricacies of how many tardinesses warranted a suspension was interrupted by a message from Mr. Corscadden, who had been called away to the front office and returned pale and shaken to report that "something was happening in the vicinity of the building." Teachers could continue the meeting, or leave. Fear rustled through the teachers as imaginations conjured up the "thing" happening. We scattered like blown leaves to our cars, driving away over the painted, tire-streaked graffiti in front of the high school: GO HOME JEROME.

But, as South Boston High School again moved into first place in the city for the third year in a row in the number of school suspensions, tardiness became irrelevant and was never mentioned again. A new word—"separation"—was coined to curb the skyrocketing suspension numbers. It was a cosmetic rather than an essential evolution, however, the difference being explained to us: Suspension is for a specified time and the letter is mailed; separation is for one day or the remainder of the day and the letter is student-delivered. But, in either case, the student is readmitted only with a parent. If students were not in class when the bell rang, sweep teams "separated" them out of the building; readmittance to the school required a parents' conference. In addition, under a new discipline code, headmasters were given the option of suspending students for 20 days for involvement in physical assault, an option until then "not available to us," Mr. Winegar said.

The myriad media representatives from around the world waited behind the white P R E S S letters painted on the sidewalk outside the iron school gates for the action that never came as the students returned to school by grades: Wednesday, the ninth grade; Thursday, the tenth grade; and Friday, the eleventh and twelfth grades for a half day. On the following Monday, when the press had gone and the whole student body returned, the violence began. Battle calls were sounded, and the school rumbled. Students rampaged over the basement, first and second floors, thudding and screaming down the stairs. One trooper called me aside while a group of white boys marched by in an angry pack. "Army maneuvers," he explained, wryly. Teachers and guidance personnel pulled students into rooms away from the herding beast. Troopers' faces were clouded with fear—wearing gloves, videotaping the fights, although Captain Kimball promised the information would be locked up and kept confidential—not pulled out in a few years and used against the students when they went job hunting. Ms. Murphy protested the videotaping under the First Amendment; Mr. Winegar agreed with the qualms of the parents about the abuse of power. The videotaping stopped.

In English class I read the seniors a short story by John Galsworthy, called "The Pack." The moral of the tale was clear: People who run in a pack lose their sense of decency. I asked the students to write a paragraph describing a pack situation. I wondered whether they would recognize their behavior in the corridors. They wrote:

> An example of people in a pack, are the kids at South Boston High. The blacks have their pack, and the whites have theirs. And when someone gets in a fight they all jump in to help their own pack.
>
> A white girl

> Two years ago when we had a riot in South Boston High including a stabbing of a white youth, and the people of South Boston got together and came up to the school to try to beat up the black students of South Boston High.
>
> A black girl

> People who run in packs sometimes don't loose their dignity. These people aren't animals when they are fighting for something that they think is wrong. When people sometimes riot in the streets in South Boston, it is for a reason. This reason is to stop forced busing, which is wrong in every way.
>
> A white boy

> A street gang: When you become a member of a gang, you do as they do whether it's stealing, fighting or whatever, but I think the people who do these things really have no sense of individuality from the beginning, so they join these groups to try to find who they really are; but end up being some one else, under the illusion that their being themselves.
>
> A black girl

The school psychiatrist commented that having the students read "The Pack" was an excellent idea because they might step back and see their behavior objectively rather than jump instinctively into the pack the next time.

On Monday, September 13, as she was leaning over a black student lying on the office cot, the nurse was knocked back against a steel file and lost consciousness. The statement of the nurse, accused last year of selling bandaids for ten cents, saved the school that day. It was an accident, she said. "I am sure he meant no harm." At one o'clock the school was put under the control of the state police. At the height of the melee, I showed a trooper my trembling hand. He said, "When the teachers go, we go." While the teachers met with Mr. Winegar in an emergency meeting after school, parents gathered outside the school and sang "Go Home, Jerome" to the tune of "Good Night, Irene."

The nurse temporarily lost the sight in her eye, and suffered periodic dizzy spells afterward. "Dr. Reid," she said ruefully, "would have hovered around me like a mother hen." She did not return to work.

Some of the school chaos originated among students who simply did not know where to go. Two of the most experienced programmers had been ordered removed by court order because they were administrators: Jack Kennedy, Mr. South Boston, and Ernie Ryan, so crippled he rarely left the programming room, who died of heart trouble before the close of the last academic year. The reading room was firebombed on July 13, 1976, and all materials destroyed or condemned because of water fungus. Mr. Fred Murphy of the reading department immediately inventoried the material destroyed and made out a requisition for repair of the room and replacement of books. Instead, Mr. Winegar spent some of his summer hours on Thompson Island watching a film on "problem solving," as reported by Muriel Cohen of the *Globe*, while he waited for Mrs. Kozberg, his $30,000-a-year curriculum development "expert," to be hired by court order.

Thus, in September and October, 1976, although there was documented evidence that a large number of students read only in the first percentile, the reading rooms were still unusable, books not purchased. Students assigned to reading programs wandered the halls and auditorium looking for their classes and teachers while teachers scouted for books.

Sister Norine Curley, a language teacher, complained about teaching in the halls. She asked Mr. Corscadden, "Would you like your children [in suburban Wellesley] treated this way?"

Before the end of October, two of the best and most experienced reading teachers had transferred.

At the faculty meeting, Mrs. Kozberg reported she agreed with a school headquarters administrator who said teachers should be "reviewed for burnout."

Mr. Winegar's other major appointment, Tim Murphy, although appointed head of the English department, made his priorities the new cluster programs, which, he acknowledged, consumed 80 percent of his time because "they *have* to be *successful* the first two years." Instead, authority to assign teaching programs was given to a business department teacher. When programs were distributed to English teachers the day before school opened and minor or major adjustments could have been made, Tim Murphy was at Boston City Hospital in the South End with a cluster program.

Although the high school clusters were assigned an average of five regular teachers, an aide, and 50 to 80 students, other classes like my senior college English class, with three months to prepare for the college board exams, had fifty-three students and not enough chairs. As problems in the English department became exacerbated, Mr. Winegar told the English teachers he would act as head of department, if we liked. He didn't see the need for centralization, ignoring the fact that there was no one to meet and direct long-term English substitutes, to select books, or to organize and assign duties, such as responsibility for the book room.

At a teachers' meeting on September 29, Ms. Murphy complained, "One fortieth of the year has gone by and nothing's happened."

I whispered to her, "One thirty-sixth."

She replied, "Round it off. That makes it memorable."

Adjustments of schedules were not made until the middle of October. In the interim, classes were supervised by substitutes. On October 6, 1976, Ms. Murphy gave Mr. Winegar the "golden doorknob award." She left the knob on his desk so he could see it while he addressed the faculty meeting after school. Afterward, Ms. Murphy explained to him that the doorknob came from room 320, which has been assigned substitute teachers all day, and was destroyed by lunchtime, with the American flag out the window and the doorknob off the door. The golden doorknob, she said, was to remind him how many subs there were in the building.

In my ninth-grade English class, my students asked, "Why do we always have substitutes?"

"What classes?" I asked.

"Math and science."

Margie, a student from my sophomore class last year, told me in the library as she sat and helped me file library shelf list cards, "I've had four teachers in history since the beginning of the year—two teachers and two subs. We are guinea pigs." When Judge Garrity came by last year, she had told me, "He don't care about us."

But while substitutes proliferated, so did administrators. Besides Tim Murphy, Ron Rosenbaum, and Mrs. Geraldine Kozberg, three more black administrators were added. In addition, several successful history and English teachers were taken out of the classroom for most of the day and put in charge of discipline, tasks formerly administered by administrators, while one male English teacher was assigned to compile and supervise the writing of incident reports. Another male teacher was taken out of his geography classes to coordinate bus and van transportation of students and faculty in and out of the school. Temporary substitutes took up the slack. Ms. Murphy complained to Mr. Winegar at the faculty meeting that the students needed male role models in the classroom. Where were the male role models? She had met a lawyer during the past summer who told her he was prosecuting six Southie youths for first-degree murder.

On October 21, 1976, Ms. Murphy had enough and demanded out. She lifted a finger and said, "Get me the van."

As federal money inundated South Boston High under the aegis of Mrs. Kozberg, ESAA (Emergency School Aid Act) programs proliferated like cancer growths, again drawing off regular staff for programs that involved a handful of students: the after-school suspension program—the "Educational Siberia" from 2:00 to 4:00 for one or two students; the "Quest" program for a small handful of "underachieving" students. ESAA money provided also for the in-school suspension program for a handful of students, four personnel and two rooms; a theater group to work with the cluster programs; trips to Thompson Island; and a poet-in-residence, James Humphrey, who worked with a few classes at a consultant fee of $75 a day. Copies of his book, *The Re-Learning*, were purchased at $2.50 apiece for students, and $1,000 was set aside for the publication of a book of student poems, although there was no money for books in regular English programs. Teachers who needed them could do without or buy their own.

South Boston residents protested James Humphrey's weary, middle-aged poems in *The Re-Learning*, his unzipping "to piss" into the clear water bowl in "Something at Night," or the poem entitled "First Communion"— about tarnished lovers, not the religious sacrament that a fifteen-year-old sophomore from a Catholic working-class community might expect. But, according to Muriel Cohen of the *Globe*, the charges by some teachers that the poems were "vulgar" and "obscene" were viewed by "one school official" as an attempt to "sabotage new programs operating under court-ordered receivership at the high school." Muriel Cohen's article cited the nomination of Humphrey's book for "two of the most prestigious prizes in

U.S. literary circles this year" — the Pulitzer and the National Book Award [He didn't win either prize] — and concluded with a quotation from the South Boston Information Center flyer being distributed in the community with selections from Humphrey's book: "The South Boston Information Center feels that the taxpayers of the City of Boston have a right to know how their hard earned Tax Dollars are being spent. . . . You Be The Judge!"

Ms. Murphy used to demand to be informed. After she left in October, the "open" administration ceased. Teachers were unable to recognize who was a part of the staff and who was not, since so many people had been added as ESAA peripheral staff, and voluntary, informational faculty meetings, where the new teachers might have been introduced, were discontinued. There were no student assemblies as there had been in the first year-and-a-half of busing under Dr. Reid — just several rooms at a time — and no senior class day show.

South Boston High School teams again won the city hockey and football championships, but the pre-Thanksgiving football rally was canceled because eggs had been brought into the school, and one landed on Mr. Winegar. Student lockers were broken into and searched for eggs. The blue-and-red school streamers festooning the walls of the auditorium drooped for days after the canceled assembly. The following Monday, classes were held in homerooms until 8:40 when enough substitutes had arrived to cover classes. In the homeroom period, Mr. Winegar spoke on the intercom, and, in a midwestern accent, congratulated the team on their Thanksgiving Day win: "We did ourselves proud on Thanksgiving. Take the battle now to Nickerson Field." He was booed in the senior homerooms.

But the battle was taken to the Division III Super Bowl playoff at Nickerson Field. There were spots from the game on TV. The Southie football players, who had been described in the pregame publicity as "Sand Bags" pitted against the Newburyport "Sea Wall" and who averaged twenty-five pounds less than the Newburyport team, were flicked off the opposing players like flies, and slithered across the field in the wet, snow-moistened mud. The audience was well behaved until half-time, when a dress band wearing pom-pom high hats marched across the field, twirling batons, blaring their instruments. The band had been hired to play in behalf of South Boston at the suggestion of School Committeewoman Pixie Palladino, but no one told the Southie fans, who mistook the band for Newburyport High's one-upmanship.

It was too much for the Southie crowd, who had not enjoyed a band, glee club, or drama society for the two-and-a-half years since busing began — just police and an ever-dwindling number of girls who "civilize the boys," as Dr. Reid once said. A red-headed Southie adult hot from a Broadway bar attacked a marching musician and was punched back; the musician was from Southie. Fights interrupted the game until the game was called 2:35 early, with a score of 41 to 0. The TV camera zoomed in on youths kicking and punching in the bleacher seats. One Boston University guard tried to break apart two opposing factions and was felled, his head bloodied, and taken out to an ambulance. Representative Ray Flynn from South Boston appeared dazed on TV. He said he had been hit with an object on the back of the head.

Mr. Winegar with Detective Famolare watched from the glassed-in press box.

The following Monday at school, a Southie student exulted, "They won the game, but we won the fight."

One black sophomore Jamie had integrated the periphery of the football team. But as tension mounted at the beginning of the year, white students were threatened, and another black player's clothes were stolen in the presence of the police. "And that was their only duty, to guard clothes at practice," Mr. Winegar expostulated. As he realized his pawn-role, Jamie managed to disqualify himself from the games. He came to English class, stood before the mirror at the back of the room, and combed his hair, explaining, "I don't want to be here." Nothing was done about the racial count of the all-white team, although Coach Perdigao last year had been removed because he did not take "affirmative action to integrate the football team."

Enrollment at South Boston High closed on Thursday, September 23, 1976, with 1,195 students registered. By January 1977, the average attendance, according to Mr. Winegar, was 650-700 students, with the L-Street Annex and the Hart-Dean Annex now closed, and all ninth graders formerly in those buildings now at the main building on the Heights. "It doesn't look that many, though," admitted Mr. Winegar, "because the co-ops are not in the school." Judge Garrity had insinuated that Dr. Reid or his staff had falsified attendance numbers, when he wrote in his "rationale" for the receivership:

> *The reported total attendance on Dec. 2 was 510. However, making allowance for between 30 and 40 mechanical drafting students who were away from the school on a field trip, the court and its law clerk and the two experts were in agreement that the number of students in attendance was substantially overstated.*

Students drop out of school; or, if they are seniors, drop out as they earn enough points for graduation. They go to work, or wait at home for college to begin. The most commonly heard comment now, from both black students and white, is "I hate this school." A Southie senior boy said, "If anyone asks me if I've ever 'done time,' I'll tell them, 'Yeah, *I've* done time.'"

When I asked the seniors to write a stream-of-consciousness paragraph about their thoughts going through the metal detectors in the downstairs front lobby, a black senior girl wrote:

> Being in a place where am not wanted. Other boring day. Wondering if the metal detective is going to buzz off. Who behind me what the boy or girl name in front of me Racial violent name calling wonder if some one frame me and they found a gun in my pocket, wondering about my baby at home do he have to go threw the same thing I do just to get a education.

It isn't the ordeal it used to be for teachers to call in sick. Formerly teachers called Dr. Reid before 7:00 A.M. at his home or Mr. Goorvich, assistant headmaster, at the school after 7:00 A.M., when Dr. Reid had already left his house. Now, sometimes Willie, a student, answers the office phone. He is a lot less formidable than Dr. Reid. "Oh, I know you," Willie told me. "I pulled the plug on your projector."

Willie, who is hyperactive, hurls himself like a cannonball against a podium on wheels and shoots around his English class, or leaps out the door and up onto his English teacher in a crushing bear hug, if his teacher, John Dowdell, doesn't hurl himself first against the wall in a protective crucifix position.

On bad days, Mr. Winegar told the teachers, he could predict which teachers would be out, and he calls school headquarters ahead of time. As a result, on some days surplus substitutes spend the day and the city's money assisting in coverage of the studies.

Last year at the receivership hearing, teachers were criticized because of their reluctance to endorse Superintendent Fahey's Instructional Task Force, the Boston University Crisis Team, and the mediating team of the Citywide Coordinating Council under the directorship of Father Michael Groden. A year later Mr. Winegar unilaterally rejected the same B.U. Crisis team, just as Dr. Reid had, because they were not integrated. He told them, "Come back when you are," and appointed a black administrator to field any further business with them. Marion Fahey's Task Force spent the month of December 1975 in the teacher's room off the school cafeteria, and left when Dr. Reid did. Father Groden verified that after two meetings with the South Boston High School white student caucus, the CCC Mediating Board concluded the students were beyond their reach; they were acting as community spokespeople, rather than individuals. It was hopeless; their team did not return to the high school. The school psychiatrist commented, "People would like to help, but, when they get here, they are at a loss what to do."

The psychiatrist left in January. Teachers would no longer meet for the Crisis Prevention seminar.

Students still sit in the cafeteria in patches of black and white, but no administrators are present, as Dr. Reid was every lunchtime. The old student feuds continue. One teacher performed a mock Indian war dance around the torn and littered hair of a white girl who had been jumped in the corridor.

Deans Dentler and Scott, the Boston University court-appointed desegregation "experts," had advised Judge Garrity during the receivership hearings that a headmaster could turn a school around "overnight." One teacher observed, "Does that include upside down?" Another added, "Or around and around?" On television, Mr. Winegar said he would need "six to seven years" to effect the changes he wanted. Some of the most successful new programs — the cooking program and Thompson Island — had been envisioned under Dr. Reid's administration and only awaited funding, but Dr. Reid was given only a year and four months, under the first impact of desegregation.

In April 1977 the Boston School Committee complained in reports to the court that costs for each pupil at South Boston High this year totaled $4,300, twice that of any other school in the city, while attendance at South Boston High School hadn't exceeded 58 percent enrollment this year; they questioned advocacy of "alternative, thematic instructional programs," while "no mention is made of the conventional classroom, ongoing student-teacher relationship," and challenged plans to reorganize the administration of the high school by eliminating assistant headmasters responsible for subject areas. Attorney Sandra Lynch of the State Department of Education countered in a brief warning that if the School Committee "continues to fail to meet its obligations, the court and the parties at some future time will be forced to consider whether the school should remain open."

At School Committee meetings, Mr. Winegar refused to comment without his lawyer, and then only in private.

At the high school, Mr. Winegar, retaining his nickname "Howard Hughes," rarely left his closed office, and regularly only to meet the buses in the morning.

Friday, May 6, 1977

The Phase 3 desegregation order for 1977-78 is out. It provides for desegregation of kindergartens; the retention of East Boston High as a district high school with 400 of its 1,200 seats set aside for a magnet business education component; and the creation of a permanent, independent Office of Implementation to insure desegregation of the Boston public schools.

Monday, May 9

At a court hearing today, Judge Garrity refused to lift the receivership of South Boston High. For five minutes the judge praised Jerome Winegar and his court-appointed team with "working around the clock to turn around what was a hopeless situation." At the same hearing, the black plaintiffs, through their lawyer Eric Van Loon, presented the judge with a list of complaints, including a suspension rate six times the citywide average, and asked the court to close South Boston High and move it to another location. To back up their demands, the blacks proclaimed a "Solidarity Day," and circulated a pamphlet urging a "week of mourning" for students forced to attend school in hostile territory at South Boston High, in a situation that was "worse than ever."

Thirty blacks from a black enrollment of 200 broke the boycott and attended school.

Tuesday, May 10

At the regularly scheduled bimonthly faculty meeting, I asked about the dismissal procedure for seniors on Friday, their last day. Couldn't the undergraduates be dismissed early, and the seniors come in at one o'clock to return books and sign out? An administrator answered, "Same as last year."

Wednesday, May 11

Black students staged a sit-in demonstration in the cafeteria and presented their demands, including "Close the school; move it to a neutral site." Mr. Winegar told the students and parents that he could not guarantee their absolute safety in the school, not even his own. Most black students then left the school building. By 10:15 there was still no announcement for classes to begin. White students, who had been in their homerooms for over two hours, started moving to the doors, huddling there.

"If they leave, we're leaving," they told me.

I answered, "If you go out the door, they'll close the door behind you."

They hesitated, and stayed. Then bands of white students swept through the corridor, past our room. A police walkie-talkie sputtered their direction: The students were meeting in the auditorium. My homeroom burst out the back door and followed.

Mr. Winegar addressed the white students in the auditorium, telling them what he had told the black students earlier: If they walked out and left the school building empty, they would just be playing into the hands of those people—who "for whatever their reasons—want to see this school closed down." The white students answered, "We don't care."

It was almost time for lunch when the bell sounded for the school day to begin. Most students slipped out the back, front, or side doors. Mr. Van Schyndel stopped some students about to jump out the rear first-floor window onto a concrete pavement below. Instead, he let them out the back door, rather than allow them to risk breaking their heel bones, as one student did last year. By the last class, the school was almost empty.

Thursday, May 12

The school was evacuated at 7:35 and searched until 8:30. One stick of dynamite was discovered in the school parking lot. Willie, the hyper-student, answered the phone when the bomb threat was called in.

Students were held an hour in the homeroom. When the bell sounded for classes to begin at 9:00, it was like sounding the beginning for round one of a championship bout. The screams from the first and second floors rose to the third floor.

A guest lecturer, who arrived in my classroom to give a comparative slide talk on the poets W. B. Yeats and Robert Frost, told my class he had found it easier to cross the border into Northern Ireland than to pass the security check in the front lobby. He told his students at the New England Conservatory later in the day, "What could be more romantic? There I was giving a lecture on Yeats and Frost while outside a revolution was going on."

There were nine injuries at the school, including a substitute's broken nose. A trooper was also rumored to have been hurt, but, like the immortals, they are never reported to have sustained an injury. Dr. Michael Donovan of South Boston described the school as a "lunatic asylum" when he was called in to help the injured.

There was an "informational meeting" after school. Mr. Winegar said, "Until this week I thought there was a chance for this school to desegregate. Ellen Jackson of Freedom House, Roxbury, visited the school this afternoon and asked me, 'When will you say the school should be closed?'"

Friday, May 13

Today was the seniors' last day. This year all students were held in homerooms for two and a half hours. Black seniors were held on the first floor and white seniors on the second. TV cameras waiting outside focused on the building. They videotaped a handful of students with diabolical expressions at a second-floor window wrenching a screen away from a window; then the cameras traced the airy descent of papers wafted from the upper windows.

Seniors were tossed caps and gowns and papers, then were corralled like cattle through police lines down and out to the street. There was no chance to return delinquent books; there were no good-byes. Bill Hamann, a senior homeroom teacher, commented, "This is not urban education. It is social degradation," and applied to personnel for a transfer.

Meanwhile, undergraduates waited in homerooms, becoming angrier and angrier as they focused on their troubles. "Why are the blacks here anyway?" one of my sophomore boys asked. They slipped over to the windows to inspect the progress. When the bell rang finally for the first class of the day at 10:20, the students exploded through the doors like race horses. The press outside, too, heard the bell ring, and then the screams.

At lunchtime, an aide told us, a white senior had her clothes ripped off her back in the lavatory, before the aide could reach her. "They kicked her and punched her over my head before I could shove her in a john until the troopers came."

Outside the school, a group of men and women gathered. The police warned them to move, to go home or be arrested. "We are home," one woman answered. "That's what we've been trying to tell you for the past three years." Eleven were arrested for ignoring police orders to move— two men, six women, three male students.

An "informational" meeting was called after school; though we were then unaware of this, it was the last formal faculty meeting of the year. Mr. Winegar told the teachers that the court-mandated Citywide Parents Advisory Committee (CPAC) had voted to close the school. Any suggestions?

At the earlier meeting of the faculty senate, one teacher from South Boston said, "Close it."

Mr. Winegar, reviewing the events of the day, said, "Three hundred students came in today, and 290 of them came in to fight. Usually the fights are over by lunchtime, but today they went on right up to and including the last period of the day." He needed the support of the parents to send their kids to school, especially with the warm weather coming, he said. Attendance should not drop below 50 percent.

At the end of the day, Mr. Winegar told thé press he felt "slightly abandoned" and asked, "Where are the so-called leaders of this city?" He continued:

> For some reason or another, small negative groups — both black and white — have been allowed to call the shots in a negative way. Initially, it was the blacks. I think it is a little of both now. They jack up the kids so all they want to do is fight.
> . . . There hasn't been a day like this since September. This school has been basically quiet and reasonable for a long time. Then all at once there was a week of mourning for the blacks at the school, and the blacks have a "Solidarity Day." The kids come to school all jacked up and ready to go. Obviously, the whites aren't going to sit back and do nothing. Then everybody wants to act that way.
> We've never had any real support from anybody. There are all kinds of people I've never met. The mayor. You wouldn't believe the people I've never met. The plaintiffs. I don't know who they are; I've never seen them.

The teachers reminded Mr. Winegar, "We've asked repeatedly to meet with Judge Garrity, but he never has."

Mr. Winegar asked parents to continue sending students to South Boston High for the remainder of the year, saying, "Even the president can't be guaranteed absolute security. But we do the best we can."

In response to his appeal, Mr. Winegar received, he said, "a tremendous amount of hate mail. . . . Some actually signed their names."

Mr. Winegar complained to the media:

> Coming from the Midwest, I always had this feeling of Boston as this great bastion of liberalism, of learning and of allowing people the freedom of doing their own thing.
> After seeing it, I will never again feel inferior about coming from the country. The whole image of Boston is changed. Boston is backwards. And I just can't believe that the people of this city just sit still and put up with all of this.

But, in the last presidential election, 1976, South Boston supported George Wallace for president; the black community supported Jimmy Carter. President-elect Jimmy Carter commented, "Liberals are too difficult to please."

Monday, May 16

Today 400 whites demonstrated outside the high school in support of keeping the building open. One hundred Boston police and 70 state troopers inside the building; Boston and state police cars; police wagons, ambulances, and police buses lined up in banks outside the high school. Six adults were arrested for "unlawful assembly," one of them Mr. James Kelly, director of the South Boston Information Center.

Looking out from my homeroom window, Mr. Van Schyndel, a bird-watcher by hobby, commented, as he watched the helmet-covered police bunched together in groups outside the school, "They look like crows in the cornfield."

Tuesday, May 17

Two hundred forty-nine students attended school today, a number that included the clusters at the Boston City Hospital. There are so many students absent that the attendance sheet now lists only those students present. The high school is empty.

Thursday, May 26

The fifteen teachers who submitted transfer papers are being called to the front office. Mr. Winegar, Mrs. Kozberg, and Mr. Corscadden interview the defecting ranks. They frame the interviews with the question, "How do you feel about desegregation?"

One teacher listed five high schools she would like to transfer to.

"But five!" they exclaimed. "Why five?"

"There were only five lines," she replied.

The old-timer science teacher, Ms. Folkart, left in September with the black history teacher, who was carried out from his shop class on a stretcher; two reading specialists and the nurse left in October; a 766 special needs evaluator in December; and a young male history teacher in April for "medical" reasons.

Later, when asked on the Bay State Forum radio program how many teachers wanted "out," Mr. Winegar replied, "I can't give the exact number," but "7 percent of the total staff."

Friday, May 27

The senior prom was last night. Forty couples attended — no blacks. The party was dull, but rallied to sing "Go Home, Jerome" when Mr. Winegar left the room for a few minutes.

There were fewer than 150 students in school today, and 24 teachers out. The bell for the first class was held for 20 minutes until substitutes arrived and classes could begin.

While I was on duty in the library, I allowed a black student to leave. A black security aide brought him back and chastised him. The boy became ugly. "You think you're somebody, but you ain't. You're nothing but a nigger like me," he answered back.

The aide was embarrassed. "That's right. You're right," he said, then left.

Tuesday, May 31

Nine buses pulled up to the high school today. I counted 115 black students get off — twelve to a bus.

School opens for the personnel: 35 troopers, 55 transitional and security aides, 120 teachers and administrators, 3 secretaries, kitchen staff, as well as ESAA peripheral personnel.

Seniors are marked "constructively present" until graduation on June 14.

Friday, June 3

Security aides have been assigned to work at the Hynes Auditorium on graduation night. There are rumors that the white seniors will have green shamrocks and RESIST printed on their gowns, the black seniors will have a clenched black-power fist on theirs.

Friday, June 10

It is cold and wet today. The school is like a gloomy morass, and the students have finally sunk below the surface. There were five white boys in my homeroom. If it weren't for the promised field trip to Lincoln Amusement Park today — canceled — no one would have come in.

The graduation has become a problem. After invitations had been distributed to seniors, Mr. Winegar walked around the Hynes Auditorium, found it was impossible to secure the building, and decided to move the graduation to the smaller New England Life Hall. Mrs. Casper, an aide and parent of one of the seniors, met with Mr. Winegar, Superintendent Fahey, the associate superintendent of safety, Mr. Kelly of the South Boston Information Center, two Justice Department officials, five black parents, and four other white parents to resolve the crisis.

Mr. Winegar had "solid evidence that people in possession of those tickets planned disruptive action at graduation," he said.

"What information?" the parents demanded.

"I can't say," he said. Details were better left to the people who had that information.

"Well, then," Mrs. Casper argued, "you can tell one of us. If there are rumors, we have a right to know what they are. We elect Mr. Joyce to hear what the rumors are, and the blacks can elect a representative to hear them."

Her request seemed reasonable to me, since even the president of the United States briefs a few members of Congress on his top secret security plans. That suggestion was ignored.

To Superintendent Fahey, who was concerned about the rumors that seniors planned to paint their gowns with shamrocks or black-power fists, Mrs. Casper reasoned, "You have so much money for programs, why not have a pile of gowns there? If the kids come in with a painted gown, give them another one to wear instead."

"That's a very good suggestion," Miss Fahey said.

Angrily Mrs. Casper concluded. The Superintendent should consider the feelings of the parents and students who had relatives coming from out of state to the graduation, and who had planned parties. "And what about the good, quiet kids who have come to this school for four years and stayed out of all the fights? What about them? Aren't they entitled to something? Never mind your feelings. What about their feelings? If you're afraid of some of the kids starting fights, keep them out of the graduation. We all know who the troublemakers are. But, if we don't have the Hynes Auditorium for graduation, we'll have our own graduation."

To me Mrs. Casper said later, "I just said that. We don't have any plans."

The Justice Department was delighted, Mrs. Casper said, that finally a group of black and white parents were working together. "But, hey," she told me, "I have to live in this community. They're not getting *me*. Besides, I don't believe in forced busing." She concluded, "They may have a lot of book knowledge, but they don't know people."

I drove Mrs. Casper to the post office to mail the graduation announcements reinstating the Hynes Auditorium with a compromise of five tickets per student instead of the original ten.

One senior homeroom teacher, disgusted, commented, "They'll put the kids and guests in a bus and ride them around to a mystery graduation."

Monday, June 13

In my homeroom, there were three white boys and one white girl. My surviving black boy is in voluntary "in-school suspension," and comes to school at 9:00 in the morning.

During my study, I talked to two black boys. Their attendance is regular, but one has a study two classes in succession. I asked them what they had learned all year.

One said, "Nothin'. All you learn in this school is to hate—whites to hate blacks and blacks to hate whites. I'm going to a private school next year." His father is a carpenter.

A black aide, when I asked her if she was working graduation night, said, "I'll have to sleep on it. Why should I go to their graduation? They haven't been nice all year." She said, disgusted, "Up there with a cap on their head, and they don't know nothin'."

Tuesday, June 14

Graduation night, Southie High, class of 1977. Boston motorcycle police lined the underground parking lane to the Hynes Auditorium. Five mounted police horses stomped outside the entrance beside the Channel 5 TV truck. Teachers, administrators, and 55 aides on duty for the night checked tickets at the entrance and "secured" the building. Five Boston police in uniform stood along the walls of the auditorium.

There was no procession of graduates across the rolled-lawn football field to their seats; no musical interlude by orchestra and chorus; no reminiscing about the sweltering day when the million-dollar air-conditioning system broke down or about the senior kissing booth on St. Patrick's Day; no edifying speech about Robert Kennedy and the enemies of mankind: racism, poverty, and I-forget-what, as there had been last week at the graduation ceremonies of suburban Newton North High; and no gratifying reminder by the mayor that President Carter had cited Newton as one of America's "ten all-American cities."

Instead, a black adult volunteer played the piano while the seniors walked up the aisle of Hynes Auditorium in their pale blue-and-maroon gowns. Mr. Joseph McDonough, briefly receiver for the high school, spoke, followed by School Committeeman Paul Tierney. The senior class president turned over a class check to Mr. Winegar without shaking his hand. Then, as their names were called, students walked across the stage, received a diploma from Mr. Winegar and shook hands with Mr. Tierney. Two of the white senior girls lifted their arms like prize fighters, then turned around, displaying their pallid blue gowns stamped with a white shamrock and the legend "Southie" and "Southie Is My ROOTS." Aides hustled them out of the auditorium.

A South Boston resident wrote his observations for the local *Tribune:* "The graduation went on, the speeches and scholarships. Police everywhere, there was a big smile on Winegar's face because no shamrocks could be seen anywhere. He thought he has successfully suppressed all attempts at displaying the symbol of South Boston. . . . Meanwhile the three girls had slipped off the plain gowns. When it was their turn to get their diplomas they walked across the stage, arms raised displaying the shamrocks. The crowd responded with a roar of applause. Many even gave them standing ovations. The girls had succeeded. As the crowd continued to applaud, the smile disappeared from Winegar's face. He had failed."

Without waiting for the closing ceremonies, clusters of seniors left immediately after receiving diplomas. Piano music played again for the recession, and the class of 1977, South Boston High, departed.

A half hour later, from the Hynes Auditorium side doors, 50 uniformed Boston police exited from the belly of the building.

Wednesday, June 15

I stopped in the front office before school. Mr. Winegar was there pointing angrily to the box of unused, plastic-wrapped gowns on the floor beside the black administrator. "It was the teachers' fault," he said. "We knew a week ago how they planned to do it."

There were few students in today.

Friday, June 24

The last day of classes. No students came in. Mr. Winegar left for the Midwest. The troopers waited until the end of the day, talking in groups or stretched out on chairs in the corridors.

No bells were sounded, no dismissal announced after the last class. A single yellow bus pulled up escorted by a police car, waited, then drove away.

Wednesday, June 29

I tabulated the year's cumulative attendance for my homeroom. It took much longer than usual because someone had stolen all the May attendance sheets listing the year's accumulated attendance from the faculty mail boxes. Some teachers are marking everybody present rather than go back and tabulate the day-to-day attendance.

Of the 35 students assigned to my sophomore homeroom, 13 did not enroll. From a possible total of 178 days, the year's attendance read:

	Number of Days		
Students	Present	Absent	Tardy
Boy (black)	95	83	0
Boy (black)	7	25	0
Boy (black)	11	11	0
Boy (white)	71	105	15
Boy (white)	121	57	5
Boy (white)	74	104	45
Boy (white)	103	75	73
Boy (white)	93	85	49
Boy (white)	102	76	31
Boy (white)	151	27	5
Boy (white)	44	132	13
Boy (white)	68	68	0
Boy (white)	107	71	0
Boy (white)	96	82	54
Boy (white)	130	48	72
Boy (other: Spanish)	2	76	0
Boy (white)	173	5	5
Girl (black)	131	47	1
Girl (black)	54	122	1
Girl (black)	48	130	0
Girl (black)	66	21	2
Girl (black)	115	61	13
Girl (white)	63	115	5
Girl (white)	113	65	10
Girl (white)	29	147	0
Girl (white)	25	79	0
Girl (white)	6	172	0

At nine o'clock the faculty gathered in the South Cafeteria for a final meeting of the year. Mr. Winegar, who had returned from his Midwest trip, was absent with a "cold." None of the other members of his "administrative team" appeared—although Tim Murphy stopped by for a few minutes at the end. Instead, Mr. Corscadden communicated Mr. Winegar's team decisions. He reported: New programs would be mailed to teachers sometime during the summer, after it was determined which teachers would be dropped into the excess pool; first order of preference would be given to special "program" teachers, whether or not they had tenure; black faculty would be added until they made up 20 percent of the staff. In response to the faculty senate petition proffered the previous Friday, it was promised that classes assigned tentatively to the auditorium and cafeterias would be moved to regular classrooms, and all classes would have assigned teachers prior to the first day of school. The question of the two rooms set aside for in-school suspension programs was not addressed. The report ended. It was time to go.

During the summer Mr. Winegar told an interviewer, Muriel Cohen of the *Globe,* that he has learned to pay no attention to the GO HOME, JEROME, YOU FAILED signs in the neighborhood: "Most people ignore me when I walk down the street. Sometimes someone yells, 'Go home, Jerome.' I turn around and wave and get a smile. . . . But anyone who thought this place could change in a year was dreaming."

However, in August 1977, Mrs. Kozberg told Muriel Cohen, "Now I really feel confident that we have turned this school around. That we are successful. I have no hard data yet, but we will have."

Epilogue

In August 1977 Mr. Winegar and his court-appointed administrative team, ignoring seniority rights, dropped thirty tenured teachers, including Mr. Van Schyndel, into the excess pool and hired new teachers, black and white, in their place; Judge W. Arthur Garrity upheld the action. In June 1977 the newly formed, court-appointed Office of Implementation asked Mr. Winegar for incident-report documentation on 200 disruptive students, then programmed them out of the high school. In June 1978 Martin Walsh of the U.S. Justice Department pronounced South Boston High School a "turnaround" and a "major victory for desegregation."[1] Three months later, on September 20, 1978, Judge Garrity lifted the receivership — the second in U.S. history — from South Boston High School. Tim Murphy and Ron Rosenbaum had left a month earlier, in August 1978. In April 1980 Geraldine Kozberg took a leave of absence and did not return. On December 23, 1982, U.S. District Court Judge Garrity, in an Order of Disengagement, appointed the Massachusetts Board of Education to take primary monitoring reponsibility for the Boston public schools and ordered the City of Boston to compensate the state board for the costs accrued.

In June 1977 I took a leave of absence from South Boston High School to finish my doctoral degree at the University of Texas. When I remained away longer than a year to complete the requirements, Mr. Winegar exercised his quite legal option and terminated my position, and I, too, was dropped — books, baggage, and Irish curriculum — into the excess pool.

When I returned, I transferred then to Boston Latin School, a citywide magnet school remote from the turmoil of the city, where the "carrot" at

---

[1] Fletcher Roberts, "S. Boston High 'Turnaround' Hailed," *Boston Globe*, evening ed., June 26, 1978.

the end of the "stick"—the bus ride—is a 350-year-old tradition of academic learning. Eventually the sound of teenagers screaming in the corridors, chilling to "Zero at the Bone," became only a memory. I relaxed,
despite the occasional egalitarian threat to dismantle the "elitist" Latin
schools—alarming, then sputtering out.

Meanwhile, the debate on the success or failure of busing in Boston
continues. In 1981 Robert A. Dentler and Marvin B. Scott, Judge Garrity's
court-appointed desegregation "experts," published *Schools on Trial,* an
"inside account" of the Boston desegregation case—a book the *New York
Times* reviewer found "extraordinary" in its "sneering sarcasm" directed
toward the Irish Catholics of Boston.[2]

In the chapter on South Boston High School, Dentler and Scott recall
that in 1975, after their brief visit there in mid-November, they found an
"educational wasteland" and advised Judge Garrity to create a new educational leadership. Not surprisingly, in 1981 they found Mr. Winegar's
new administration and leadership had "transformed" the high school,
generating a climate of hope through "programs and fairness." Even the
students' "dress, grooming, posture, and bearing" had "visibly improved,"
they observed.

However, in a nationwide survey of schools for the school year 1981-82,
Boston was found to have worse student attendance than any other big city
school system. South Boston High School, with a daily attendance average
of 55.6 percent, was more than fourteen percentage points lower than any
other school in Boston.

Incredibly, Dentler and Scott underscore the prejudice in their observations by repeating their allegation of falsification in the teacher-attend-
ance roster uncovered by their own "head count" during their mid-November 1975 tour of the high school—an allegation Dr. Reid had denounced
as a "lie" and requested the attorney general to investigate.

Acknowledging that South Boston High had, by 1981, been "taken away"
from the people of its neighborhood, Dentler and Scott extolled the change:
"Its [the high school's] programs extend beyond the district into other parts
of the city and they no longer reinforce the *status quo* of the self-enclosed
enclave in which most of South Boston's adults reside. The programs teach
that there is life beyond the enclave of one's heritage. It teaches that respect
is due all humans and cannot be parcelled out according to ethnicity, class,

[2] Martha Bayles, review of *Schools on Trial,* in *New York Times Book Review,* Sept. 6, 1981.

or residence."[3] In contrast with the court-appointed "experts," Boston public schools Superintendent Robert Spillane in June 1983 called South Boston High School a "sore" with a "non-productive educational program." If it were within his power, he said, he'd close the school.[4]

In a more sweeping indictment, Edward J. Logue, director of the Boston Redevelopment Authority from 1960 to 1967 and who, in 1965, first proposed the formation of the successful METCO program, denounced Judge Garrity to an MIT audience in April 1983 as "the worst disaster to have befallen Boston in the last sixteen years." Assailing as "immoral" and "irresponsible" a busing system that had polarized the city by forcibly exchanging poor black and white low-income families while excluding the affluent, liberal, and suburban whites, he concluded, "To put it most unpleasantly about Garrity: Where there was unquestionably passive prejudice, he created active hate. And that's hard to forgive. To this day, I do not think he knows he's done that."[5]

Thomas I. Atkins, plaintiff attorney, had high praise for Judge Garrity's action, however, describing Boston as "the single most significant school desegregation case since the 1957 confrontation in Little Rock," and "probably the greatest assertion of federal judicial authority in a school district in the country's history."[6] Atkins also noted, "The impact of desegregation on children has been to save both this immediate generation and succeeding generations from growing up in ethnically isolated neighborhoods and schools, thinking that there are gross differences between people based on insignificant factors.... The city still has a distance to go in eliminating barriers of racial hostility and animosity, but it has made a good start.... Nobody knew the case would last this long because no one knew it would take the administrators of the Boston School Department this long to learn that one wars against the U.S. Constitution futilely."[7]

The changes in the school system, reflected statistically, have been dramatic.

Eleven years ago, before busing began, the total enrollment of 93,647 students in the Boston public schools included 53,593 whites; 31,963 blacks;

---

[3] Robert A. Dentler and Marvin B. Scott, *Schools on Trial: An Inside Account of the Boston Desegregation Case* (Cambridge, Mass., 1981), 182.

[4] Joe Sciacca, "'Southie a Sore, I'd Close It,'" *Boston Herald*, June 16, 1983.

[5] Edward J. Logue, "Garrity's Impact and Other Thoughts on Boston," *Boston Globe*, May 2, 1983.

[6] John Birtwell, "The Great Busing Debate Lives On," *Boston Herald*, Sept. 3, 1985.

[7] Peggy Hernandez, "New Times, Old Feelings," in a section entitled "The Desegregation of Boston's Schools," *Boston Globe*, Sept. 4, 1985.

and 8,091 others. By January 1986 the student enrollment had dropped to 57,694 students: 27,483 blacks; 15,536 whites; 9,921 Hispanics; 4,502 Orientals; and 252 Indian-Americans.

In 1974 there were 5,000 teachers in the system, 400 of them black (135 of them in non-permanent positions); by October 1985 the number of teachers had dropped to 4,356, among whom there were 3,013 whites, 936 blacks, and 407 others. Seventy-eight school buildings had closed, including Roxbury High School and the Prince School in the Back Bay, which had been sold to developers for conversion to shops and elegant condominiums.

As of January 1986 the official enrollment at South Boston High School was 952, a number that included 189 bilingual students, 168 special needs students, and 189 students in a work-study ORC (Occupational Resource Center) program. The racial mix of the enrollment was 361 blacks; 295 whites; 118 Orientals; 170 Hispanics; and 8 Indian-Americans. Eleven years after the first impact of desegregation, race is no longer cause for conflict. "After all," commented Barbara Colbert, teacher in the school-within-a-school program there, "these kids have been in the same classrooms with each other since first grade. Many of them aren't even aware of the high school's desegregation history."

Enrollment at South Boston Heights Academy, the alternative community school, was also down from its opening-year enrollment of 576 students in 1975 to 150 children in grades 1-12 in 1986.

In January 1984, former state representative Raymond Flynn, a graduate of South Boston High School, who describes himself as "the son of a longshoreman and the son of a cleaning woman as well," succeeded Kevin H. White as mayor of Boston on a populist platform.

During his last scheduled press conference, outgoing Mayor White, in retrospective mood, turned to the most traumatic period of his four-term administration, the desegregation of the Boston public schools. He regretted, he said, the "excessiveness" with which busing had been implemented in Boston and wished that, in the spring and summer of 1974, instead of "going around with the antibusing mothers convincing them the imbalance law would work," he had urged Judge Garrity to ease up on the plan, to be "more generous" or "softer." Alluding to Phase 2 he said, "I think busing would have worked except when they threw Jeremiah Burke [high school students] into Southie. It was too much in pain, and I missed it. And I went down to fight Garrity. . . . I did it too late."[8]

[8] Ed Quill, "Mayor Is Packing Up, Looking at His 16 Years," ibid., Dec. 29, 1983.

In June 1985 Superintendent of Schools Robert R. Spillane resigned at the end of a four-year term. Disappointed that Judge Garrity had not yet disengaged himself from the Boston school desegregation case, Dr. Spillane criticized him for trying to manage the schools himself instead of appointing a master who would report back to him. "He [Judge Garrity] became the focus, so blacks and whites would go to the court to get answers. Once he's out they will be forced to sit together. He had a paternalistic mentality that all goodness and all knowledge flow from the federal court."[9]

The Boston School Committee, which during Dr. Spillane's tenure had grown from a body of five at-large members to a thirteen-member board of nine district and four at-large members, then elected Dr. Laval S. Wilson, superintendent of schools in Rochester, New York, as superintendent. Dr. Wilson, the first black to head the Boston school system since its creation in 1851, the twenty-first superintendent to hold that office, and the eighth superintendent since 1974, was elected by a 9 to 4 multiracial majority vote (which included Joseph Casper, committeeman from South Boston).

On September 3, 1985, on the day Laval Wilson assumed office, Federal Judge W. Arthur Garrity issued his 415th—and final—order and returned control of the school system to the Boston School Committee. Although relinquishing control, Judge Garrity left in place the court's requirements, which the School Committee must adhere to in operating the school system. This final judgment required the school department to:

1. Implement a unified facilities plan, which prescribes a repair and renovation schedule for many school buildings. An accompanying memo explains that "the dilapidated condition of many Boston schools has been an obstacle to their desegregation." First priority is to be given to renovating the Jeremiah E. Burke High School and South Boston High School. Not approved were the construction projects for the Latin schools, which Dr. Spillane characterized as "a linchpin all these years for the promise of quality in the future of Boston."

The Court simply wanted "written specifications" for renovations at the Latin schools, Judge Garrity later explained; it was not "holding out" on them.[10]

2. Never again discriminate or segregate on the basis of race in any school facility.

3. Assign students to schools so that the racial-ethnic mix reflects the

[9] Irene Sege, "Parting Words from Spillane," ibid., June 28, 1985.
[10] Peggy Hernandez, "Garrity Says Many Tasks Still Ahead in Schools Case," ibid., Sept. 24, 1985.

student population of each school district or, with respect to magnet schools and programs, of the city. Starting in 1986-87, a second option permits the adoption of a citywide plan, allowing the percentage of any race at any one school to vary by 25 percent, plus or minus, from the total percentage of that racial group systemwide.

4. Continue to promote and adequately fund the Citywide Parents Council for a minimum of three years.

5. Desegregate the faculty and administration until they are at least 25 percent black and 10 percent other minorities, gradually increasing black percentages by at least one-half percent a year and other minority groups by not less than one-quarter percent annually.

6. Maintain the Department of Implementation to oversee all aspects of desegregation.

7. Carry out all previous orders.

8. Consult the state board of education, the attorney general, the mayor, the Citywide Parents Council, the NAACP, and the Council of Administrators of Hispanic Agencies before modifying any of Garrity's orders.

9. Put into effect a unified vocational education plan that assures blacks and other minorities are not discriminated against.

"Final orders," however, did not mean "final judgment." In a memorandum dated November 1, 1985, citing the 1975 *Swann vs. Charlotte-Mecklenburg Board of Education* case in North Carolina as precedent, Judge Garrity explained that he was retaining "standby jurisdiction" on five critical areas—student assignments, faculty desegregation, vocational education, school facilities, and parent councils.[11]

Of Judge Garrity's "final orders" in early September, Mayor Flynn had said, "The judge's withdrawal will symbolize an end to a period of time that everybody wants to put behind and will close a chapter on a time that Bostonians want to forget. Everybody wants to open a new chapter of good will for the city."[12]

---

[11] Muriel Cohen, "Garrity Cites 'Unfinished' School Issues," ibid., Nov. 2, 1985.
[12] Muriel Cohen, "Flynn: People Want Peace," in "The Desegregation of Boston's Schools," ibid., Sept. 4, 1985.

SYNC06-OJPRISM   JBLKJ   JLCKJSent   MOD   SID: 00500   J J
RF   I L
1 field(s) modified.

ILL 11:2290445   Record:1 of 1

"ILL: 2290445   "Borrower: FAU "ReqDate: 930209 "Status: WILL SUPPLY
"OCLC: 12551925   "NeedBefore: 930311 "RecDate: "Renewal Req:
"Lender: *UNH,GRN,CTL,NHP,CTW   "DueDate: 930315 "NewDueDate:
"CALLNO:
"AUTHOR: Malloy, Ione, 1931-
"TITLE: Southie won't go : a teacher's diary of the desegregation of South
Boston High School / Urbana : University of Illinois Press, c1986.
"IMPRINT:
"VERIFIED: OCLC
"PATRON: barrett,rena   STATUS: ug   REQ#:   DEPT: TYPE: b
"SHIP TO: ILL/Nyselius Library/Fairfield Univ./Fairfield, CT 06430
"BILL TO: Same
"SHIP VIA: C CAR-4 in CT   "MAXCOST: @n/any   "COPYRT-COMPLIANCE-CCG
"LENDING CHARGES: "SHIPPED: "SHIP INSURANCE:
"LENDING RESTRICTIONS:
"LENDING NOTES:
"RETURN TO: Interlibrary Loans/University of New Haven Library/300 Orange
Ave./West Haven, CT 06516
"RETURN VIA: Ccar 5 in Ct.

Bibliography

Anglin, Robert J. "Four Policemen Are Suspended in Rabbit Inn Case." *Boston Globe,* Feb. 6, 1976.

————. "15 Pupils Arrested for Fighting at S. Boston High." *Boston Globe,* Oct. 25, 1975.

"Atkins Says Integration Moving 'on Schedule.'" *Boston Herald,* Dec. 28, 1974.

Bayles, Martha. "On Busing in Boston." *Harper's,* July 1980.

————. Review of Robert A. Dentler and Marvin B. Scott's *Schools on Trial. New York Times Book Review,* Sept. 6, 1981.

Birtwell, John. "The Great Busing Debate Lives On." *Boston Herald,* Sept. 3, 1985.

"Boston: Back to School." *Newsweek,* Jan. 20, 1975.

Botwright, Ken O. "Not Bitter at Judge; Reid Says He Did His Best." *Boston Evening Globe,* Dec. 16, 1975.

Breslin, Jimmy. "Jimmy Breslin on Boston." *Boston Globe,* Sept 8, 1975.

"Brooke to Fight 'Day, Night' Prohibition of Forced Busing." *Boston Globe,* Dec. 24, 1975.

Buell, Emmett H., Jr., and Richard A. Brisbin, Jr. *School Desegregation and Defended Neighborhoods: The Boston Controversy.* Lexington, Mass.: Lexington Books, 1981.

"Bulger Rips 'Outburst' by Garrity." *Boston Globe,* Feb. 20, 1976.

Bullard, Pamela, and Judith Stoia. *The Hardest Lesson: Personal Stories of a School Desegregation Crisis.* Boston: Little, Brown, 1980.

Burke, Alan Dennis. *The Fire Watch.* Boston: Little Brown, 1980.

Ciccone, John. "South Boston Information Center News." *South Boston Tribune,* June 23, 1977.

Cohen, Muriel. "Dentler Optimistic about S. Boston's Future," *Boston Globe,* Dec. 18, 1975.

————. "Winegar Due Soon at S. Boston." *Boston Globe,* Mar. 3, 1976

————. "Banned Poetry Book Stirs S. Boston," *Boston Evening Globe,* Apr. 6, 1977.

————. "Committee Objects to S. Boston School Plan." *Boston Globe,* Apr. 8, 1977.

————. "Winegar Encouraged after First Year." *Boston Evening Globe*, July 5, 1977.

————. "Southie High's Gerry Kozberg—Her Success and Frustration." *Boston Globe*, Aug. 3, 1977.

————. "Flynn: People Want Peace," in "The Desegregation of Boston's Schools." *Boston Globe*, Sept. 4, 1985.

————. "Garrity Cites 'Unfinished' School Issues." *Boston Globe*, Nov. 2, 1985.

Coleman, James S. "Presentation to Massachusetts Legislature." Mar. 30, 1976.

"Coleman on the Griddle." *Time*, Apr. 12, 1976.

Colvario, Mary G. "Recollections of South Boston High School Before and During Its First Year of Desegregation." May 1, 1978.

Cottle, Thomas J. *Busing.* Boston: Beacon Press, 1976.

Croft, George, and Jerome Sullivan. "3 Students Arrested As Tension Grips Charlestown, S. Boston High Schools." *Boston Globe*, Oct. 10, 1975.

————, and Robert J. Anglin. "Reid Disputes Explanation for Takeover." *Boston Globe*, Dec. 18, 1975.

Dentler, Robert A., and Marvin B. Scott. *Schools on Trial: An Inside Account of the Boston Desegregation Case.* Cambridge, Mass.: Abt Books, 1981.

Doherty, James. "Boston's Federal Experiment." *Boston Union Teacher*, Dec. 1975.

Dumanoski, Dianne. "Jerome Winegar: New Man at Southie High." *Boston Phoenix*, Apr. 20, 1976.

Duncliffe, Bill. "Reid Critical of Garrity's Action." *Boston Globe*, Dec. 11, 1975.

Eisner, Alan. "Scuffles Cut Short Black Student Seminar." *Boston Herald*, Oct. 8, 1974.

————. "Reid Charges Garrity Lied." *Boston Herald*, Dec. 18, 1975.

Fields, Carmen. "'Someone Tried to Kill Me with American Flag.'" *Boston Globe*, Apr. 7, 1976.

Filteau, Jerry. "Ethnic Expert Views Busing as 'Hypocrisy.'" *Pilot*, Dec. 12, 1975.

"The First Year." *Boston Sunday Globe*, May 25, 1975.

Garrity, W. Arthur. "Garrity's Text Lists Reasons for Taking Over South Boston High; Judge Explains Rationale for His Ruling in South Boston Case." *Boston Evening Globe*, Dec. 17, 1975.

Griffiths, Gary. "Louise Day Hicks (1961-1976) R.I.P." *Real Paper*, Oct. 30, 1976.

Hassett, Robert L. "Bitter House Flays Attack on Black Man." *Boston Herald*, Apr. 7, 1976.

Hernandez, Peggy. "New Times, Old Feelings," in "The Desegregation of Boston's Schools." *Boston Globe*, Sept. 4, 1985.

————. "Garrity Says Many Tasks Still Ahead in Schools Case." *Boston Globe*, Sept. 24, 1985.

Hillson, Robert. *The Battle of Boston.* New York: Pathfinder Press, 1977.

"Hispanic Pupils to Boycott South Boston High," *Boston Herald*, Jan. 13, 1976.

"Hundreds of Hyde Park Pupils in Melee." *Boston Globe*, Jan. 22, 1976.

Husock, Howard. "Kennedy on Violence, Racism, and the U.S. Flag." *Boston Phoenix*, Apr. 27, 1976.

"Is Judge Garrity Failing?" *Real Paper*, Jan. 14, 1976.

Jenkins, C. David, and Robert W. Tuthill, Saul I. Tannenbaum, and Craig R. Kirby,

"Zones of Excess Mortality in Massachusetts." *New England Journal of Medicine,* June 9, 1977.

Jones, Arthur. "Explanations Differ for 3 Weeks of Relative Calm in Boston." *Boston Globe,* Nov. 3, 1974.

Kelleher, John. *Southie.* Dublin: RTE; Boston: WGBH, 1977. Film.

Kenneally, Katie. *South Boston:* The Boston Neighborhood Histories Project, 1976. With acknowledgment to Ms. Deborah Insel and Her Bicentennial Class at SBHS, 1974.

Kenney, Charles. "Busting Poetry at Southie." *Real Paper,* May 28, 1977.

Kent, Richard. "Takeover Order 'New Law,'" *Patriot Ledger,* Dec. 18, 1975.

Kifner, John. "3 Boston School Officials in Contempt over Busing." *New York Times,* Dec. 28, 1974.

Lodge, Emily S. "Busing: A Vat of Trouble." *Beverly Times,* Jan. 2, 1976.

―――――. "S. Boston Parents Angry over Gilligan's Remarks." *Beverly Times,* Jan. 5, 1976.

Logue, Edward J. "Garrity's Impact and Other Thoughts on Boston." *Boston Globe,* May 2, 1983.

Longcope, Kay. "Jury May Get Hub Murder Case Today." *Boston Globe,* May 20, 1976.

Lukas, J. Anthony. *Common Ground.* New York: Alfred A. Knopf, 1985.

Lupo, Alan. *Liberty's Chosen Home.* Boston: Little, Brown, 1977.

MacNeil/Lehrer Report. "Update: Boston Schools." Library #713. Full text from a film produced by Shirley Wershba and Pamela Bullard, June 21, 1978.

Morgan, Tallulah, et al, Plaintiffs, v. John J. Kerrigan, et al, Defendants; Morgan v. James W. Hennigan, et al, Defendants (1972 to July 1974). Civil Action No. 72-911-G.

Morgan, Tallulah, et al, Plaintiffs, v. John A. Nucci, et al, Defendants. Memorandum Regarding Final Orders by W. Arthur Garrity. November 1, 1985. Civil Action No. 72-911-G.

"NAACP, State Warn on So. Boston High." *Boston Globe,* Apr. 15, 1977.

Patterson, Rachelle. "Kennedy, Brooke Back Garrity Fiat." *Boston Evening Globe,* Dec. 12, 1975.

Payton, Brenda. "Black Students React to School Reopening." *Bay State Banner,* Jan. 16, 1975.

"Please Don't Make It Impossible." *Pilot,* Oct. 25, 1974.

"The Power of Our Judges: Are They Going Too Far?" *U.S. News and World Report,* Jan. 19, 1976.

Quill, Ed. "Mayor Is Packing Up, Looking at His 16 Years." *Boston Globe,* Dec. 29, 1983.

Reisig, Robin. "Who Does Judge Garrity Listen To?" *Real Paper,* Dec. 24/31, 1975.

Richard, Ray. "A Headmaster Feels Abandoned." *Boston Globe,* May 14, 1977.

Roberts, Eleanor. "Reid 'Cautiously Optimistic.'" *Boston Sunday Herald Advertiser,* Sept. 7, 1975.

―――――. "For Bill Reid, It's Farewell to Southie." *Boston Sunday Herald Advertiser,* Dec. 21, 1975.

————. "Superintendent Fahey Speaks Her Mind." *Boston Sunday Herald Advertiser,* Feb. 1, 1976.

————. "Year of Fear Ends for 121." *Boston Sunday Herald Advertiser,* June 6, 1976.

————. "Changes Coming at Southie." *Boston Sunday Herald Advertiser,* June 20, 1976.

Roberts, Fletcher. "S. Boston High 'Turnaround' Hailed." *Boston Globe,* June 26, 1978.

Sciacca, Joe. "'Southie a Sore, I'd Close It.'" *Boston Herald,* June 16, 1983.

Sege, Irene. "Parting Words from Spillane." *Boston Globe,* June 23, 1985.

————. "Garrity Gives Terms of Pullout." *Boston Globe,* July 6, 1985.

Shanker, Albert. "Little Rock, 1959, Boston, 1974: Same Thing?" *Boston Union Teacher,* Jan. 26, 1975.

Sisyphus. "School Busing—A Detour." *Commonweal,* Oct. 24, 1975.

"South Boston Hi Seeks Support." *Federation Paper,* June 1978.

"Ted, Brooke Back Garrity." *Boston Herald,* late ed., Dec. 12, 1975.

Toomey, John, and Edward P. B. Rankin. *Old South Boston.* Boston: The Authors, 1901.

Ward, Robert. "DiGrazia 'Unhappy' over Reid Dismissal." *Boston Evening Globe,* Dec. 11, 1975.

Note on the Author

Ione Malloy is a teacher of English in the Boston public school system. She taught at South Boston High School from 1970 to 1977, when she left to finish her Ph.D. She presently teaches at the Boston Latin School. Her college degrees include: Ph.D., University of Texas (1979); M.A., Boston College (1964), M.Ed., State College at Boston (1961); and A.B., Emmanuel College, Boston (1953).